REDEVELOPING INDUSTRIAL SITES

REDEVELOPING INDUSTRIAL SITES

A Guide for Architects, Planners, and Developers

Carol Berens

JOHN WILEY & SONS, INC.

This book is printed on acid-free paper. ∞

Copyright © 2011 by Carol Berens. All rights reserved.

Published by John Wiley & Sons, Inc., Hoboken, New Jersey.
Published simultaneously in Canada.

No part of this publication may be reproduced, stored in a retrieval system, or transmitted in any form or by any means, electronic, mechanical, photocopying, recording, scanning, or otherwise, except as permitted under Section 107 or 108 of the 1976 United States Copyright Act, without either the prior written permission of the Publisher, or authorization through payment of the appropriate per-copy fee to the Copyright Clearance Center, Inc., 222 Rosewood Drive, Danvers, MA 01923, 978-750-8400, fax 978-646-8600, or on the web at www.copyright.com. Requests to the Publisher for permission should be addressed to the Permissions Department, John Wiley & Sons, Inc., 111 River Street, Hoboken, NJ 07030, 201-748-6011, fax 201-748-6008, or online at http://www.wiley.com/go/permissions.

Limit of Liability/Disclaimer of Warranty: While the publisher and author have used their best efforts in preparing this book, they make no representations or warranties with respect to the accuracy or completeness of the contents of this book and specifically disclaim any implied warranties of merchantability or fitness for a particular purpose. No warranty may be created or extended by sales representatives or written sales materials. The advice and strategies contained herein may not be suitable for your situation. You should consult with a professional where appropriate. Neither the publisher nor author shall be liable for any loss of profit or any other commercial damages, including but not limited to special, incidental, consequential, or other damages.

For general information on our other products and services, or technical support, please contact our Customer Care Department within the United States at 800-762-2974, outside the United States at 317-572-3993 or fax 317-572-4002.

Wiley also publishes its books in a variety of electronic formats. Some content that appears in print may not be available in electronic books.

For more information about Wiley products, visit our web site at http://www.wiley.com.

Library of Congress Cataloging-in-Publication Data:

Berens, Carol.
  Redeveloping industrial sites : A Guide for Architects, Planners, and Developers / by Carol Berens.
     p. cm.
  Includes bibliographical references and index.
  ISBN 978-0-470-39824-1 (cloth : alk. paper); 9780470649305 (ebk); 9780470649312 (ebk); 9780470649329 (ebk); 978-0-470-95017-3 (ebk); 978-0-470-95041-8 (ebk)
1. City planning–Case studies.
2. Industrial sites. I. Title. II. Title: Strategies for reclaiming the urban landscape.
  NA9053.I53B47 2010
  711′.5524–dc22

                                      2010007961

Printed in the United States of America

10 9 8 7 6 5 4 3 2 1

CONTENTS

Acknowledgments vii
Introduction ix

SECTION 1: THE INDUSTRIAL LEGACY

Chapter 1: Patterns of Industrial Settlement — 3
Industry Arrives — 3
Transportation — 16
Why Industry Left and What It Left Behind — 18

Chapter 2: The Emergence of An Industrial Architecture and Aesthetic — 21
Industrial Buildings—Early Developments — 21
Industrial Architecture and the Modern Movement — 33
Industrial Aesthetic and Renovation — 39

SECTION 2: REDEVELOPMENT—AN OVERVIEW

Chapter 3: Project Planning Strategies — 45
Public Outreach: Requests for Proposals, Competitions, and Other Tools for Public Participation — 46
Government-Initiated Projects — 49
Owner/Developer-Initiated Projects — 58
Community-Initiated Projects — 65

Chapter 4: Public policy and Urban Evolution — 75
Urban Evolution, Rezoning, and Development Controls — 75
Retaining Industry — 88
Art as an Economic Development Engine — 95

Chapter 5: Environmental Remediation and Development — 115
Environmental Regulation — 115
Sustainability Issues — 121

Remediation and Landscape Architecture ... 122

Chapter 6: Development Financing Programs ... 131
Tax Credit Programs ... 132
Conservation Easements ... 140
Tax Increment Financing for Brownfields ... 144

SECTION 3: PROJECT TYPES

Chapter 7: Cultural Projects ... 149
Architecture as Advertising ... 149
Museums of Industry ... 150
Adaptive Reuse ... 171

Chapter 8: Residential, Commercial, and Mixed-Use Developments ... 183
Pioneering Projects ... 184
The Role of Single-Purpose Entities or Development Corporations ... 206
Self-Contained Projects ... 223

Chapter 9: Open Space and Parks ... 229
Creating New Parks—An Overview ... 233
Retaining History through Design ... 245
Waterfront Parks ... 257

Afterword ... 269
Appendix: Resources ... 271
Bibliography ... 273
Index ... 275

ACKNOWLEDGMENTS

Writing is said to be a solitary experience; however, writing a book requires the help and support of many people. For their encouragement, valuable comments and suggestions, I would like to thank Julie Pecheur, Judith Bing, Ellie Becker, and Tom Doramus. Jacqueline and Dick Loehr patiently listened to me and also trudged out to take some photos. Paula and Philip Forman were, as always, stalwart supporters, and Anne Asher, Patricia Zedalis and Michael Strasser continually encouraged me. My travels would have been much less enjoyable and productive if it weren't for the kind generosity of Diederik and Dana Advocaat in London and Bert and Malou Bakker in Amsterdam. In Paris, Patricia Bungener was always ready to set out to explore a new project. Patrick Weiller, Caroline and Jean-Francois Kindermans played hosts, guides, and translators in my journeys.

I greatly appreciate those who shared with me the details of their projects and the long paths to completion. Their recounting of the vagaries of the market, the endless public sessions, and the deadlines almost missed supplied invaluable information and conveyed the commitment required to undertake these projects. T. Allan Comp explained the complexities of establishing AMD&ART in Pennsylvania and the roles his impressive team played. Sarah Parker and Wendy Holmes of Artspace expressed their enthusiasm for and knowledge of creating artist housing. Tom Meyer and Jeff Scherer of Meyer, Scherer & Rockcastle, Ltd. outlined the perseverance required to sensitively renovate historic industrial structures to enhance today's use, while Ligeia Uker kindly endured my requests for images. John Grady at the Philadelphia Industrial Development Corporation explained the redevelopment process of converting a naval base to become a new part of its city. Anath Ranon of Cho Benn Holback + Associates Inc. patiently led me through the renovation of the flamboyant American Brewery building into a center for Humanim, and Henry E. Posko, Jr. and Cindy Plavier-Truitt of Humanim described the nail-biting experience of being first-time developers. Kara Cicchetti of the Architectural Heritage Foundation helped me understand how the renovation of the Washington Mills Building No. 1 was achieved. The enthusiastic recountings of Emma Keyte at Wilkinson Eyre Architects and Richard Bevins of the National Waterfront Museum in Swansea, Wales, made their project come alive. Aurèle Cardinal of the Groupe Cardinal Hardy explained how Montreal approaches redevelopment and the transformation of its waterfront, while Eve-Lyne Busque shepherded the images for me. The team at West 8—Adriaan Geuze, Jerry van Eyck, Nicolette Pot, and Dianne van

Essen—untangled the story of the redevelopment of Amsterdam's Eastern Harbor. Regina Meyer explained the massive rezoning process in Brooklyn, and Brian Coleman and Paul Parkhill of the Greenpoint Manufacturing and Design Center traced the history of their development efforts to protect industry in a corner of Brooklyn. Tim Jones of Artscape in Toronto shared the importance the support of art and artists to his city, and Liz Kohn helped greatly in finding the images to support that claim. Norman Hotson of Hotson Bakker Boniface Haden architects + urbanistes remembered how the design and planning ideas embodied in Granville Island were new and untested at the time and Noreen Taylor helped unearth some old images. Steve Soler of Georgetown Land Development Co., LLC explained how he worked with the local community to seek approvals. Scott Erdy from Erdy McHenry Architecture shared the urban vision of the developer of Piazza at Schmitds and Kristine Allouchery helped me with the images. Tom Ogara, a local developer, and Dan Reardon of the Trust for Architectural Easements walked me through a project that showed that it is as economical to renovate as to tear down.

In addition, I am indebted to all those individuals who went out of their way to help me with photographs and permissions: Dana Kelly of Bruner/Cott & Associates; the Mairie de Noisiel, France, and Nestlé France S.A.S.; Fiona Small of Urban Flash and Richard Cooper from Photoflex Studios; Lisa Rics from the Albert Kahn Family of Companies; Ellen Flanagan Kenny with Cummings Properties; Mikko Heikkinen of Heikkinen-Komonen Architects; Caroline Leroy at the Pavillon de l'Arsenal; Mathieu Génon at the ville de Nogent sur Marne; Stefania Canta at Renzo Piano Building Workshop; Timothy Sullivan at Design Collective, Inc; Iwan Baan and the Friends of the High Line; Paul Januszewski; Ronald L Glassman; Emily Winslow at Greenpoint Manufacturing and Design Center; Richard Johnson at the Torpedo Factory; Ron Solomon; Michael Van Valkenburgh and Adrienne Heflich from Michael Van Valkenburgh Associates, Inc.; Jeroen Hendriks of cepezed; Karen Utz at the Sloss Furnaces National Historic Landmark; Galia Solomonoff and Steven Harper of Solomonoff Architecture Studio; Andrew Zago and Laura Bouwman from Zago Architecture; Jo Oltman with Cambridge Seven Architects; Annie O'Neill; Brian Rose; Silke Schmidbartl at Latz + Partner; Shelley Seccombe; Lara Swimmer; Scott Fraser at Granville Island; Porter Gifford; Rob Watkins; Kevin Weber; Teresa Lundquist; Jill Slaight with the New-York Historical Society; and last but not least, Philippe Besnard.

INTRODUCTION

In New York City, along the Hudson River's edge where longshoremen once unloaded cargo and scows plied the waters, golfers now practice their drives and bikers cycle. In London, contemporary art hangs in a former power station. In Omaha, lofts and studios echo with the sounds of rock bands, not livestock. Throughout America and Europe, where smokestacks and warehouses once defined neighborhoods and even cities, today shade trees overhang park benches, museums attract streams of visitors, and new housing and office buildings bustle with activity.

For the last several decades, industry has been leaving the metropolitan centers of America and Europe in search of cheaper or more efficient places to produce goods. The swaths of derelict land and crumbling buildings left in its wake challenge architects, planners, politicians, and all those who are interested in the vitality of their cities. *Redeveloping Industrial Sites* describes the strategies that cities, towns, and determined individuals have used to turn their formerly uninhabitable and economically bereft land and buildings into parks, cultural destinations, commercial complexes, and vibrant neighborhoods.

Headlines mourning industrial abandonment have an eerie similarity; stories of reinventions, too, though varied in design and use, are related in process and intent.

These projects show how three powerful forces guiding development today—environmental concerns, renewed urban cores and historic preservation—work together to redefine the post-industrial city. The many successful strategies recounted in *Redeveloping Industrial Sites* have entailed decades of effort, multitudes of consultants, and concerted political will, to say nothing of extensive financial resources.

* * *

Although the course of industry has never been static, after WWII the advent of multi-laned highways swept industries from densely developed cities toward more sparsely populated suburban and rural areas where new industrial facilities had acreage over which to spread out and easy transportation access via the new arterial networks. Container ships demanded deeper, more mechanized ports than the traditional harbor cities could provide. It became cheaper to manufacture goods beyond the shores of America and Europe for consumption at home. Industrial ruins soon pocked cityscapes. Abandoned buildings with broken windows sagged amid the weeds on their bleak, forlorn grounds. Rotting piers silently testified to the past dynamism of waterfronts. Cities, former economic powerhouses of production and trade, reeled from these physical and financial blows. Cities, however, have proven more resilient than the naysayers' warnings.

Now there are decades-worth of achievements ranging from well-publicized projects to those only known by their neighbors. The problems and ultimate solutions of the often long and arduous development process are examined in this book. One of the puzzling questions that arose is determining how the redevelopment of industrial sites differs from the standard development project, if at all. The difference, however, isn't in process as much as in necessity. The vacant land and abandoned property of long-gone factories and failed projects stifle growth and effectively seal off sections of towns.

To look at some of the pioneering projects in the book is to see not only an apparently simpler era, but also to glimpse back at a time when economists and sociologists declared that "The City" was no longer a viable or even a necessary entity. Urban crime was rising, cities were going bankrupt, and urban investment evaporated. The uniform answer was to tear down what wasn't being used, a policy influenced by government funding. Urban renewal created new high-rise housing in low-rise neighborhoods or left parcels vacant when the money ran out.

Slowly, with the help of a few strong personalities, the post-industrial urban center was redefined. New York's artists rescued SoHo's nineteenth-century cast iron factories, and in so doing unwittingly created a new approach to economic development. Vancouver's Granville Island combined recreation, art, shopping, and industry to show that a layering of uses creates an active place people want to return to again and again. Paris turned industrial sites into parks in its eastern section to attract residents to formerly dreary neighborhoods. Baltimore's Inner Harbor brought people close to the waterfront.

While we may take these projects for granted today, they forecast differences in approach to urban redevelopment of their time and point the way to some of the large themes of successful conversions. Far from being the result of anonymous change, I was struck by how many projects were the visions of strong personalities who saw beauty and possibility where others saw deterioration and hopelessness. With every conversation I had with the people behind these developments, I was struck by how determined they were to achieve what they did, and that without this personal commitment and advocacy, these projects would not have gotten done.

The projects in the book were chosen for their transformative nature. Contrary to those in vibrant neighborhoods or exurban areas, these projects are critical to a city's financial health and urban fabric. Abandonment and ruin, often in strategic urban areas and comprising many acres, motivate the conversion of industrial sites. This is not an easy proposition, as these projects involve multiple layers not only of regulation and complicated financing, but also of history, emotion, and sometimes Byzantine land ownership patterns. These complexities lead to projects that entail government involvement as well as the cooperation of all development actors and can take years, even decades to complete. A long view and patience is required by all parties.

* * *

To look at these early projects and the more recent ones that have followed them, I've divided the book into three sections: A review of the industrial legacy, an overview of the redevelopment process and how it applies to industrial sites, and finally an examination of three broad project types—cultural, mixed-use, and parks and open space—and how they affect their cities.

The Industrial Legacy. Where industry settled and what kind of land it required play important roles in how these sites are redeveloped. Early industry needed water, either from the rivers or man-made canals and raceways, to power looms and other machinery. Cities developed around these economic generators as the workforce they attracted settled nearby. As a result, waterfronts in many industrial cites were inaccessible, reserved for working ports or factories. These areas now are in the greatest demand for recreation and residential use.

Industrial needs also spurred the development of new materials and building types for factories and the accommodation of machinery. The resulting spare forms of industrial buildings, their means of construction clearly expressed and not covered up, along with the prevalence of mass production of building elements greatly influenced designers and theories of modern architecture. Years after function or market changes rendered these buildings obsolete for their original use, the simple, wide-open spaces of factories and warehouses with their exposed structures ignited the imagination of new generations, who since the 1960s have been rescuing these buildings. Although there are many reasons for the reuse of these buildings and sites, the allure of the industrial aesthetic cannot be dismissed, and in many instances, is crucial to the success of their redevelopment.

Redevelopment Overview. Another overriding theme that arose in conversations with developers, architects and project proponents is that development has become more complex and expensive since those first transformative projects. Some of the early actors look back and are amazed at how simple, at least in memory, the process was when they first started tackling reuse issues. While the process might have been easier, the concepts were novel, requiring innovative thinking.

Some of the programs that evolved in response to redevelopment issues have added numerous layers of approvals, and mechanisms such as tax credits, which may make these projects economically feasible, but at the cost of complicated financing requiring a roomful of consultants. The rise in public participation in the form of community meetings and forums, as well as the increase in the use of competitions and requests for proposals for both design and development schemes, has led to a greater transparency and control of local projects, but has also added various approval levels and subsequently time to the development process. How well this process is managed is a key to success or failure. This more open public outreach has given individuals who see a potential project a way to galvanize their neighbors and the government. It also presents the same tools to their opponents.

Often, cities evolve on their own while government policy plays catch-up, legitimizing what's already taken place without its prior approval. The initially illegal colonization of SoHo in New York City by artists has had an immeasurable effect on the economic development approaches of cities, to say nothing of zoning laws. Almost every hub city in America today has an arts or warehouse district. This "SoHo Effect"—both the spontaneous establishment of new neighborhoods "discovered" by artists as well as their dislocation because of the rise in value of the surrounding real estate—has molded public policy as well as methods to deal with it. Both Minneapolis's Artspace and Toronto's Artscape were established to provide affordable artist space so that artists wouldn't be pushed out and have since expanded their development mandate. Other cities have changed their zoning laws to allow live/work areas and artists overlay districts to encourage artists to settle there.

As beneficial as the arts economy may be for cities, encouraging it must be balanced with other public policy decisions that relate to the character of the post-industrial city. Not everyone can be an artist. When a factory leaves, it also abandons its employees. How does a city maintain its tax base and middle class and retain industry? Several cities have addressed this problem through zoning and special industrial areas, with varying success. Should the property remain zoned industrial or has the march of time made that futile? Questions of public policy infuse these projects that affect more than their neighborhood but the character of a town.

Two major environmental milestones have facilitated, and in the best cases normalized, the redevelopment of industrial sites. The first is that after several years of pilot projects in the mid-1990s, federal brownfield legislation addressed legal liability and cleanup issues directly. In general, subsequent owners of property on which others caused pollution are not liable if an analysis is done beforehand and an agreement concerning cleanup can be reached with the authorities. The federal government as well as the states have initiated programs for voluntary cleanups in order to make these properties useful again. Along with these policies are grants to do this initial due diligence.

The second is the rise in green building techniques, such as LEED certification, that encourage the redevelopment of existing sites. Former industrial sites often have easy pedestrian access to existing transportation compared to new buildings on a new sites outside a city. LEED certification also promotes the reuse of existing materials and structures. Ironically, while environmental concerns with respect to industrial sites can be daunting, they're often more easily addressed than the larger issues such as retaining population, city identity, and finding a marketable use.

At one time, almost all projects were conventionally financed; however, it is striking how complex financing has become today. The days of the simple bank loan are past. Almost all projects now have multiple funding sources, many of which make the project feasible but also add complexity and lawyers' fees to the cost. The availability of tax credits for properties that are historical, old, or in underserved areas has had an inestimable effect on restoring industrial sites that fit in one of the allowable categories. Discussions of both environmental and financial aspects, however, are clouded by the variation in state and federal laws that are continually in flux as well as the ever-changing lending environment.

The increased role of not-for-profit groups in the redevelopment of industrial sites is noticeable. These groups, whether in the arts, social services or industry, are taking the initiative and becoming developers of their own projects. Rather than sitting back, they are building their own facilities. Groups with specific needs and outreach programs can use buildings that confound other developers. The Baltimore social service provider, Humanim, saw a building that stood vacant for over 30 years in an underserved neighborhood, undertook the renovation itself and invested the developer fee into the project. The Greenpoint Manufacturing and Design Center saw artisan manufacturing businesses squeezed out of their neighborhood in Brooklyn, struck a deal with the city to take over a rambling old rope factory, and became so good at what it does that it recently finished developing its fifth building. Stories of such not-for-profit group undertakings are scattered throughout the book and are an inspiration to those people and groups with little experience but a lot of drive.

Project Types. The projects in this book range from conversion of a small warehouse into a contemporary art gallery, to the remaking of the Amsterdam and London waterfronts, to the creation of a riverfront parks along the Hudson River in New York. Whether cultural, mixed-use or parks, change seldom comes quickly or without controversy. Some projects reflect investment spear-headed by government which is often the European model. Others are accomplished through collaborative efforts of government and private developer initiatives. In America, by far the most common story is that of a lone visionary or group of like-minded locals who see a rotting pier or an abandoned factory and then refuse to accept "no" as an answer in order to renovate it. From New York City to the small canal town, individual pioneers often initiate projects.

Two powerful economic development partners, art and tourism, often work together to rescue abandoned industrial buildings and sites and infuse life into moribund areas. Museums now operate in former mills, factories, and industrial wastelands in North Adams, Massachusetts; Tacoma, Washington; Minneapolis, Minnesota; and Swansea, Wales—just a few of the many cultural venues around the world that have pinned their hopes on being the key to their local and regional economic development renewal. Both large and small cities use their adaptive reuse projects—especially in the myriad mill museums that recount how things were made by the areas ancestors—to maintain a neighborhoods' sense of history in hopes of attracting visitors who will not only come for the exhibits, but remain to eat, shop, and perhaps stay overnight.

The large spans and raw spaces of these former industrial buildings are comfortable spaces for contemporary art, with its large sculptures that often don't fit into traditional museums. The unfinished surfaces of these converted buildings resemble artists' studios and are a perfect backdrop for this type of art.

Other cities pinning their hopes on creating tourist destinations opt for attention-getting structures that use their architecture as advertising. Merging the world of the culture and economic development, high-profile museums and cultural centers lure visitors to once run-down former industrial areas with attention-getting buildings. Because of the large areas and huge infrastructure investment required, these projects are almost always government-initiated with the costs and efforts justified by projected job generation and the economic benefit gained through increased tourism and newly burnished image.

In America, the availability of land has traditionally fuelled growth, with companies and people accustomed to picking up stakes to start afresh in less populous or polluted areas. In Europe and more densely populated American areas where open space is scarce, the call for refurbishing blighted urban areas and existing underutilized facilities more easily resonates. In these areas, there may be a strong desire to restrict building and keep undeveloped land undeveloped.

The last half century saw people and resources move from cities to newly created suburbs and beyond, especially in America. While this outflow has not abated, the allure of urban living spurred in part by the revitalization of formerly undesirable areas that offer previously unavailable services and amenities now attracts the young as well as retains those with growing families. Projects are fueled in no small part by the revival in importance of urban public space. Not long ago, the urban landscape consisted of private spaces and often dangerous streets. With the rise of urban crime, the will to maintain or support public space diminished, or indeed was disparaged as an inappropriate public goal. The increased safety of certain cities coincided, and in some ways was due to, reclaiming the public realm for the public.

The mixed-use and parks projects address this American urban resurgence that has encouraged the market for redevelopment of industrial properties within its cities, making the real estate investment worth the risk. This turnaround has also left communities thirsting for more public space and amenities. The modern urban lifestyle now includes active outdoor pursuits such as biking and kayaking as well as visiting museums, shopping, strolling in parks, or eating at an outdoor café.

The fine line between neighborhood improvement and gentrification is a recurring theme heard throughout the planning and redevelopment process of these sites, both in America and Europe. With some exceptions, neighborhoods adjacent to these industrial sites fall into two large categories: Either they are the last refuge of affordable housing in their cities or they were severely underused and then unofficially homesteaded by a particular group such as artists or newly arrived immigrants. As houses, stores and parks replace boarded-up factories, existing nearby residents and businesses fear becoming strangers in their own neighborhoods, unable to afford or adapt to changes and concerned that future stores and services will appeal to a different class or group of people. There is no fixed response to this situation, whether based on an unspecified fear of change or deep-seated class antagonism or other concerns, as will be seen throughout the projects presented. Even though these issues arise time and time again, they must be addressed specifically with each project.

The large issues of deindustrialization and globalization are directly tackled on local levels as individual communities are left to deal with the effects of these macroeconomic issues. Often what appears to be a controversy over a specific development is at root an argument about the past and what used to be, not purely a fight over the future. The stage is set for conflict. Each project creates its own advocates and opponents—union workers pitted against nearby residents or newcomers versus long-timers, for example—that may not be obvious at the outset as each project confronts anew the fallout of sociological as well as economic change.

* * *

Until the late 1950s, packages for Uneeda Biscuits and Oreos, printed in a factory in Beacon, New York, were loaded onto trains and delivered to the Nabisco Bakeries on West 16th Street in New York City. Today, that bakery is the Chelsea Market, a rambling mixed-use food market and office building, that printing plant is the museum, Dia:Beacon, and part of that railroad is called the High Line, New York City's newest park. How these and other projects were accomplished are explored in this book.

SECTION 1

THE INDUSTRIAL LEGACY

CHAPTER 1

PATTERNS OF INDUSTRIAL SETTLEMENT

Industry Arrives

Starting with the first factories, facilities for manufacturing and distributing goods produced indelible marks on the physical layout and sociology of cities, and indeed countries. Although the whys and wherefores of the Industrial Revolution are complex and beyond the scope of this book, the changes wrought by this historical event shaped the built environment, influencing how and where cities developed. The story of the impact of industry's arrival and establishment can be read from their remains today—urban population concentrations, patterns of transportation networks, and the evocative ruins of factory and warehouse buildings. Industry's monopolization of urban waterfronts, the wide swaths of land consumed to accommodate machines and production, and the system of roads, canals, and rails over which supplies and finished merchandise flowed shaped and often created these cities.

For trading purposes, industry first settled where it had easy access to rivers and oceans. When manufacture was local and craft-based, port cities, traditional centers of activity, received raw materials and distributed products through cavernous warehouses situated directly on the harbor. As technology developed, especially in America and in Britain, industry claimed waterfronts in order to harness water power. Mills that produced cotton, paper, lumber, and flour, among other items, needed water for energy, superseding the men or animals who previously turned the wheels. Initially, the mills took advantage of naturally occurring waterfalls that produced energy to power their waterworks. Developments that manipulated and controlled nature for more energy and consistent results quickly followed, as waterways were dammed and raceways created in order to moderate the effects of drought and generate a constant flow of power throughout the seasons.

Cities developed around these economic generators as the workforce they attracted settled nearby. Several cities and regions claim the mantle of the birth of the Industrial Revolution as manufacturing developments happened quite rapidly and often simultaneously, imposing similar physical effects on landscape and urban developments. It is commonly agreed, however, that Great Britain forged an important lead in the advancement of manufacturing, fueled in large part by an effective merchant fleet, natural resources, and dense population centers. In addition to these advantageous factors, inventions for cotton spinning and the mechanisms to power them propelled Britain into the forefront of textile manufacture and the development of cities. Manchester, quickly

HIGHLIGHTS OF INDUSTRIAL DEVELOPMENT	
1761	Bridgewater Canal built
1765	James Watt's patent of improved steam engine
1769	Richard Arkwright patented spinning yarn machine
1780s	Widespread use of steam power
1785	Edmund Cartwright's power loom
1791	*Panic of 1791*
1792	SUM and City of Paterson
1812+	Textile mills in Waltham
1819	*Panic of 1819*
1822	Lowell established
1825	Erie Canal opens / Lachine Canal opens
1825	Menier factory in Noisiel built
1880s	Town of Pullman started
1902	Ebenezer Howard's *Garden City* plan published
1917	Tony Garnier's *Cite Industrielle* plan published
1955	Air Pollution Control Act
1956	Federal-Aid Highway Act of 1956
late 1950s–1960s	Rise of container shipping
1963	Rachel Carson's *Silent Spring*
1963 & 1970	Clean Air Acts
1972	Clean Water Act
1974	Love Canal evacuation
1982	Times Beach evacuation
1980	"Superfund" Act
mid-1990s	Brownfield pilot programs
2002	Brownfield Revitalization and Environmental Restoration Act

dubbed "Cottonopolis," is a good example of how technology and manufacturing transformed an area from a sleepy town to a major industrial hub.

In America as in Britain, textile production led the way and the textile mills of New England were the vanguards of industrial development. The rest of the country quickly followed, adapting the milling process as industrial and agricultural progress dictated. The natural landscape was transformed to accommodate industry's needs, and towns formed or grew exponentially in response to this rise in development. Social and physical changes occurred as towns expanded around these mills, thus enabling laborers to live close to the factories where they worked. Some enclaves were built by mill owners, who established company towns complete with workers' housing, stores, and community facilities, while others occurred naturally and incrementally. The first centers of American industry, however, were planned.[1]

Although New England became America's major mill center, the first industrial planned town was located further south, in New Jersey. As early as 1791, Alexander Hamilton and a group of investors founded the Society for Establishing Useful Manufactures (SUM). It was created to implement his Congressional *Report on Manufactures*, which stressed the importance of creating an independent American manufacturing capacity to establish economic autonomy from Britain. Its first and only industrial foray created Paterson, New Jersey, high above the 77-foot-high Great Falls of the Passaic River (Figure 1.1). In 1792, SUM purchased approximately six acres from three existing landowners and, supported by a charter from the New Jersey State legislature exempting it from local taxes, hired Pierre Charles L'Enfant, the architect of Washington, DC, to design the town and develop a means of controlling the water power to run mills. His plan was ultimately scrapped as too complicated and costly, but an alternate series of canals and raceways was built to provide water storage to ensure adequate and uniform water power to the cotton mills.

INDUSTRY ARRIVES

Figure 1.1
At 77 feet high and 280 feet wide, the powerful Paterson Falls on the Passaic River in Paterson, New Jersey, were a source of power for some of the first mills that were developed on the East Coast. The 1912 SUM Hydroelectric Plant is on the left.
Photo by Martha Cooper, 8/15/1994 Working in Paterson Project Collection (AFC 1995/028), Archive of Folk Culture, American Folklife Center Project, Library of Congress

SUM's life span as a producer of goods was cut short by overreaching and mismanagement. Although no longer engaged in manufacturing after 1796, it controlled the land and leased water rights. The number of mills grew, requiring new sites and a reworking of the raceway and reservoir system to keep pace with the expansion. By 1910, the existing power was inadequate and SUM built a central hydroelectric plant, employing Thomas Edison's Electric Company, and increased production to 6,500 horsepower. The city of Paterson bought SUM's business and holdings in 1946.

When SUM exited the manufacturing arena others stepped in, and factories producing paper, firearms, silk, railroad locomotives, and other items soon joined the original cotton mills. In the 1840s, Paterson started fabricating silk, and when high tariffs were placed on imported textiles after the Civil War, it became the center for the domestic manufacture of silk ribbons and cloth. By the late 1880s Paterson was responsible for about half

Figure 1.2
Essex Mills Building in 1973, built in 1870s in Paterson, New Jersey, shows the drop from the middle to lower raceway.
Historic American Engineering Record, NJ-2-9; HAER NJ, 16-PAT, 16, Jack Boucher, Photographer, 1973

the domestic production of silk, giving rise to its moniker, "Silk City."

Meanwhile, in Waltham, Massachusetts, in the years after the War of 1812, another textile manufacturing community started, taking advantage of the power of the Charles River and British textile advances brought back to America by Francis Cabot Lowell, who had toured the textile mills in England.

Although perhaps an urban legend, the establishment of the Industrial Revolution in America may also be one of the first instances of industrial espionage. During a tour of England, Lowell is said to have memorized the design of Edmund Cartwright's power loom and then recreated and refined it with the help of others in Waltham, thereby bringing the method of manufacture to America's shores. Not only did the owners build upon the progress and standardization of the British manufacturing system and maintain comparatively clean and organized mills, they established boarding houses for their workers, in this case almost

Figure 1.3
Waltham, Massachusetts' Boston Manufacturing Co. building as it looked in 1979 from across Moody Street dam. The 1814 wing is on the left, the 1816 mill is on the right, and the 1843 addition connects the two.
Historic American Engineering Record, MA-54-5; HAER MASS, 9-WALTH, 4-5, Steve Dunwell, 1979

all women, or "mill girls" as they were called. This housing was comparatively safe, but strict rules for living and conduct were enforced and boarding fees charged.

The practice of providing housing and services for workers near mills, thus creating an industrial district, became known as the "Waltham System." It became the "Lowell System" when the community moved to Lowell in 1822 to take advantage of the more powerful waters of the Merrimack River, which was harnessed through a series of canals and dams. At the time of the relocation, Lowell's population was small and agricultural,

Factory Girls

The story of working conditions, the rise of the labor movement, and the influx of immigration obviously parallels the story of the arrival and departure of mills and factories and the impact on urban development. Despite their importance, these subjects are beyond the scope of this book. From time to time, however, it is valuable to acknowledge the people behind the machines who made the goods and materials and who were responsible for the rise of industry. The history of the labor movement is rich in song, and sometimes the simple lyrics bemoaning workers' fates illustrate difficult lives better than text. For example, while owners claimed their provided housing was a service, having their lives ruled by the factory bell and expensive boarding fees made the workers' lot difficult. Perhaps the truth of the mill girls' lives can best be visualized in songs, which they sang while working because they could not be heard above the din of the machines. An example of one of the many songs, entitled, "Factory Girl" follows:

No more shall I work in the factory, greasy up my clothes;
No more shall I work in the factory with splinters in my toes.
Pity me, my darling, pity me I say;
Pity me my darling and carry me away.[2]

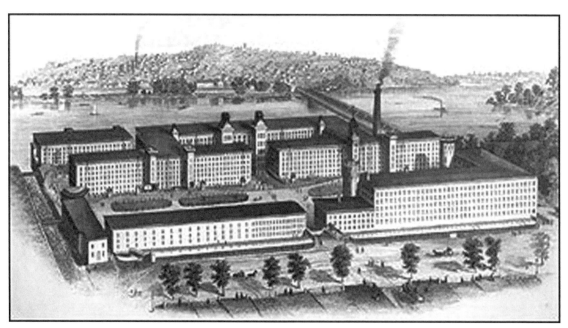

Figure 1.4
Lithograph of Boott Mills in Lowell, Massachusetts, shows the large mill complex sited against the Merrimack River. Many of the buildings have been converted to housing or are sites in the Lowell National Park (see Chapter 9).
Library of Congress, 1852

Figure 1.5
The design of this brick block on Dutton Street in Lowell, Massachusetts, is attributed to Kirk Boott and was one of the original boardinghouses built as part of the Merrimack Manufacturing Company (since demolished).
Historic American Building Survey MA-1151-1, Richard Graber Photographer, 1960s

and the boardinghouses and services were a recruitment tool to entice workers to this new area. The building of canals, whose owners leased water rights to the mills, also created a magnet for laborers, both from the northeast region and new immigrants, mostly from Ireland. Within 25 years, Lowell was the second-largest city in Massachusetts and America's largest industrial center. Its 5.6-mile-long canal system produced enough horsepower to support 40 mills. Not only were there over 10,000 workers in these mills, but they created the need for more support and other industrial developments as well as spurring the creation of other industries and putting Lowell at the front of industrial technology. In fact, Lowell is considered "the first major city in the United States designed and built for the needs of production."[3]

Figure 1.6
Slightly later version of the boardinghouses built in Lowell, Massachusetts, often sited near a canal or the river (circa 1840s; since demolished).
Historic American Building Survey MA-1153-2, Richard Graber Photographer, 1960s

The building of one or two mills was soon followed by other factories, making either the same or totally different goods. This was a pattern repeated throughout Europe and America. New factories tended to be built near each other, drawn by physical attributes such as a convenient energy source from a rapids-filled river, planned sites along man-made canals, conveniently located transportation, or the availability of a large number of factory workers, both skilled and unskilled. With each new factory more workers arrived, requiring places to live and shop, thereby fueling the development of industrial towns and cities. And thus the cycle repeated itself.

* * *

Figure 1.7
Worker housing in Pullman, formerly outside Chicago, Illinois, though plain, was sturdily built of brick and had cross-ventilation, gas service, and indoor plumbing among its amenities.
Historic American Building Survey IL-173-2, Jack E. Boucher, photographer, December 1977

In response to these changes to the environment and society, utopians and pragmatists, whether philosophers, ideologues, or factory owners, formed theories and established communities to address the location of industry in relation to other urban uses in order to provide a better life for workers and more "rational" cities. Many of these communities, including Lowell, not only aspired to the physical betterment of workers in terms of hygiene and education, but many also contained a moral component and a concern for propriety. The balance of work and leisure, as well as the contributions of workers to the industrial products, was the goal. Some also addressed the design of industrial buildings and physical layout of towns to accommodate workers and factories.

During the early 1880s, about 60 years after the city of Lowell was founded, George M. Pullman established his eponymous town in Pullman, Illinois, on approximately 4,000 acres about 13 miles south of Chicago. The town was built to support the factory that produced luxury sleeper railway carriages, with the expectation that quality housing, far from city pollution, would create a happy and productive workforce free from labor strife and agitation. Pullman was a planned industrial town, with factory buildings for manufacturing railway

Figure 1.8
Pullman, formerly outside of Chicago, Illinois, was a complete town that contained public buildings as well as factory and worker housing started in the 1880s. This is the Hotel Florence.
Historic American Building Survey IL-1018, Cervin Robinson, photographer, August 19, 1963 (ILL, 16-CHIG, 20-1)

cars using the steel of Chicago's mills, and also housing, public buildings such as a hotel, churches, schools, and parks. Meticulously planned by the architect Solon Beman (who designed all the 1,300 original buildings) and landscape architect Nathan Barret, the town plan was a grid with landscaped elements arranged throughout and provided for planted circles at some intersections, front yards, and tree-lined parkways, supplied by plants from its own greenhouse and nursery.

The more than 500 houses accommodated workers as well as professionals and company officers. Although designed in different styles to reflect class status as well as to lend visual variety to the streets, buildings were all constructed of brick and designed to have cross-ventilation, gas service, indoor toilets, and running water—a step above most worker housing of the day. Executive homes, located closest to the carriage plant, contained more ornament and detail than the plain worker houses.

Pullman expected the residents to be as fastidious as his town and controlled their lives by forbidding newspapers, speeches, and free public life. The town was maintained by the Pullman Company, which charged

INDUSTRY ARRIVES

Figure 1.9
Worker housing built by the Menier family in Noisiel, France, was part of a company town that included a town hall, school, and other public buildings that supported its chocolate factory. Photo circa 1900.
Collection Nestlé déposée en mairie de Noisiel. © Nestlé France et mairie de Noisiel

rent but also inspected homes and evicted renters for breaches of cleanliness. As a result of the Panic of 1893, business declined, and by the next year many employees were let go; however, their rents were not proportionately reduced. In an exemplification of the fact that architecture cannot trump sociology, the resulting Pullman Strike was a violent landmark in labor history; federal troops were brought in to break the strike because it disrupted rail and federal mail service. In 1898, the company town became part of the city of Chicago, when the Illinois Supreme Court ordered the Pullman Company to divest its ownership, a result of a commission's ruling after the strike that the town was "un-American."

In 1960, when Pullman was scheduled to be demolished for the construction of an industrial park, the Pullman Civic Organization formed to save the area. Subsequently, it became the Historic Pullman Foundation and has been working to restore the buildings and grounds and maintain public access. Pullman was designated a historic district by the National Park Service in 1970. It is now called the Pullman State Historic Site and the Illinois Historic Preservation Agency owns portions of the original Pullman factory, as well as the Hotel

Florence. Although the subject of continuing preservation and restoration work, people live there, some of whom are descendents of long-ago residents.

Europe also had planned industrial towns. When Menier Chocolate established itself in Noisiel, France, in 1825, it found itself in the same situation as the early Lowell factories. The town itself had few inhabitants, resulting in a labor shortage. Menier's solution was to create a workers' city—"a society of the future"—based upon progressive social ideals. Beginning in the 1870s, the Meniers launched an enclave complete with schools, library, stores, town hall (where a member of the Menier family would be mayor until 1959), and hotel. The public buildings were arranged around a central town square. Thirty years after its start, a home for retired workers was built. Soon, the company owned the whole town, and the Meniers considered their town the ideal workers' city and showcased it at the Universal Exposition of 1889 in Paris.

Brick housing was constructed along parallel streets, with the buildings staggered to allow as much air and light into the residences as possible. Approximately 300 houses were built, each containing two apartments with separate entrances, many with side and rear gardens. The wide tree-lined streets were lit by gas. Tenants were not allowed to purchase their houses, as Menier wanted to control their use for his factory workers. Rents, deducted from wages, were approximately 10 percent of the annual earnings of the heads of household. It was a paternalistic arrangement in which renters received free education for their children and free medical care, as well as access to public baths and entertainment venues.

In 1960, the housing was sold to a real estate developer, and today this former workers' housing is locally coveted houses. The European Route of Industrial Heritage considers it one of the best-preserved industrial communities in Europe.

The nineteenth century produced a hotbed of ideas and approaches to city planning and social theories aimed at taming the problems of industry's rise and saw no lack of utopian communities. Reacting to what was seen as the physical degradation of the land as factories encroached upon the rural landscape, these schemes also attempted to redistribute wealth and resources. The ideas behind Ebenezer Howard's Garden Cities and Tony Garnier's Cité Industrielle can been seen in today's concepts of zoning and city planning. That industrial areas are often set apart from the rest of their cities stems from these zoning approaches, and their integration into the urban fabric can be a major challenge to redevelopment.

The basis of Howard's idea of community control of land and profits was an attempt to integrate town and countryside, a method of controlling the movement of the urban, industrial population into the rest of the country. Dirty industry and overcrowded slums would be eliminated in these new cities, which were to be started from scratch. His 1902 *Garden Cities of Tomorrow* proposed towns built in concentric circles connected by axial roads. Public buildings and a commons were in the center, surrounded by grand avenues, housing, and industry. Farms were at the outer ring, a link to the untouched landscape. Residents would be assured of air and light and be close to work.[4]

Tony Garnier's Cité Industrielle, first exhibited in 1904 and later published in 1917, was a comprehensive proposal for the regulation of towns that clearly separated the city into areas reserved for work, living, traffic, and leisure, with each element isolated to allow for expansion. A green belt separated industry from the town. Garnier's town was sited on a river, the power source for a hydropower plant, and although connected by a railroad, the city was self-contained, the local economy capable of providing all. Garnier's Cité was a socialist haven; the public realm was responsible for the distribution of land, food, and necessities. There are great similarities between his plan and the workers cities such as Noisiel, specifically in the provision of housing and public facilities, such as schools and libraries, as well as the need for a river and rail transportation. Garnier's Cité was owned by the people, whereas workers cities were owned and controlled by industrial families.

Although neither of these plans was tested by reality, the ideas behind them periodically are revived and can

Chimney Pot Houses

Today renovated worker houses play an important role in addressing affordable housing issues, and though they are small and pose challenges, they have been converted, some quite cleverly. Chimney Pot Park in Salford, England was recently renovated by Urban Splash, an English company that renovates all types of industrial buildings mostly for residential use. Salford, along with its neighbor Manchester, was an early center of textile manufacture, especially of cotton and silk fabrics. These 349 houses, built during the nineteenth century, were typical of the cramped units created for mill workers in the nearby factories. Because of its distinctive rooftop landscape, it had a screen life as a working-class backdrop—first as the setting in the 1961 film *A Taste of Honey*, and then during the opening credits for the British television show *Coronation Street*.

Scheduled for demolition in 2002, local groups came to its rescue and it was recently renovated into ingenious housing, backed by government support and an innovative developer. The designers retained the exterior, in particular enhancing its name-giving chimneys and streetscape but gutting the interior. Siting two bedrooms on the ground floor and the living spaces on the second floor with kitchens and a newly created mezzanine level, this scheme opens up the attic to give the 1,000-square-foot houses a greater sense of space. The former rear yards contain a parking area which is terraced over to create communal backyard accessed from the upper floor living spaces. It received the government-bestowed Housing Design Award in 2008.

Figure 1.10
The renovation by Urban Splash of the Chimney Pot Park row houses in Salford, England, maintained the streetscape and modernized its namesake feature.
Image by Robert Cooper, Photoflex, Liverpool

be seen in the New Towns of the post-World War II era as well as some suburban enclaves. The principals of city zoning underline the need for rational development, the separation of uses, and integration of green space and development. As will be seen in the following chapters, the strict separation of zoning uses can make reuse of some industrial sites difficult, another barrier to overcome.

Transportation

Industry demands the ease of movement of ideas and goods: raw materials need to get to the factory, finished merchandise must be distributed, and fuel has to be delivered to factories to fire their furnaces. Before the rise

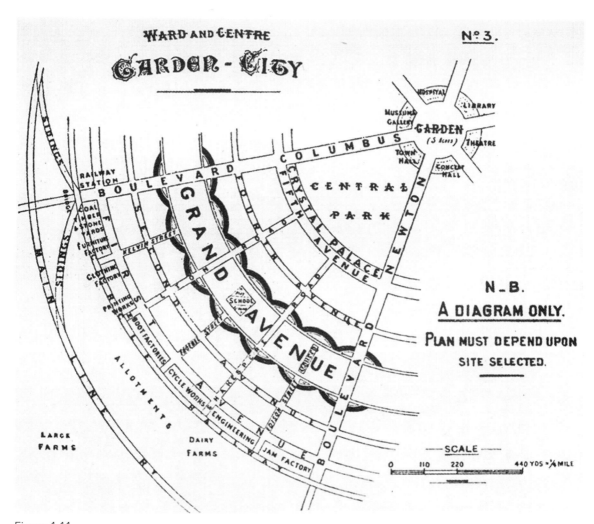

Figure 1.11
Ebenezer Howard's Garden City Plan proposed that towns be designed in concentric circles connected by axial roads that separated uses.

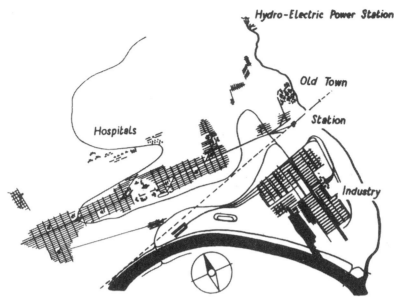

Figure 1.12
Garnier's Cité Industrielle was an early twentieth-century plan that also proposed separation of uses.

of industry, river boats and horse-drawn carriages along muddy roads sufficed for local trade. Entrepreneurs and budding industrialists lcreated canals to tame existing rivers and channel new routes for the inland movement of bulk goods. In Britain, canal construction soared, and in turn, created pockets of industry along its path. Canal boats were capable of moving more goods quickly and smoothly compared to any previous system that relied on the horse and cart.

Although canals were known and used by the Romans, and most obviously by the Dutch to control flooding in low-lying cites such as Amsterdam during the 1600s, it was the rise of industry and its unquenchable desire for trade that spurred canal building and refinement in both Europe and North America. The advantages of a navigable water network became evident as soon as the first canals were built. Between the end of the eighteenth century and the beginning of the nineteenth, canals transformed the countryside and transportation systems, easing internal commerce wherever they were built.

British canals were originally designed to connect rivers, by supplementing and feeding into the existing transportation network. As these waterways became more linear and sophisticated, their network changed the face of the country's landscape. The first canals, such as the Bridgewater Canal that opened in 1761, were quite effective in hauling coal from the mines in northern England to fuel the factories of Manchester's burgeoning textile industry. Horses trod along towpaths on the sides of the canals and hauled barges, an economical and smooth way of moving heavy as well as fragile goods. In England, as in other European countries, canals were privately built and tolls were collected to repay investors. These canals were not built according to any master plan, but according to the will and finances of private companies, often providing redundant services and creating conflicts. (The canal system was nationalized in 1948, along with the railways.)

In 1825, when New York Governor De Witt Clinton opened the Erie Canal, the most famous man-made waterway in the United States, he connected the Hudson River and New York City in the east with Lake Erie in the west, and along with it the agricultural riches of upstate New York and the heartland. Originally 363 miles long, 40 feet wide, and only 4 feet deep, the canal's success demanded that it be expanded many times. It and other American canals not only transformed their termini, but also all points in between, attracting industries and immigrants along their routes.

Concerned that the Erie Canal would draw the American Midwest trade to New York City, the Canadians built the Lachine Canal to connect the Great Lakes with the Atlantic Ocean, thereby avoiding the Lachine Rapids and simultaneously changing the character of Montreal. Finished the same year as the Erie Canal and financed by the founder of the Bank of Montreal, it originally spanned 8.7 miles and needed seven locks (subsequently reduced to five) from the port of Montreal to Lake Saint-Louis. However, more trade and larger boats demanded progressive expansion that lasted until the 1880s. As with the Erie Canal, the Lachine spawned smaller canals, such as the Welland Canal, that connected Lake Erie with Lake Ontario and allowed ships to bypass Niagara Falls.

The Lachine Canal allowed Montreal to progress from a trading city to an active industrial base and one of the largest ports in North America. The changes in elevation that required the locks on the Lachine Canal also provided hydropower for burgeoning industry. A system of headrace and tailrace hydraulic canals was built on both sides of the Lachine Canal. Along these canals and falls, industrial lots were developed and sold for the building of wood, flour, and cotton mills, and factories specializing in iron and tool manufacture. Later into the twentieth century, larger industries specializing in chemical and steel production flourished. The industrialization of the banks of the Lachine Canal typified industrial expansion and the concentration of industry into clusters in certain areas with access to easy trade routes and cheap power. Industrial districts formed as businesses needed each other's goods and could benefit from the available pool of workers.

For several decades, Montreal was the industrial powerhouse of Canada, with nearly 15,000 ships passing through the Lachine Canal annually before the Depression of the 1930s. Although industry still has a presence along the canals, much of the industry that grew on its banks eventually led to the canal's demise: industrial development hogging its edges prevented canal expansion. The St. Lawrence Seaway to the east opened in 1959 and siphoned off much of the maritime trade from both the Erie and Lachine canals. The Lachine Canal closed to shipping in 1970.

* * *

With the increase in both the volume of goods and the need to transport them faster and over longer distances, canals became outmoded and were soon superseded by railroads, many of which were built along canal rights-of-ways. The surviving canals, however, remain an evocative and still-working remnant of the pervasive push toward industrialization. As will be seen in subsequent chapters, some of these renovated channels are among the more successful recreation and tourist attractions, their banks filled with strollers and picnickers rather than barge-pulling mules and horses, and the old warehouses and factories replaced with housing and museums.

Why Industry Left and What It Left Behind

Industry and change have been synonymous since the spinning jenny produced its first thread. Populations move. Markets are fickle. Technology sows seeds of its own progress and forces industry to adapt as one innovation quickly supplants another. Different technologies and patterns of behavior continually replace the old. A trip along the Erie Canal, for instance, is an interesting microcosm of how industry has changed over the years, a catalog of now-defunct nineteenth- and twentieth-century products. One passes towns once famous for making brooms (Scotia), rags (Amsterdam), cotton sacks and paper bags for shipping on the canal (Canajoharie), matches (Frankfort), bushels for apples (Middleport), knit goods (Utica), and salt for food preservation (Syracuse). A prickly plant formerly required to finish wool fabric propped up the New England textile industry, and put Skaneateles on the map for just enough time to produce a few local moguls. Now only its namesake, Teasel Street, remains. The typewriter (Syracuse) will soon join this list. Over the past 60 years this process has continued, and accelerated.

* * *

Technological advances after World War II combined with a population boom and a desire to apply these advances to improve everyday life. Industry flourished, supplying war-weary populations with the means for becoming modern.

Unfortunately, this newly energized activity was accompanied by the blatant disregard to the land, sea, and air around it. Rivers became de facto sewage systems when industry merely dumped one chemical byproduct after another into them without looking back. Drums of waste products were buried on factory properties and chimneys spewed soot into the air. Slowly, postwar sensibilities became aware of a newly energized sense of the environment, emphasizing the dangers of pollution and environmental degradation.

As lifestyles and expectations changed, industries that had built up these cities were seen as interlopers in their own neighborhoods. At the same time, the roads that improved the movement of goods also served to disperse the population. In America, government policies encouraged the building of suburbs, further emptying cities. Industry acted as the population did—if still viable, it left urban centers and resettled miles away from its traditional base. If obsolete, it merely closed its doors. In either case, it became easier to abandon decaying industry than to clean it up and replace it.

The heavy industry that had changed the face of North America and Europe since the Industrial Revolution moved en masse to other continents over the latter years of the twentieth century, its products either superseded or now extinct from lack of need. This movement of industry as it searches for cheaper or more convenient places to operate continues apace. As a result of changes in manufacturing and transportation spurred by World War II, ships became larger, requiring deeper ports. More efficient methods to increase cargo capacity and prevent theft at the docks hastened the need for container ports, which required not only larger harbors but acres of land rather than mere port-side warehouses. Original city ports could not provide the facilities now required. As a result, the ports moved elsewhere—if only across the river.

Government policies in America, quickly imitated in Europe, encouraged the building of larger roads to avoid the small towns and cities, changing traffic patterns for both residents and commerce. Delivery by truck became more efficient, quickly making obsolete the cities that had made their mark first by the waterfronts of the sea and canal and then by rail.

Industry's exodus has dealt a severe blow to urban areas, now empty shells of their former selves, pockmarked with vacant, deteriorating buildings, victims of the transformation of the labor force and changing methods of distribution of goods. Left in their wake were rotting piers, abandoned factories, and empty, collapsing warehouses, often near city centers. How cities have been restoring these properties involves many steps and much time, as will be seen in the following chapters.

ENDNOTES

1. In America, whether to industrialize or not was a subject of controversy and disagreement between Hamiltonians and Jeffersonians, the latter envisioning an American economy based upon agriculture,

importing manufactured goods from Europe and avoiding the pitfalls of industrialized urban hubs. According to Thomas Jefferson, manufacture, when it existed, should be local and cater to the agrarian economy.
2. Evelyn Alloy, *Working Women's Music* (Somerville: New England Free Press, 1976), p. 8.
3. Dennis Frenchman and Jonathan S. Lane, *Discussion White Paper: Assessment of Preservation and Development in Lowell National Historical Park at Its 30-Year Anniversary* (2008), p. 3.
4. This idea is being revisited today in an effort to promote "smart growth" and to prevent suburban sprawl. Some towns in agricultural areas are promoting a similar "conservation area" designated to remain open and unbuilt at the outskirts of the town center, so that one enters the town through a country landscape, not a road lined with strip malls.

CHAPTER 2

THE EMERGENCE OF AN INDUSTRIAL ARCHITECTURE AND AESTHETIC

As the products and processes of manufacture developed and changed, buildings and physical plants assumed new forms and used new materials and methods of construction to respond to evolving needs. The resulting spare forms of industrial buildings and clear expression of materials and equipment, along with the prevalence of mass production of construction elements greatly influenced designers and theories of modern architecture. The history of industrial architecture is beyond the scope of this book; however, a short review of the milestones of early industrial building design and goals sheds light on the structures and complexes encountered in the redevelopment process today. The innovations developed by both Albert Kahn and Ernest L. Ransome are explored as examples because they illustrate how architects brought about some of the advances of the industrial age.

The industrial aesthetic has often been more admired by architects and artists than the public at large; however, the clean lines and expansive volumes that were an outgrowth of these design ideas now please the modern eye and aesthetic, a key to renovation success.

INDUSTRIAL BUILDINGS—EARLY DEVELOPMENTS

Industrial architecture has two main goals: efficiency and safety. Improved economy in turning raw goods into manufactured items and in the construction of the buildings themselves, as well as the prevention of fire with the resulting loss of life and materials propel the design of warehouses and factories. The germ of the modern industrial aesthetic is seen in the simple mill buildings of England and New England that date from the late 1700s. The first mills, precursors of the modern factory, were straightforward wooden or masonry buildings with repetitive forms and rhythmic openings. As lone buildings, these mills fit into the landscape, their scale and materials making little impact on their surroundings. The conglomeration of these mills when expanded into manufacturing hubs, however, monopolized and blocked the rivers and canals that fed the millwheels that provided power for their machines.

These first mills reflected building technology of their time and responded to the realities of fire and workplace safety. In the days before electricity, flooding workspaces with as much daylight as possible was of paramount importance. In both England and America, the first centers of mill activity were in the north, where days are short and natural light limited in supply during a good part of the year. Long and narrow, these buildings had open and unobstructed internal spaces to accommodate as many machines and workers as possible. Their narrowness not only allowed light into their centers, but also efficiently enabled machines on both sides of the building to be powered from a single shaft down the center of a floor.

Relying upon water power from adjacent rivers or canals, these buildings by necessity sidled up against the riverbanks or nestled in the landscape. Their size was determined by machinery as well as the strength and size of the waterwheels. The taller the building, the greater the energy needed to reach the top floors, and the bigger and more powerful the wheel.

Millwrights and engineers generally built these structures; however, architects were also involved in their design. Early industrial buildings were simple because their utilitarian nature placed them low in the social—and therefore aesthetic—hierarchy. From the earliest times, buildings generally reflected their social importance. The more esteemed a building's function, such as churches, public buildings, and royal structures, the more ornament was used; service buildings were strictly no-frills.

Most eighteenth- and early-nineteenth-century mills were multistoried buildings that combined brick or masonry bearing walls with heavy timber structural frames to obtain the largest column-free interior spaces possible. As the ultimate utilitarian places, their design features not only encouraged an efficient work process but aimed to prevent fires. The fear of fire was so prevalent that insurance companies shaped much of the early architecture. The Factory Insurance Associations' 1905 guidelines for building design and materials sound like a modern manifesto. They discouraged interior wall coverings as well as

HIGHLIGHTS IN PRE-WAR DEVELOPMENT OF INDUSTRIAL ARCHITECTURE

1837	*Panic of 1837*
1840s	Use of cast iron
1854–1858	Les Halles built in Paris
1857	*Panic of 1857*
1871	Chicago Great Fire
1873	*Panic of 1873*
1870–1880s	Cast Iron SoHo
1872	Menier Mill at Noisiel
1879	Invention of the fire sprinkler
1880s	Rise in use of steel
1884	*Panic of 1884*
1889	Eiffel Tower opens
1893	*Panic of 1893*
1897	Ransome's Pacific Coast Borax building
1901	*Panic of 1901*
1902–1906	Larkin Complex–Buffalo
1903	Ransome's United Shoe building Founding of Ford Motor Company
1905	Kahn's Packard Building No. 10
1906	San Francisco earthquake and fire
1907	*Panic of 1907* Founding of Deutscher Werkbund
1908	Adolf Loos, *Ornament and Crime*
1908	Ford Highland Park Plant
1908–09	Behrens' AEG High Tension Factory (Berlin)
1911	Fagus Shoe-Last Factory
1913	Gropius article on American tour
1916–1932	Kahn's Rouge River Plant
1919	Founding of the Bauhaus
1923	*Vers une architecture* (1927 in English)
1929	*Stock market crash; Great Depression*
1936–39	Wright's Johnson Wax Company

ornament on building exteriors; sought open, partition-free interiors to facilitate extinguishing fires; advocated flat roofs and frowned upon attics; encouraged large windows to facilitate fire suppression; and recommended that floor areas be separated from interior stairs. The resulting stair towers simultaneously freed up floor space and, more importantly, lessened the possibility of fires from spreading floor to floor.[1] Flat facades punctuated by a stair tower became a familiar building type, especially in New England. Whatever ornament, if any, was located at the towers, which were sometimes capped with fanciful roofs or cupolas to declare the owners' identity.

Even with these precautions, the risk of fire in these mills intensified, especially in textile factories when oil from machines dripped and leaked through the wooden floors and combined with cotton dust and lint. All major cities saw multiblock conflagrations, which spurred the development of fire and safety codes. In addition to the introduction of internal sprinkler systems in the late 1880s, the search for affordable fireproof or retardant materials led to the use of concrete and steel (when encased), both of which had the added advantages of being able to support more weight.

The Rise of Cast Iron

An interesting way station between wood and steel in the search for fire-resistant material that could support heavy loads is cast iron.[2] Mainly seen now in nostalgic pictures of iron and glass pavilions of international expositions or in various historic neighborhoods, such as New York's SoHo Historic District, cast iron was a popular material for many types of commercial and industrial structures built in the mid-1800s throughout America and Europe. Cast iron, an iron alloy with a high carbon content, is easily molded at high temperatures into a wide variety of decorative and structural forms. The use of cast iron in industrial buildings is modern more in engineering than in architectural style, as it was molded into fanciful shapes or those recalling the forms and details of classical architecture.

Much stronger in compression than in tension, slender columns made from cast iron could support heavy loads. When used in textile mills, the exterior of these buildings remained brick or stone and the cast iron was used on the inside. Although often encased with masonry or tile in order to be fireproofed, even exposed it was a major step toward safety above wood. Its ability to be shaped and cast into repetitive units and installed at the site was invaluable for commercial or public buildings. Especially under the development of its primary promoter, James Bogardus, cast iron epitomized methods of prefabrication, mass production, and use of identical interchangeable parts.[3] It became a favorite for pavilions at international exhibitions because it was easy and quick to assemble. Cast iron enabled the large open structures such as the 1851 Crystal Palace in London, in which the construction was clearly expressed.

Because of its ability to sustain large loads, cast iron became a desired material for urban storefronts because it allowed large street display windows and was easy and inexpensive to assemble. Many American downtowns were filled with these facades, most of which have been demolished during urban redevelopment efforts. Some cast iron districts remain, however. In addition to SoHo, the National Trust for Historic Preservation estimates that 44 percent of the buildings in the Strand/Mechanic National Historic Landmark District of Galveston, Texas, have cast iron

Figure 2.1
Cast iron, although a modern material, often was molded into classical forms as seen in this SoHo storefront detail in New York City.
Carol Berens

Figure 2.2
The diagonal puddled wrought iron bracing supports the decorative glazed brick and tile of the 1872 Menier Chocolate factory in Noisiel, France, whose elaborate design disguises one of the first curtain walls.
Carol Berens

storefronts or facade elements. Its mid-nineteenth-century buildings were seriously damaged by Hurricane Ike in 2008, and its endangered cast iron architecture made the National Trust for Historic Preservation's 2009 list of Most Endangered Historic Places. Also on the National Register of Historic Places are the West Main District of downtown Louisville, Kentucky, and Portland, Oregon's Skidmore/Old Town Historic District, both of

Figure 2.3
The refurbished rotunda is located in an early twentieth century reinforced concrete building called "The Cathedral" constructed on the former Menier Chocolate factory complex in Noisiel, France and now the headquarters Nestlé France.
Nestlé France S.A.S.

whose concentration of cast iron buildings rivals New York's.

One of the more structurally innovative buildings to use iron—both cast and wrought—is the mill at the Menier Chocolate factory in Noisiel, France, designed by Jules Saulnier in 1872. The building, and indeed the entire complex, breaks the industrial standard of unornamented buildings. The building spans the Marne on transverse and longitudinal tubular beams with riveted flanges on top of stone piers. The two first stories have two rows of interior cast iron columns running down the center, however, the top floor,

> the third, is column-free, suspended from the attic floor from roof trusses. The highly decorative and polychromatic facade of glazed brick and tile is an early curtain wall that assumes no weight but its own and is held in place by an exposed diagonal grid of puddled wrought iron bracing. Not only is the structure exposed, but it also plays an important decorative role and is incorporated into the design. The site is now a corporate headquarters for Nestlé France and is a national *Monument Historique*.
>
> Several years later in 1886, Gustave Eiffel started his eponymous tower in Paris that, although not an industrial building, influenced the mass production methods of building as well as pointed the way toward an aesthetic that glorified unadorned, exposed structures. Created for the 1889 Universal Exposition celebrating the centennial of the French Revolution, the tower was a "kit of parts," composed of fabricated angles, standard sections, flat bars, and tee sections of cast and puddled iron manufactured in Eiffel's factory and assembled and riveted onsite. The tallest structure in the world when it was built was constructed in three years and remained unsheathed—"naked" to the eyes of the time. Originally scorned as unfinished, it and other engineered buildings of its time pointed the way for an aesthetic that extolled the clear expression of structure.

Albert Kahn and Ernest L. Ransome

New ways of producing energy spurred the growth of both buildings and machinery, necessitating structures that could support more weight, span greater distances and, of course, be better fireproofed. In addition, the manufacturing process was expanding beyond textiles, demanding more flexible and adaptable layouts. The answer would come from a material that had been known centuries before but had been forgotten and whose strength needed the addition of a new element, steel, that would enhance its function: reinforced concrete.

Few architects in America had more influence over the aesthetics and development of industrial buildings and the glorification of the functional than the self-educated Albert Kahn, along with two of his brothers, Julius and Moritz.[4] Born in 1869 in Germany, Kahn came to America with his family in 1881 and settled in Detroit, the soon-to-be home of the automobile industry. After a year of European travel, he started his own firm with partners in 1895. His younger brother, Julius, was an engineer and inventor who made his mark developing a construction system which he patented as the Kahn System of Reinforced Concrete. Julius also was an entrepreneur and started the Trussed Concrete Steel Company (later to become the Truscon Steel Company, and then the Republican Steel Corporation).

Although he had little experience designing factories, one of Albert Kahn's first industrial clients was the Packard Motor Car Company. (Kahn had recently remodeled the house of its president.) With the help of his brother, he employed the Kahn System of Reinforced Concrete to create the 1903 two-story Packard Building No. 10, the first automobile factory to use reinforced concrete. (The previous nine Kahn-designed buildings were of standard mill construction.) The building boasted of 30-foot spans which provided great flexibility for changes in production on the interior. This concrete frame, clearly expressed on the exterior, had glazed openings to the

Figure 2.4
Packard Building No. 10 (1903) in Detroit, Michigan, by Albert Kahn was the first automobile factory to use reinforced concrete. Originally two stories, the top two were added at a later date.
Photo courtesy of the Albert Kahn Family of Companies

ceiling permitting as much daylight onto the factory floor as possible. Its best characteristic, of course, was that it was fireproof.[5]

Kahn designed buildings with an eye toward interior flexibility in order to complement and enhance the manufacturing process. The building's exterior was a continuation of the interior. Kahn was a businessman's architect and was concerned with the work process and ease of material flow. Kahn's approach to designing for manufacturing anticipated Henry Ford's, and he was ideally suited to become Ford's architect. In 1909 Ford commissioned Kahn to do the Automobile Assembly Building in Highland Park outside Detroit. During these early days of manufacturing there were two main theories of building for industry—housing different operations in separate buildings specifically designed for those operations or having the entire plant in one building. Kahn preferred the latter as it allowed for more flexibility, and

Figure 2.5
Ford Motor Company—Highland Park (1909–1918) facility by Albert Kahn was a concrete frame building with steel sash windows and a pitched glass roof and clerestory at the top floor.
Photo courtesy of the Albert Kahn Family of Companies

by eliminating the number of exterior walls, these larger buildings were cheaper to build.[6]

Building factories in which workflow determined operations demanded flexible layouts that could change as the manufacturing process changed. Kahn soon championed single-story buildings for their flexible and adaptable use. Light entered through clerestories or monitors on the roofs which were supported by wide-span structural grids. These buildings required more acreage (in fact, the early Model T factory was on a 230-acre plot) and also a change of material—thus the rise in the use of steel. Steel not only was mass produced but could span great distances compared to cast iron or concrete, thereby providing the flexibility required for the ever-changing manufacturing processes.

Electric and coal-fired power combined with advances in mass production developed for the heavy steel and automobile industries allowed greater flexibility for buildings and their siting. Soon the one-story factory that spread over many acres was deemed more efficient than multi-storied buildings. Perhaps one of the most influential was Ford's River Rouge factory, designed by Albert Kahn and spread over 2,000 acres on previously untouched bottomland—property that Henry Ford had bought. Industry indelibly changed the landscape and population patterns, especially in America,

Figure 2.6
Ford Motor Company's Rouge Plant embodied Kahn's belief in having the entire operations occupy one building which allowed for flexibility of manufacturing. Light entered through roof-top monitors.
Photo courtesy of the Albert Kahn Family of Companies

but also throughout Europe, by moving outside compact cities to where land was plentiful. This relocation demanded a new and expanded road and rail system for materials and workers, a phenomenon reviewed in Chapter 1.

During the early 1900s, Kahn wasn't the only architect adapting reinforced concrete for industrial buildings and making strides in increasing spans and weight-bearing capacity. Ernest L. Ransome is generally credited with being the architect of the first reinforced concrete factory building, the Pacific Coast Borax Refinery in 1897 in Bayonne, New Jersey. This simple utilitarian building is not architecturally distinguished, but it could accommodate heavy machinery on all floors. It achieved fame for surviving a 1902 fire in which all elements of the building were destroyed except the concrete structure, thereby

INDUSTRIAL BUILDINGS—EARLY DEVELOPMENTS 31

Figure 2.7
Ford Motor Company—Rouge Complex by Albert Kahn which occupied over 1,200 acres was a defining moment in the development of the assembly line. Various operations were within one-story buildings, requiring the plant to spread over a lot of land and be located outside the city center.
Photo courtesy of the Albert Kahn Family of Companies

cementing this material's importance in industrial architectural development.

In 1903, Ransome started a project for the United Shoe Machinery Corporation in Beverly, Massachusetts, and created a building that clearly expressed its structure on the outside and sported simple decorative details. The wide window bays are filled with industrial sash windows to allow natural light into the building. Looking back in 1977, the New York Times' architectural critic, Ada Louise Huxtable, admired the building's quiet importance and stated that it had a "singular assurance and surprising grace."[7] This building also played an important role in the cross-Atlantic development of the modern movement due to its relationship with the owners of

Figure 2.8
Ernest Ransome's 1903 sprawling, reinforced concrete factory for United Shoe Machinery Corporation in Beverly, Massachusetts, is a proud backdrop to the assembled employees. Around 1910, as well as during WWII, the factory employed approximately 4,500 people (*photo date unknown*).
Photo courtesy of Cummings Properties

Figure 2.9
Cummings Properties renovated "The Shoe" into an office complex in Beverly, Massachusetts in 1996 through Tax Incremental Financing (TIF) and worked with the Commonwealth of Massachusetts to create an Economic Opportunity Area to offer benefits to tenants. Although the courtyards are gone, the original structure peeks out in between the glazed infill wings.
Photo courtesy of Cummings Properties

the German Fagus shoe last company. The founder's son worked at United Shoe for a year before bringing ideas back to Germany to be incorporated into a new factory, which, although constructed entirely differently, was designed by Walter Gropius and Adolf Meyer, proponents of the International Style.

Industrial Architecture and the Modern Movement

Industrial forms, materials, and aesthetics had an incalculable influence on architects and the direction of early modern architecture. Industry and its processes inspired and continue to engage the imagination of artists and architects: from the screed against ornament by Adolf Loos to the design explorations of the Bauhaus and the sleek lines of the International Style to the explicit expression of construction elements in the work of Rogers Stirk Harbour + Partners.

Industrial architecture, especially in America, showcased a simplicity that was expressed on the exterior by unadorned flat surfaces, whether in brick, stone, or wood. While these buildings were obviously required for the rise of industry, their designers were often anonymous and these structures remained outside the purview of traditional architectural practices. Until the beginning of the twentieth century, architectural theory and styles concentrated on important civic and commercial buildings or private residences.

As industrial uses grew in complexity and importance, schools of design and architectural theory emerged to respond to the challenges that this development posed. Charged with defining new forms for the ever-changing factories, industrial storage, and transport facilities, architects carved pathways toward defining the future. Around the early 1900s, the factory was seen as a building type deserving of architectural treatment in order to enhance the production of goods and dignify the workplace, as well as forge corporate identities.

In 1907, the Deutscher Werkbund was founded to improve the quality and design of Germany's manufactured goods to compete with its European neighbors. The Werkbund stressed the importance of good design, including architecture, to companies as a way of conveying their identity as a form of advertising.[8] Although the Werkbund was originally based upon craft and art, many of Germany's most influential architects passed through it including Peter Behrens, Walter Gropius, and Mies van der Rohe. During its existence, two influential industrial buildings were designed by its members: Peter Behrens' AEG turbine factory and Walter Gropius and Adolf Meyer's Fagus shoe last factory.

Behrens, as architect and designer to the German national electric company, AEG, built the high-tension turbine factory (1907) in Berlin. Regarded as a "temple to industrial power"[9] this building had a monumentality based upon neoclassical principles. For the Fagus factory, Gropius and Meyer eschewed this masking of structure, however grand, and strove to clearly express its materials, an important hallmark of the modern aesthetic as applied to all buildings, not just factories. As a result, in discussions of industrial buildings, it is often difficult, or in fact immaterial, to separate architectural advances from engineering ones.

One year later, in 1908, Adolf Loos, a Viennese architect, wrote in his provocative essay titled "Ornament and Crime," that industrialization had changed the nature of the relationship between objects and their creators as well as the users. Craftsmen produced individual objects and imbued their work with ornament and designs that represented who they were. With mass production, the generation of the design idea was transferred to the makers of the mold from which the products were made. The change of process should, according to Loos, cause a change in aesthetic. As he stated, "I have discovered

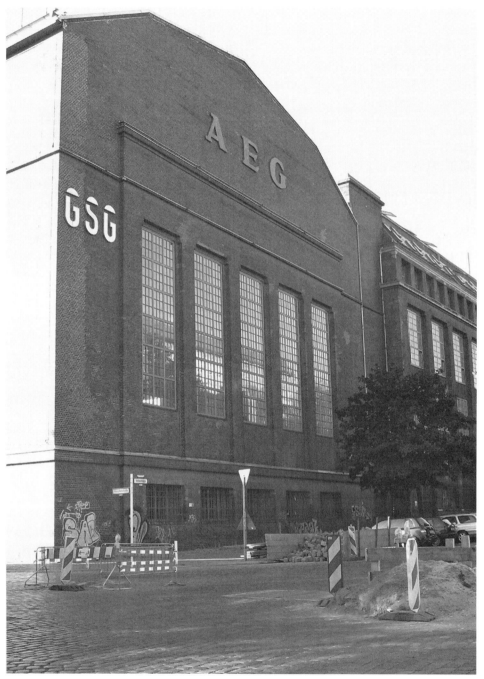

Figure 2.10
Peter Behrens turned his 1907 AEG turbine factory in Berlin, Germany, into a neoclassical monument, extolling the electrical industry while hiding the structure.
Carol Berens

the following truth and present it to the world: *cultural evolution is equivalent to the removal of ornament from articles of daily use.*"

The controversy that ensued revolved around his assumption of a progressiveness to human aesthetic development—the less educated and the lower classes (he included his countrymen as well as those in the developing world) needed their objects to have more ornament; the more educated preferred the simpler, machine-made lines. The "crime" referred to products that did not reflect their production. According to Loos, decoration should not be applied but could derive from the innate nature of the materials—for example, through the use of highly veined stone or grained wood.

This essay set up a dynamic that continues to resurface. Those who like simple, unadorned buildings and objects with exposed structure are assumed to be an elite group of artists and architects. When Gropius organized a collection of photographs of American architecture, he concentrated on industrial buildings and bemoaned that "people simply don't understand that plain, utilitarian buildings can be beautiful."[10]

While America looked toward Europe for theory and precedent, it greatly impressed some European architects such as Le Corbusier, Walter Gropius, and Erich Mendelsohn, who praised American industrial architectural achievements and chronicled them in their writings. Exploring how to respond to industry continued at the Bauhaus, a German arts school that was founded after the First World War. Although it had several phases and its aesthetic approach was not monolithic, its influence is still seen in designers' responses to mass production of everyday products. Its machine-celebrating spare lines and structural expression still infuse discussions of modern design. Le Corbusier, in his seminal *Vers une architecture* (1923), proclaimed that the industrial era required new attitudes and aesthetics for architecture based upon function and pure form and exhorted architects to embrace the modern age.

Artists also looked upon complex machinery and hulking buildings and saw beauty. Charles Sheeler glorified industry in art, creating numerous photographic and oil studies of Ford's River Rouge automobile factory. More recently, Hilla and Bernd Becher's photographs of abandoned machinery and buildings, memorials to the simple and elemental forms of the industrial past, helped educate the modern eye in honoring the industrial aesthetic in redevelopment.

Grain Elevators

The grain elevators around Buffalo, New York, are featured prominently in the commentaries of the European modernists such as Le Corbusier and Gropius although their admiration of these monumental structures derived mostly from photographs, not from their travels. It's interesting to take a detour to admire this pioneering use of reinforced concrete. The ever-present danger of fire spurred technological developments of grain elevators as grain dust is volatile, known to spontaneously combust when stored in tight, enclosed areas.[1] Fires can smolder inside grain storage facilities and then violently explode without warning from a buildup of heat generated by the dust.

At the beginning of the twentieth century Buffalo prospered, benefiting from its location between the bread basket of the Midwest and the markets of the east. These silos, lined up along the Buffalo River banks to receive goods from Great Lakes ships to be distributed via rail, are still impressive today and continue to inspire photographers and artists. Deemed

Figure 2.11
Frontier Elevator, Buffalo, New York. (Great Northern Elevator in the background.) Pictures of Buffalo's grain elevators rising from the river inspired European architects at the beginning of the twentieth century.
Historic American Engineering Record NY-249-3, Jet Lowe Photographer, Summer 1994

ugly by the locals, pictures of these structures, which circulated in Europe, highlighted their abstract, unadorned forms serving as ideal advertisements for proponents of the new modern era in architecture. Photographed heroically emerging from the river, they appear as witnesses of a brave new era of technology and rationality.

Because of their austere geometric forms and massive presence, storage elevators are difficult building types to convert to other uses. An early, though perhaps a bit forced, transformation took place in Akron, Ohio, where 36 grain storage silos built in 1932 and originally used by the Quaker Oats Company were turned into a hotel, restaurant,

Figure 2.12
In this 1994 photo, the Perot Elevator is on the left, American on the right. The cylindrical shape originated in Minneapolis; however, it became a symbol of Buffalo's importance as a supplier of grain.
Historic American Engineering Record NY-244-3, Jet Lowe Photographer, Summer 1994

and shopping center in the 1970s. The building was listed on the National Register of Historic Places in 1975. The hotel rooms are in the silos and maintain the round shape in their interior. In 2007, the University of Akron bought the complex and will use some of the rooms as a dormitory.

A more elegant renovation of vegetable and grain silos into offices in Helsinki, Finland, was accomplished by Heikkinen-Komonen Architects in 2003. The goal was to preserve the industrial character of the complex, which anchors its city block and is located in an industrial district. The client, Senate Properties,

Figure 2.13
The renovation of vegetable and grain silos in Helsinki, Finland, into offices uses the silos for elevator shafts and service cores. The new brick addition that faces the street is the same proportion as the existing warehouse.
Jussi Tiainen

a government agency that develops and manages state properties, converted the structure and also built an addition for its own use and to house the Headquarters for the National Research and Development Centre for Welfare and Health. The silos, in two rows of six, were turned into elevator shafts and service core, with the offices opened to the courtyard behind. Interior industrial details, such as the mushroom column capitals of the warehouse, were retained, infusing present-day offices with a sense of the history of the structure.

[1] In January 2008, the New York City Department of Buildings evacuated 150 people from an 11-story loft building in Brooklyn because there was an illegal matzo factory in the basement, leading to fear of fire.

Figure 2.14
The Helsinki, Finland, warehouse had low ceiling heights and stout mushroom capital columns. Heikkinen-Komonen Architects employed industrial materials and details throughout the building's renovation into offices.
Jussi Tiainen

Industrial Aesthetic and Renovation

Seeing beauty in industrial buildings has been critical to their renovation. Years after function or market changes rendered these buildings obsolete, the simple, wide-open spaces of factories and warehouses, with their clear expression of construction materials, ignite the imagination of new generations who, since the 1960s, have been rescuing these buildings. Although there are many reasons for the reuse of these buildings and sites, the allure of the industrial aesthetic cannot be dismissed, and in many instances, is crucial to the success of their redevelopment.

The conversions of loft buildings into housing during the late 1960s and early 1970s, whether the textile mills of New England or the cast iron buildings of

Figure 2.15
The Centre Pompidou's unabashed exposure of structural and mechanical systems represents the apotheosis of the industrial aesthetic.
Richard Loehr

SoHo, was a defining moment for industrial renovation. The expansive interior spaces with large windows invited homesteaders to formerly unused buildings while maintaining a sense of history through reuse and renewal. Interior design and lifestyle magazines ran spreads about urban pioneers inhabiting sparsely furnished lofts with expanses of white walls and polished wood floors. Editors extolled "Industrial Chic," a style which showed how nonloft residents could bring a bit of industrial grit and exposed materials into more traditional apartments and suburban homes—be it kitchen shelves, furniture, or accessories with exposed functional details.

The term "industrial aesthetic" can refer to the deliberate exposure of structural and mechanical elements as well as the repurposing of the objects of manufacture. Industrial architecture and design extolled the economical use of material and methods of construction that were often not hidden or camouflaged—from the clear expression of the reinforced concrete frame of the daylight factories to the exposed metal trusses of steel factory buildings and the early exhibition halls and train stations. Today, that approach is being used aesthetically in all types of buildings, not necessarily just factories and warehouses.

Clear expression of structural elements, as well as building systems such as mechanical and electrical services, developed into its own aesthetic. This aesthetic perhaps achieved its apex in 1977, when the nonindustrial Centre Pompidou, designed by Richard Rogers and Renzo Piano, opened in Paris, France. Often compared to the Eiffel Tower, which stunned many at the time because its structure was left exposed, the building of the Centre Pompidou is all steel frame, ducts, and pipes. Famous for its exterior escalator that climbs up the plaza façade and affords a wonderful view of Paris, the building makes architecture out of industrial elements, though it's unclear how much of the structure and services are simply "uncovered" and how much exists for the overall effect and design.

Thirty years after this trend started, there is no sign of its abating. In fact, textile mills and factories from Connecticut to Los Angeles continue to be converted for residential and commercial use, their beams and pipes left exposed. In addition, in cities that did not have an existing stock of industrial buildings, new housing has been built to mimic the loft form. What started as a small trend among artists in search of large studio space has now mushroomed into a string of conversions into different uses and scales. The appeal of these buildings as places to live has saved a huge percentage of the industrial patrimony.

ENDNOTES

1. Louis Bergeron and Maria Teresa Maiullari-Pontois. *Industry, Architecture, and Engineering*. New York: Harry N. Abrams, Inc. 2000, p. 187.
2. Although visually similar, cast iron is molded and strong in compression; however, it is too brittle to be used in tension. Wrought iron is forged and worked with tools such as hammer and anvil and, because it can bend, is strong in tension. Puddled iron is wrought iron derived from cast iron and is particularly strong in tension. Many iron building elements use both cast and wrought iron, especially in trusses which use both forces.
3. "The Maintenance and Repair of Architectural Cast Iron," John G. Waite, AIA Historical Overview by Margot Gayle, Technical Preservation Services, National Park Service, 27 Preservation Briefs, www.nps.gov/history/HPS/tps/briefs/brief27.htm accessed December 3, 2009.
4. According to George Nelson in *Industrial Architecture of Albert Kahn, Inc.* (New York: Architectural Book Publishing Company, Inc. 1939), Kahn was one of the most prolific architects of his time, with projects global in scope. In 1938, his firm's commissions represented 19 percent of all industrial buildings designed by architects.
5. Just a year before Packard Building No. 10, the nascent Ford Motor Company built its first factory, the Model T on Piquette Avenue. The building was a traditional mill-style building with a load-bearing brick facade and wood interior columns and beams. The building was sectioned by three firewalls.
6. A younger brother, Moritz, worked in London at the Truscon office and then was to take over the Russian operations of Kahn's firm. In 1907, he published *The Design and Construction of Industrial Buildings* in which he gave pointers on how to build efficient factories with an eye toward expansion and flexibility.
7. Ada Louise Huxtable, *On Architecture*. "Personal Landmarks Along the Highway." p. 461. Originally published in the *New York Times*, June 26, 1977.
8. Using architecture as advertising will again become a strong element in the revival of cities, as will be seen in Chapters 9 and 10.
9. Kenneth Frampton. *Modern Architecture, A Critical History*. New York: Thames and Hudson. p. 111.
10. Gropius to Karl Osthaus as cited in Annemarie Jaeggi. *Fagus Industrial Culture from Werkbund to Bauhaus*. New York: Princeton Architectural Press 2000. p. 50.

SECTION 2

REDEVELOPMENT—AN OVERVIEW

CHAPTER 3

PROJECT PLANNING STRATEGIES

Even in the centuries-old locations it previously defined, industry often turns into an incongruous intruder as cities change. Industrial sites that dominated once-active waterfronts now block views and impede recreation. Forlorn factory districts become dangerous and incriminating reminders of the past. Living cheek by jowl with struggling industries can at best seem tenuous or at worse hazardous. While there is usually agreement that "This derelict area is forbidding" or "They should do something about this," defining the "who" that should do it and the "what" that should be done is not easy.

As obvious as it might sound, the first step of any project is to identify it as one—not a simple task in the case of industrial sites with often complex ownership patterns, and the idea for a project is not necessarily generated or shared by the property owners. Developing a program and design for industrial sites varies according to ownership or initiator. If a company still owns its facility and is interested in adapting it for another use for itself, the following strategies are not pertinent, as the company can pursue its plans, such as a renovation of an existing building, on its own. It's the rare industry, however, that has the capability or need to adapt nineteenth- and early-twentieth-century structures into modern factories and offices.

The complex nature of development today, as well as the need for either public funds or powers, requires public outreach and often involves the provision of public amenities. Many of these industrial sites are vacant or abandoned, encompass large swaths of land, or are lonely outposts in changing districts—factors that necessitate a comprehensive approach, rather than a simple or discrete renovation. As many redevelopment projects reinvent older urban areas, whose factories, railroads, and other relics of their industrial past render them uninhabitable or inconvenient, they are often charged with the heavy burden of redefining or recreating a new economic *raison d'etre* for their cities or neighborhoods. Planning must take into consideration the long-term economic repercussions and future directions of a city as well as the normal concerns and aesthetics of a project. Whether to build housing, a cultural destination, or recreation facilities, or to encourage new industry are economic planning questions that are best addressed from the outset.

Redevelopment goals vary with the economic needs of the community, the nearby residents and businesses, the characteristics of the project location, and ownership of the property. For example, popular opinion often opts for parks rather than factories as the use for many of these sites, especially those on waterfronts. Such new public use, however, not only changes the character of a neighborhood but also the urban balance sheet from one of income from business and jobs to one of expense for construction and maintenance. While such an amenity can be welcomed, it does not address the underlying economic requirement of providing employment for residents and a solid tax base.

Identifying goals and capturing the imagination of those who can effectuate change is best done by first developing plans that inspire the public, business community, and government. Subsequent steps advance support and persuasively advocate for either the need for or the proposed scope of the project. Predicting the success or failure of initial ideas for projects is difficult during the planning stage. These first designs or development efforts are seldom in evidence at ribbon cuttings, but nonetheless are critical in spearheading projects. Over time a dialogue evolves between the forces that first presented redevelopment ideas and those who oppose or respond with alternatives. The "whos" and "whats" of projects become clearer through this planning stage.

A striking aspect of many of these projects is how often their genesis stems from the ideas and actions of one person or group. These project advocates imagine how these abandoned buildings can be revived and pursue the goal of renewal and reuse though the web of approvals and financial and regulatory hurdles. They are often visionaries, seeing the underlying beauty of these industrial relics and utility when others can't get past the images of crumbling bricks and contamination. By force of personality or position, the champions for these renovations bring others on board to work toward their dream of transformation. Whether others consider the change a dream or nightmare often determines the length and fervor of ensuing battles.

This possibility of such personal effectiveness in industrial site redevelopment coincides with the rise of public involvement and the expectation that the planning process will include community outreach and the provision of easily accessible information. Government involvement requires these procedures (with various levels of transparency and compliance), and others such as public hearings. If done perfunctorily, however, they seldom engage dialogue, but become one-way discussions in which audience members comment and government officials listen with no obligation to respond.

In fact, successful projects embrace a team approach at the earliest stage possible and include development consultants, site engineers/evaluators, public outreach professionals, public officials, and of course, vocal local personages. As a result, new consulting professions that bridge real estate, public relations, and lobbying have been created to guide governments, developers, and community groups through this predevelopment process from defining the project, writing Requests for Proposals (RFPs) and evaluating their responses, assembling teams as well as negotiating development agreements, and even garnering good press. Urban and community planners have expanded and redefined their work to routinely include public forums, meetings, and information programs in project schedules. Planning department curriculums now include courses on handling public participation and building consensus.

Although public participation has often been described (not necessarily positively) as "civic theater," ignoring this critical step has sidelined many projects.[1] The public now expects meaningful project outreach and influence. Many community groups have become quite adept at employing the tools developed for such participation and use them to thwart projects they don't want or believe need modification.

PUBLIC OUTREACH: REQUESTS FOR PROPOSALS, COMPETITIONS, AND OTHER TOOLS FOR PUBLIC PARTICIPATION

Public Planning Tools

- Charrettes—to foster public involvement and propose design ideas

- RFPs—to assess market interest and to solicit development and design ideas
- Competitions—to solicit designs and engender excitement about project
- Task forces and committees rather than large public hearings
- Panel discussions
- Website updates

Public outreach is labor intensive, potentially expensive, but almost always necessary today. Soliciting ideas for projects and seeking support for them are two main reasons for public information efforts and require different methods. Coincidental to the increase in the number of redevelopment plans is the increased use of design and development competitions and RFPs as planning tools to develop programs and explore financial viability and market interest. The RFP, formerly the provenance of government entities, has joined the vocabulary of private developers and community groups as a method for generating new ideas and public support.

Although sometimes used interchangeably, RFPs and competitions differ with respect to end product. As a rule, owners of property (often government) issue RFPs to seek proposals from developers for project ideas and purchase price. For instance, an RFP can request that developers propose a program of its choice that it believes will be economically successful—i.e., offices or housing—along with its design team and business terms. Responses present how much the developer will pay for the property, such as for outright purchase or long-term lease. RFPs are also issued with specific programs and design guidelines or goals for the project and responses are then evaluated accordingly. An RFP can also test the market to determine developer interest and property value.

Competitions are usually mounted to seek design ideas and approaches for the owner to implement. Sometimes, competitions seek broad-based design approaches—either a master plan with the idea that other architects will be hired to build the buildings or for a specific design that will be honed by the submitter. Design and/or ideas are usually the basis for judging competitions.

In order for submissions to be responsive and withstand the rigors of building, the more site information known, the more complete the proposals will be. As will be seen throughout this section, information about the extent of pollution, remediation required, zoning parameters, and public support all play a part in determining the possibilities of not only a redevelopment, but hopefully a successful one.

As with all public outreach, the balance between openness and chaos is a tenuous one. Total transparency and good design often do not coexist. An effective way to achieve responsive projects is to develop requirements for the RFP from discussions with the community, in public meetings or small task forces, to establish design and use guidelines that responses need to address. A task force consisting of major constituent community groups and not merely political appointees can be constructive. Fleshing out basic requirements for a project in small meetings rather than large public venues avoids excess pontificating while the ground rules for an RFP and other guidelines are debated and evaluated. Review of responses can then be rationally made by comparing how well they respond to the guidelines issued.

Public forums, informational websites, newspaper inserts, and polling all risk being manipulated by single-minded activists or excluding segments of the public that will feel ignored. Associations such as the International Association for Public Participation (IAP2) can provide assistance for designers as well as neighborhood groups with, among other services, an easy-to-understand chart to help evaluate the effectiveness and possible pitfalls of various information-sharing and design-generating techniques.[2]

From a design point of view, charrettes,[3] an architectural term that initially meant working on deadline and now denotes intensive group design workshops to engage the public, have become popular. The National Charrette Institute has tools for conducting these workshops. Although not a panacea for community acceptance, these sessions can be helpful as educational tools. Projects' programs and goals, however, should be fairly well defined before the public involvement can be helpful on a design level. The problem of rising expectations rears its head—the project designed in a charrette may never get built or may not incorporate ideas generated.

GILBERT & BENNETT MANUFACTURING COMPANY SITE

NAME: GILBERT & BENNETT MANUFACTURING COMPANY (FORMER SITE)

LOCATION: REDDING, CONNECTICUT

FORMER USE: 55-ACRE WIRE MILL FACTORY

PROJECT: NEW CONSTRUCTION PLUS RENOVATION OF HISTORIC MILL BUILDINGS; MIXED-USE, TRANSIT-ORIENTED DEVELOPMENT TO INCLUDE OVER 400 DIVERSE HOUSING UNITS, 300,000 SQ. FT. COMMERCIAL SPACE, PERFORMING ARTS CENTER, REOPENED TRAIN STATION

DEVELOPER: GEORGETOWN LAND DEVELOPMENT COMPANY

PUBLIC INVESTMENT: ENVIRONMENTAL GRANTS, INFRASTRUCTURE (RAIL AND HIGHWAY) IMPROVEMENTS, ESTABLISHMENT OF SPECIAL TAXING DISTRICTS

PUBLIC OUTREACH: CHARRETTE, PUBLIC HEARINGS FOR LOCAL AND STATE APPROVALS

TIME LINE: FIRST CHARRETTE IN 2003, PROJECT DELAYED BY INSUFFICIENT FUNDS FOR OFFSITE INFRASTRUCTURE REQUIREMENTS

Under certain situations, charrettes can be quite effective. Stephen Soler of Georgetown Land Development Company credits a 2003 charrette led by Duany Plater-Zyberk & Company for fostering public involvement and design ideas for his mixed-use development on the 55-acre site of the Gilbert & Bennett Manufacturing Company, a former wire mill and brownfield nestled amid upscale Connecticut valley towns. This polluted property had remained forsaken since 1989 when the last window screen left the factory. In order to make redevelopment and cleanup financially viable, the new owner believed a development of 1,000 residents was required. Redding, where the site was located, had a population of only 8,000, and saw itself as a low-density area.[4]

The one-week charrette was a highly scheduled event that involved hours of meetings, presentations, and workshops with town officials and residents who participated in the programming and design sessions. The project planners and architects were on hand as 1,000 people attended over the course of the week. On the first night, the charrette leaders, who are proponents of the "New Urbanism"[5] urban design theory, presented their ideas about what makes a successful community, highlighting the importance of a pedestrian-friendly town. The second night was devoted to elected officials who voiced their wishes and concerns as well as heard ideas about how development could take place. The next presentation, open to all, was an explanation of the not-insignificant contamination and other environmental issues (such as wetlands) and a detailed exposition of the constraints as well as the advantages of the site. State and federal environmental officials attended. The purpose was to create a baseline mapping of the property in order for a realistic plan to be developed.

A series of meetings and discussions that focused on transportation, public works, safety, and local issues followed. These sessions revealed, among other things, that the community has an artistic bent and was interested in the inclusion of a cultural component. As a result, space in the resulting master plan has been reserved for a black box performing arts center to be run by the newly created Wire Mill Arts Foundation. The importance of maintaining the industrial buildings, some of which have 14-foot ceilings as well as large windows, was also stressed. The last gatherings contained pin-up presentations and invited public feedback on the concept plan created by the planners and architects that incorporated the design and program concerns expressed in the previous week's discussions.

Mr. Soler strongly believes that without such orchestrated public outreach, the project would not have been approved nor be as appropriate for the community. He believes that everyone who became involved at this planning stage learned early in the process how decisions were made and didn't feel they were playing "catch-up." As he stated, "Everyone had ownership" of the project. In early 2006, the project area became the Georgetown Special Taxing District and was designated by the U.S. Treasury Department as a qualified green building and sustainable design project, making it eligible to issue $72 million in tax-exempt bonds. The phased development was fully permitted in 2008.

The project has received various brownfield cleanup grants, including the U.S. Environmental Protection Agency's (EPS) Brownfield Targeted Site Assessment Grant and Brownfield Cleanup Grant as well as various state block and economic assistance grants. Before the first resident has moved in, the project has won numerous approvals and awards. In 2005, the EPA gave the Town of Redding its National Award for Smart Growth Achievement (Small Communities) citing the extensive public process as well as the design goal of "draw(ing) people back to the old commercial center of Redding, reducing the need to drive elsewhere for entertainment and shopping."[6] Despite a public policy supportive of transit-oriented development, this project has been delayed, waiting for state funding for offsite transportation improvements for a new highway intersection and construction of a new train station and associated parking.

This project highlights the complexity of industrial site redevelopment and the strengths as well as limits of public outreach. The need for rehabilitating this blighted area was agreed to at various government levels, and concerted community discussions garnered strong local support. Raising funds required to integrate the site into the surrounding transportation system has proved difficult.

Government-Initiated Projects

Projects generated by government can be among the most controversial, especially in America where an innate fear of unfettered government power, coupled with the distaste for higher taxes, runs deep. The scale and ownership patterns of many projects, however, require the economic or political heft of government. Often viewed as unfeeling and out of touch, tinged at times with hints of corruption, government-generated projects risk being viewed as autocratic visions that do not benefit the surrounding areas. In America, projects that acquire property through eminent domain,[7] whether from small homeowners or large or even defunct businesses, trigger suspicion and mistrust.

The power of government is not absolute, and its plans go awry as often as they succeed. Given these projects' long time lines, several mayors and city councils can run out their terms before the pioneering tenants unpack or the first pick-up basketball game is played. Government usually gets involved in redevelopment either because it originally owns the property or its powers are needed to assemble land because of disparate ownership, bankruptcies, or abandonment.

GRANVILLE ISLAND

NAME: GRANVILLE ISLAND

LOCATION: VANCOUVER, CANADA

FORMER USE: SAWMILL, SHIPPING INDUSTRIES, HEAVY CONSTRUCTION

PROJECT: MIXED-USE URBAN PARK WITH ADAPTIVE REUSE OF INDUSTRIAL BUILDINGS FOR CONTINUING INDUSTRIAL USE WITH PUBLIC MARKET, RESTAURANTS, MARITIME STORES

DEVELOPER: CANADA MORTGAGE AND HOUSING CORPORATION

PUBLIC OUTREACH: MINIMAL

TIME LINE: ONGOING SINCE 1972

At Granville Island in Vancouver, Canada, government ownership was helpful in the redevelopment of this former 37-acre industrial area, which was first home to sawmills and shipping interests. World War II gave its heavy construction and maritime industries a boost, a boom that did not survive the postwar era. In 1972, the federal Canadian government obtained the land rights to Granville Island through its Canada Mortgage and Housing Corporation and pursued plans for its revival through the Granville Island Trust. Many of the highlights of the design are taken for granted today, but the concepts of mixed-use as well as renovation of old industrial buildings were novel, unproven at the time.

The executive architect, Norman Hotson of Hotson Bakker Boniface Haden architects + urbanistes stated that not only did the single government ownership simplify the development process, it was a great advantage that the entity in this case had final authorization and did not need to seek local approvals.[8] Although there were several public hearings and the project was presented to the City Council, design only required the approval of one entity and public involvement was minimal. In this case, as luck would have it, the entity had funding, a vision of a new type of urban park, and was willing to take a chance on innovation. In contrast, the little opposition that materialized revolved around wanting the whole island to be a park and for all buildings to be torn down. Mr. Hotson observed that the era of Granville Island's development was an adventurous one for new ideas and good thinking with respect to community planning and an eagerness to experiment. Today, the process has become more bureaucratic with added complexity.

Early in the design process it was determined that a mixture of uses would draw tourists as well as nearby residents to the island. Attracting locals was critical not only because of the potential

GOVERNMENT-INITIATED PROJECTS

for return visits but also for helping to keep the island "real," that is, preventing it from becoming a theme park. The mixed-use approach was not acceptable under local zoning, which is based upon the separation of uses. In addition, the local transportation department would never have approved retaining certain industrial characteristics that have become major design features: the absence of curbs, sidewalks, and gutters, none of which existed during industrial days in order to accommodate heavy trucks and easy movement of wares. As a result, today there is a free flow of pedestrian traffic and an open atmosphere. (Cars are allowed on the island; however, there is little conflict with island visitors.) Some of the old railroad tracks are still imbedded in the streets.

Granville Island has an active street life—its farmers market, restaurants, theaters, parks, and maritime stores destinations. These new venues, many located in retrofitted industrial buildings, are intermingled with some remaining working industries, such as a drill bit maker and concrete factory that still uses barges and tugs to transport its goods, the last water-based industrial use in the area. Artist studios and workshops are interspersed throughout the island, and hat makers, glass makers, goldsmiths, leather workers, woodworkers, weavers, and other artisans sell their wares from their stores, which also double as their studios.

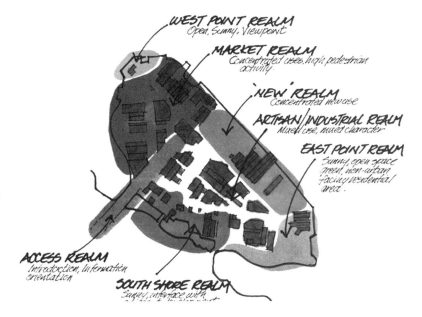

Figure 3.1
The designers of Granville Island in Vancouver, Canada, in the 1970s insisted that the area be mixed-use and developed several centers of activities.
Drawing by Hotson Bakker Boniface Haden Architects

Across from Stanley Park on the mainland, Granville Island is easily accessible from Vancouver by car or public transportation via a bridge or by water via ferry or boat. The island is roughly divided into six zones of activities and different types of public spaces and experiences, ranging from an open green area, new visitor services, and concentrated industrial and artisan uses. There are also programmed activities for all ages including a water park. The working industry is also an attraction for children who can

Figure 3.2
Granville Island, Vancouver in 1974 had been home to heavy construction and maritime industries when it was acquired by the Granville Island Trust to transform it into an urban park.
City of Vancouver Archives

see how things are made. Over 30 years later, development is ongoing, with five sites yet to be programmed. The project was phased and intended to be incremental in order to adapt to changes in visitor needs and also to reflect how cities really develop—over time and organically.

This variety of experience garnered honors from the Project for Public Spaces, which in 2004 cited Granville Island as its first "Great Neighborhood and District" as a result of the wide variety of things to do, many of which relate to the island's original use. The island is not seen as overly commercial or kitschy because of the numerous community spaces for local institutions, existing industry, and the public. The Project for Public Spaces encourages a multiplicity of

GOVERNMENT-INITIATED PROJECTS

Figure 3.3
One of the streets on Granville Island that shows the gutterless, curbless streetscape and renovated warehouse buildings.
Photo by Norman Hotson

uses for areas and commented that the "public market and adjoining area perfectly illustrate a concept that is at the core of our Placemaking principles and the new Great Cities Initiative: 'The Power of Ten.' This means ensuring a wide variety of things to do in a place (ten seems the magic number) and then creating a variety of these kind of places within a district as a whole. People's enjoyment of a place seems to increase exponentially based on the variety of things to do and see."[9]

Les Halles

NAME: LES HALLES

LOCATION: PARIS, FRANCE

FORMER USE: WHOLESALE FOOD MARKET

PROJECT: PARK, REGIONAL TRANSPORTATION NODE, SHOPPING CENTER

DEVELOPER: CITY OF PARIS

PUBLIC OUTREACH: 1970S: NONE; 2004: COMPETITION, PUBLIC POLLING, WEBSITE

TIME LINE: 1970S, 2016 ESTIMATED CONSTRUCTION COMPLETION

A legendary example of a misguided government-initiated project is Les Halles in central Paris. The wholesale food market's move to the outskirts of Paris in Rungis in 1969 initiated an irrevocable shift in neighborhood character. Ignoring a local movement to adapt the buildings for cultural uses, in 1971 the government destroyed most of architect Victor Baltard's nineteenth-century cast iron and glass food halls during the annual August holidays that empty out Paris, ensuring few protestors. The growth of Paris around Les Halles made the raucous wholesale market that provided Parisian stores and restaurants with the raw ingredients for its fabled cuisine a stranger in its own neighborhood. The area—a few steps from the Louvre and tourist hotels—was congested with produced-laden trucks converging and blocking traffic on narrow cobblestone streets. Its central location and industrial atmosphere—elegance and working-class roughness rubbing against each other—was part of its allure, part of what makes cities interesting.

The controversy was aptly symbolized by the large hole that rebuked Paris throughout the 1970s as debate swirled around half-finished redevelopment. Intense opposition forced alterations to the proposed design which nevertheless resulted in a multileveled, subterranean horror of a shopping mall. The adjacent gardens are a pleasant, if ordinary, respite from what became, in tandem with the nearby Centre Georges Pompidou, a major tourist center. Contributing to the change in neighborhood character was the coordination of the redevelopment with the creation of a major transportation hub that connects the intracity metro with regional rail lines.

What was built in the early 1980s shocked many and had few advocates. (The Project for Public Spaces went so far as to put it in its "Hall of Shame.") The situation was made worse when the streets around the shopping mall were closed to traffic, supposedly to form a pedestrian-friendly district, but created an unsafe area instead. Fiasco begat change and spurred long-range reform in how public projects in Paris are planned and designed. But will this new process produce a better project? Can an open public process and design coexist? The verdict is still out and will be tested with yet a new Les Halles.

The story of Les Halles demonstrates that community involvement is now expected, and that doing projects by government edict and traditional authoritarianism is fading somewhat, even in Europe. Formerly, the government decided in secret what was to be built, deaf to local concerns. With this new project, change was announced, a competition held, exhibitions mounted, informal votes taken, and an official website (since expired) kept all up to date.

Figure 3.4
Les Halles in Paris was the site of a thriving food market from the middle ages until 1972 when the market moved to Rungis on the city's outskirts. Victor Baltard's pavilions were built between 1853 and 1858 and each had a specialty such as meat, poultry, cheese, etc. (photo date unknown).
Collection du Pavillon de l'Arsenal, Ville de Paris

The 2004 invited competition for an overall master plan pitted four firms: Rem Koolhaas of OMA; MVRDV; Jean Nouvel; and David Mangin, of SEURA. Local polling chose David Mangin's design, the least visionary of the four, which keeps the stores and creates a formal, even classical, landscaped park. The American architectural press was not kind—whether because of the superficial desire to see a "star" architect chosen or for the craving for innovation rather than low-keyed "contextual" design is unclear. New design directions seldom arise from a democratic process.

In reality, Mangin's plan excited few people. His garden design was maintained, but a new invited international competition was held to redesign the shopping mall. The French architectural firm of Patrick Berger and Jacques Anziutti was chosen in 2007. Their design maintains most of the complex underground construction with

Figure 3.5
The arched trellises of the park at Les Halles today are a sad replacement of the original buildings. Beyond the arches is the Forum des Halles, a five-level deep shopping center and a local and regional train station on the bottom level. The area is being redesigned, however, the shopping center, albeit reconfigured, will remain.
Carol Berens

added cultural features, all under a low structure called "The Canopy," which allows views of the nearby Eglise St. Eustache and Commodities Exchange from the surrounding area. To this day, the presence of the destroyed pavilions hovers over all discussions of what this area in the heart of Paris should be. It's impossible to write about its future without reviewing its past.

BALTARD'S PAVILIONS

No one was happy with the transformation of Les Halles. Even decades after its removal, the original exists in the minds of many as the best of old Paris, based upon literary allusions and movie images of revelers greeting the dawn with onion soup and yet another *vin rouge* at *Au Pied du Cochon* and other bistros. Far from being solely a nostalgic artifact, Les Halles was a prime example of a time when Paris and the French embraced the

GOVERNMENT-INITIATED PROJECTS

Figure 3.6
The last existing Les Halles Baltard-designed pavilion was reconstructed in Nogent-sur-Marne as a venue for spectacles and other special events. Although stripped of its old neighborhood and market activity, the cast iron and glass structure stands as a wonderful testament to a hallmark in engineering history.
Mathieu Génon/ville de Nogent sur Marne

future. Commissioned by Baron Haussmann under Napoleon III and built between 1853 and 1857, Les Halles helped transform Paris into a modern city. Baltard did not look toward the past for inspiration, but designed the glass and then-new cast iron in a way that combined beauty and utility, influencing succeeding industrial buildings. (Ironically, at the time of Les Halles' destruction, a few blocks to the east the Centre Pompidou was under construction, the twentieth century's apotheosis of the industrial aesthetic initiated during Baltard's era.)

All but one of the pavilions (*Pavilion No. 8*, egg and poultry merchants) were destroyed in the early 1970s during the conversion. In 1972 the sole survivor was rescued and transported to Nogent-sur-Marne to be a venue for spectacles and special events.

Owner/Developer-Initiated Projects

Owner and/or developer-generated projects are pursued by developers who enjoy challenges or who have much experience in renovation or by the original industrial owners who choose to transform their factories rather than destroy or abandon them. There is a certain amount of autonomy that comes from owning the property, although in many instances that freedom can be illusory. Given the private nature of the development, these places risk becoming overly commercial and touristy, adding yet another shopping mall to the urban landscape. There are examples, however, of owners and developers who are striving for more historically sensitive projects that integrate the life of the surrounding city and public space. As seen throughout these projects, industrial sites present complex redevelopment pictures, especially with respect to rezoning and neighborhood impact. Private development doesn't preclude public involvement through the planning process, and the success of the projects based upon help and support from government through tax benefits and dealing with the subsequent liability issues.

Fiat Lingotto Factory

Name: Fiat Lingotto Factory

Location: Turin, Italy

Former Use: Automobile factory

Project: Mixed-use project: a convention center, exposition hall, concert hall and theaters as well as a hotel, retail stores, company and city offices

Developer: Fiat

Public Outreach: Invited competition for design and reuse

Time Line: 1982–1996

Although the arc of industry continually repeats as if on a film loop, as individual narratives each repetition demonstrates its own poignancy and importance—both architecturally and civically. A prime example is Fiat's auto factory in the Lingotto neighborhood of Turin. The nascent auto industry's exuberant expression and optimism translated into the architecture of its factory. Between 1917 and 1921 Fiat founder Giovanni Agnelli with the engineer Giacomo Mattè Trucco built a concrete behemoth that embodied the manufacturing process. Built on the outskirts of a town, the expanding city grew to encompass the complex, albeit separated by moats of railroad tracks and parking.

Combining Futurism with a classic industrial concrete structure, the building sports little ornament, its beauty residing in the clear articulation of its concrete structure and the clean repetition of its openings. Urban legend ascribes its design inspiration to Agnelli's trip to the Ford Motor Company's Albert Kahn Detroit plant. The five-story building (1,665 feet long by 79 feet wide) contains four large internal courtyards separated by service cores. The production line snaked along the perimeter: Raw materials entered at the ground floor and were progressively assembled into automobiles, which advanced through the building and up helical ramps until they arrived at the banked oval rooftop to be

Figure 3.7
This aerial of the Fiat Lingotto factory in Turin, Italy, before it was renovated, not only shows its famous test drive roof, but also how parking and railroad siding isolated the building from the fabric of the city.
© Lingotto courtesy of Renzo Piano Building Workshop

test driven. (The test track can be seen in the 1969 movie caper, *The Italian Job*.) Even Le Corbusier was impressed enough to end his book *Vers une architecture* with three photographs of the building.

After more than 50 years of production, the outmoded factory became another potential empty shell reflecting the downturn of Italy's former industrial north. But when the last Lancia rolled down the ramps and onto the street in 1982, Agnelli's commitment to Turin and the cultural life of the city prevented the automobile family from abandoning the building that had become an instant landmark. Fiat mounted an invited architectural competition to work with the city not only to retain the building but to develop another use that would integrate it into the life of the city. The competition proposals, including those by Richard Meier, James Stirling, and Aldo Rossi among the 20 participants, were displayed and comments from the public solicited. The Renzo Piano Building Workshop won, with its restrained proposal that maintained the "bones" of the original building, and presented uses that would give the building an important role in the postindustrial redefinition of Turin.

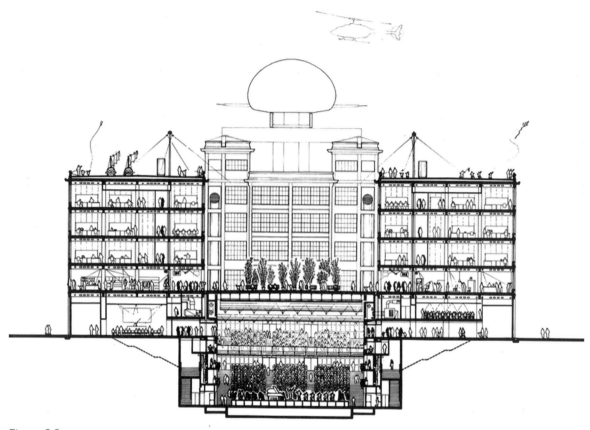

Figure 3.8
The interior of the Lingotto building was bathed in light that entered the wings through four interior courtyards.
© RPBW, Renzo Piano Building Workshop

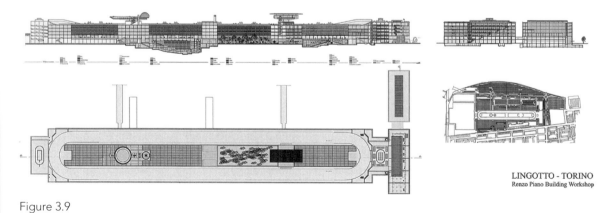

Figure 3.9
The multiuse renovation integrated the building with its surroundings, but also added two controversial rooftop additions—a conference room and the Agnelli museum.
© RPBW, Renzo Piano Building Workshop, March 2001

The 14-year, three-phased, multiuse project consists of a convention center, exposition hall, a concert hall, and theaters, as well as a hotel, retail stores, and offices for the city of Turin and Fiat. The extensive rail yard at one side of the building was removed to create inviting public spaces and outdoor plazas. The original building is indeed cleaned up and intact; however, the Building Workshop did add some strikingly modern additions (some would say too striking). A domed conference center perches atop the rooftop track, and at the other end of the roof, the Giovanni and Marella Agnelli Art Gallery publicly displays the Agnellis' private collection, as well as changing exhibitions. While renovation stories that rely upon an extraordinary building as well as the foresight and concern of a forceful corporate owner are not easily duplicated, it's helpful to recognize the importance of being able to work with city officials, as well as being flexible through the long development period.

Piazza at Schmidts

NAME: PIAZZA AT SCHMIDTS

LOCATION: PHILADELPHIA, PENNSYLVANIA

FORMER USE: BEER BREWERY

PROJECT: RESIDENTIAL, COMMERCIAL, AND PUBLIC SPACE

DEVELOPER: BART BLATSTEIN OF TOWER INVESTMENTS, INC.

PUBLIC OUTREACH: PUBLIC HEARINGS, COMMUNITY MEETINGS

TIME LINE: 2000 (PROPERTY PURCHASE); PROJECT ONGOING

In Philadelphia, Pennsylvania, Bart Blatstein of Tower Investments, Inc., spent nearly 10 years, countless public hearings, and several development plans to convert the former Schmidt's brewery and warehouse in the Northern Liberties neighborhood into housing, offices, gallery spaces, and artist's studios. The neighborhood's story has become all too familiar—working-class district's factories leave, interstates cut connections to the center city, neighborhood declines, and artists move in. What breaks the standard plot line, however, is that this privately developed project creates a pedestrian-friendly active public space. On a formerly nearly vacant lot, new construction forms a plaza with one of the brewery warehouse's walls as backdrop to what the developer has dubbed the Piazza at Schmidts, modeled after Rome's Piazza Navona. The landscaped, 80,000-square-foot paved plaza is highly programmed with free events, including an outdoor film series.

Schmidt's Brewery, founded in 1860, occupied a large portion of this industrial neighborhood when it was the tenth largest brewery in America. It fell into bankruptcy soon after it was sold in 1976 and operations ceased in 1987. When Mr. Blatstein, a shopping center developer, bought the brewery property in 2000 at a foreclosure auction, he originally intended to build retail on the site, an idea that outraged the small but tight-knit neighborhood of

Figure 3.10
The new buildings at the Piazza at Schmidts in Philadelphia, Pennsylvania, define the public plaza, which has many openings and entrances into it to create an active public space.
Erdy McHenry Architecture

artists who feared a change in character of their neighborhood. After several failed attempts at development—either from lack of market interest, bad press, or difficulty in getting planning approvals—he hit upon the idea of making an urban public place where people could gather. Although his first plans were panned, he had received approval to build a defined amount of square footage. During the debates about the future program, Mr. Blatstein accepted the proposals of local architects Erdy McHenry Architecture to design the area to be pedestrian-friendly and to contain a multiplicity of uses. As was the case at Granville Island, local zoning encourages the separation of uses and the developer had to convince local officials that uses need to be overlapping in order to create a vibrant area.

OWNER/DEVELOPER-INITIATED PROJECTS

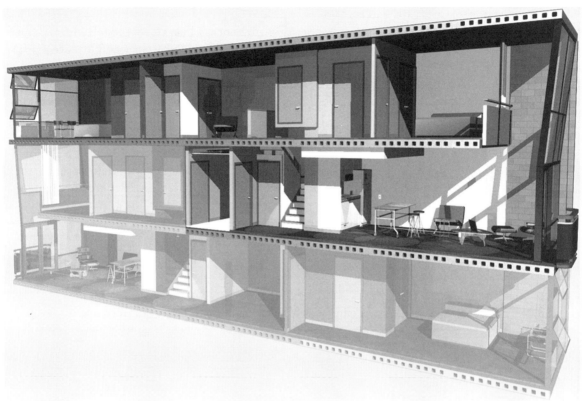

Figure 3.11
The new apartment buildings at the Piazza at Schmidts have a skip-stop configuration with the duplex townhouse units that interlock, saving corridor space.
Erdy McHenry Architecture

The existing warehouse was converted to offices, and it as well as residences—both renovated from former industrial buildings and newly constructed modernist residential buildings—form a plaza that opened in 2009. The height of new buildings around the plaza is restricted, and in the European tradition there are several entrances to the plaza so that it doesn't feel too enclosed and to allow visitors to "filter into the piazza," in the words of the architects. The surface of the plaza is composed of various materials and textures, with places for outdoor cafes and restaurants. The new apartment buildings, designed by Erdy McHenry Architecture, simultaneously recall the industrial heritage of the neighborhood and Le Corbusier's Unité d'habitation with its concrete grid facade that alternates voids and planes to add texture and visual openings within the building block on the plaza. The apartment units are all duplex townhouse types within the skip-stop buildings: The units interlock so that half the units are entered at the top floor, the other half on the lower floor.

Each unit has exposure on both the plaza and street sides. In addition to creating smaller, more neighborhood-like semi-public spaces at the elevator lobbies, this scheme reduced the built corridor area by 36,000 square feet, permitting the construction of an additional building, the oval-shaped office building, within the allowable square footage.

The ground-floor retail of the new buildings consists of small, boutique-sized spaces to encourage independent designers and artisans to rent the spaces and restaurant operators hand-picked by the developer to create a young and hip ambiance. Chain stores are forbidden. All residential tenants sign waivers acknowledging that the plaza will be noisy. It is still too new to determine the long-term success or failure of this venture; however, it shows that private developers can transform neighborhoods by listening to the community. This project also demonstrates that to succeed, the determination of a driving force who pursues his vision—in this case the developer, who was involved in every decision—is required.

TIDE POINT

NAME: TIDE POINT

LOCATION: BALTIMORE, MARYLAND

FORMER USE: SOAP FACTORY

PROJECT: OFFICE COMPLEX WITH PUBLIC ACCESS TO WATERFRONT

DEVELOPER: STRUEVER BROS. ECCLES & ROUSE

TIME LINE: 1999

In Baltimore, Maryland, within sight of the Inner Harbor, the former Proctor & Gamble 400,000-square-foot soap factory, built in 1929, is now offices for the developer Struever Bros. Eccles & Rouse. For over 60 years until 1994, Tide, Ivory Soap, Joy, Cascade, and Dawn were made in the factory from the raw materials shipped in from the harbor and then left on the railroad on the other side of the site. The developer engaged Design Collective, along with landscape architects W Architecture and Landscape Architecture, and dubbed the building Tide Point. The community was fearful of gentrification and rising rents, so it was adamant that only office use would be allowed, and not housing.

Access to the waterfront is integral to the landscape design of this 15-acre parcel. Some of the soil contamination was allowed to remain in place under existing concrete and not be disturbed, thus saving redevelopment funds. While much of the existing industrial flavor of the building has been retained, the area was decontaminated, outbuildings were removed, and art and public access to the waterfront now exist. As will be seen in the next chapters, benefits accrued to the project by the building's being listed on the National Register in order to be eligible for Historic Tax Credits and was also subject to the state's Voluntary Cleanup Program. The project won the 2001 Maryland Smart Growth Award.

Figure 3.12
Tide Point on the Baltimore, Maryland, harbor transformed a soap factory into corporate offices and opened up the waterfront to the public.
Design Collective

COMMUNITY-INITIATED PROJECTS

Community input is a double-edged sword. Community activism can initiate as well as impede, prevent, or change projects—whether for the better or worse is quite subjective. The redevelopment process has become more open and, in America and even in Europe, government seldom swoops down on a street or neighborhood and declares what should be, at least not without notice as was often done in the past. Despite the unsightliness of deteriorating sites and the deadening effect they have on whole areas, whatever is proposed will have its opponents. Sometimes this works out for the best for the community—the proposed project does not address the needs of the neighborhood. Other times, as can be seen from the story of Hudson River Park (see Chapter 9—Open Space and Parks), controversy delays the project and the enjoyment of a new development for all.

Community activists can be proponents, not only reactors. As will be described throughout the book, fired-up individuals or groups of people can indeed make their marks on their neighborhoods and are necessary components to many projects. As advocates, local communities tend to demonstrate for parks, not for more factories or museums. (The exception is a group composed of unions, workers, or local businesses.) Presenting a design to coalesce public opinion is the usual first step. Hiring a pro bono landscape architect or planner to present alternate ideas to the proposed project has become standard procedure now for groups to show other possibilities and to demonstrate that they are not against development per se, but against what was proposed.

THE HIGH LINE

NAME: THE HIGH LINE

LOCATION: NEW YORK CITY

FORMER USE: ELEVATED RAILROAD TRACK

PROJECT: PARK

DEVELOPER: NEW YORK CITY, FRIENDS OF THE HIGH LINE

PUBLIC OUTREACH: INFORMATION MEETINGS, PUBLIC FORUMS, COMPETITIONS, WEBSITE UPDATES, ACTIVE PUBLICITY THROUGH NEWSPAPER AND MAGAZINE ARTICLES

TIME LINE: FROM 1999; FIRST PHASE COMPLETED 2009; ONGOING

The High Line in New York City, an abandoned 1.5-mile-long elevated railroad built from 1929 to 1934 to ease traffic and prevent pedestrian deaths, sliced through the far west side of Manhattan in the Chelsea neighborhood and was scheduled for demolition. The last train ran on the line in 1980. Inspired by Paris's Promenade Plantée, a group of local residents and business owners with a smattering of celebrities marshaled interest in restoring the High Line through a clever campaign that drew the attention of city officials and inspired the broader community. These efforts changed the city's mind about the future of this industrial artifact, and the first phase of this new park and public space in New York opened in the summer of 2009 to overwhelming interest and crowds.

In 1999, Friends of the High Line formed a not-for-profit 501(c)(3) corporation to preserve and reuse the rail line through the federal government's "rail-banking" program.[10] Its public outreach program was multipronged. In 2001, a photo essay by Joel Sternfeld in *The New Yorker* appeared,[11] showing an evocative wilderness of weeds and savage areas with a backdrop of city skyscrapers. One year later, New York City sought a Certificate of Interim Trail Use for the structure from the federal government. Concurrently, the City Council allocated money for conversion planning while the area, which spanned three community districts, was being rezoned with plans that included the High Line's reuse.

Throughout this period, public forums, coupled with positive op-ed pieces in major newspapers, were orchestrated. Brochures were printed and meetings organized involving influential planners and cultural leaders who spoke at panel discussions to define goals and share ideas about the High Line's future. With no commitment from land owners or government that the railroad would be saved and money allocated, Friends of the High Line mounted an

COMMUNITY-INITIATED PROJECTS

Figure 3.13
The High Line in 1934 snaked through the west side of Manhattan to bring goods to the factories and warehouses and limit truck deliveries and traffic congestion.
Courtesy of Friends of the High Line

Figure 3.14
Saving the High Line and its conversion into one of New York's newest parks were accomplished by the concerted efforts of a group of savvy locals. The park opened in 2009.
Iwan Baan © 2009

international "ideas" competition that attracted 720 responses—architects, artists, and ordinary people from 36 countries. A selection of proposals was exhibited in Grand Central Terminal in July 2003 along with a video that explained the history of the rail line and steps for transforming it.

Building upon the publicity and overall awareness from this exhibition, the project was able to obtain city, state, and federal funding for planning and construction along with critical rezoning. Four final master plan designs, a result of a 2004 invited competition, were publicly unveiled at New York's Center for Architecture, and the team led by Field Operations with Diller + Scofidio & Renfo was awarded the design. Throughout this process, "Community Input Forums" were held and articles appeared in

COMMUNITY-INITIATED PROJECTS

Figure 3.15
New York's High Line artfully allows nature to invade man-made surfaces, recalling its state before the conversion. Buildings have been constructed over and around it—this building is a hotel.
Carol Berens

newspapers and magazines. It was not until 2005 that the city of New York acquired the structure from the entity that owned it, the CSX Corporation. Construction started in 2006 with New York City funds.

Dreams of this park are over a decade old. That it is becoming a reality is the result of persistent hard work on the part of the grass-roots advocates who knew how to coalesce the design and local communities and to involve the decision makers and government officials who provided funding. They were also lucky. During the late 1990s and early into 2000, the then-mayor, Rudolf Giuliani, with the concurrence of adjacent property owners, wanted to tear the structure down. The value of the property could not be determined and demolition proved problematic and too expensive. The timing of renewed efforts for a park project coincided with a change in neighborhood character, as well as

Figure 3.16
The Gansevoort Street entrance to the High Line in New York City avoids the pitfalls of the constrained, uninviting Promenade Plantée entrance.
Iwan Baan © 2009

the election of a new mayor, Michael Bloomberg, who was more amenable to public projects. While the project was being discussed, a natural conversion of the adjacent meat market into a new "in" neighborhood of design stores and restaurants was taking place, a reshaping that worked well with the solidification of its northern neighbor Chelsea as New York's art gallery center. With these two transformations, the change of lower Manhattan from an industrial culture to one of leisure and consumerism is nearly complete.

Images of this new park immediately spurred high-end development before the first phase of the project was even finished, with some of the new apartment buildings being attached to the structure or bridging over it. (One of the new buildings is a hotel that has become locally (in)famous for exhibitionist guests.) The jury is still out on the success of the High Line and how it will transition from the evocative relic that everyone romanticized in his own way to a modern park that will endure past its opening as the latest vogue. The initial design is sensitive to this. Given the new real estate developments, the High Line risks becoming the private backyard of the selected few who can afford to live nearby.

Figure 3.17
The Promenade Plantée in Paris wends its way from the Bastille to the Bois de Vincennes; however, entrances to the park above are problematic and ungracious.
Carol Berens

Figure 3.18
The Promenade Plantée in Paris is isolated from the city in most parts and is often deserted.
Carol Berens

THE PROMENADE PLANTÉE

Sometimes learning from the mistakes of pioneers benefits projects that follow. High Line park proponents cited Paris's Promenade Plantée as an inspiration. Built during the 1990s on an old rail bed that connected the Bois de Vincennes to the Bastille, this park is, despite the claims of the Friends of the High Line, one of the least interesting of the new Paris parks. The Promenade Plantée's constrained and difficult access as well as its separation from the city it hovers above pose major problems. The park is entered through narrow, hidden staircases in which it's difficult to see where one is going. The park's elevated structure does not offer the spectacular views as the High Line, and its disconnection from the city can be disconcerting. In addition its design is static, inhibited by its narrowness and isolation. Consequently, it is not much used and is often deserted. There are open areas that are more welcoming; however, they are broad swaths at grade level and more integrated within the city and are more heavily used.

As can be learned from the above examples of industrial transformations, careful and strategic planning is required over a long period of time. Whether the project is initiated by government, private developers, or community activists, patience and a determination to work with local planning officials, as well as neighborhood groups, to resolve problems is a long-term enterprise. Projects that take long-underused or deteriorating property and turn it into public spaces or tax-paying, working buildings again, are Herculean feats, not for the weary or easily discouraged.

ENDNOTES

1. For a detailed discussion of the "civic theater" of community participation in projects see *Designing Public Consensus*, Barbara Faga, FASLA (Hoboken: John Wiley & Sons, Inc., 2006).
2. International Association for Public Participation (www.iap2.org), 3030 W. 81st Avenue, Westminster, Colorado 80031, 800-644-4273.
3. *Charrette* is a French word for cart. Years ago at Paris's Ecole des Beaux Arts, final course designs were drawn on boards that were collected by carts and wheeled from studios to the presentation room. Since last-minute work was often necessary, students would hop on the carts to put the finishing touches on their presentations. Thus, in architecture schools, the term came to mean the nonstop working for a project's deadline.
4. Telephone interview with Stephen Soler of Georgetown Land Development on July 17, 2008.
5. New Urbanism is an urban design theory that promotes the building of traditional neighborhoods with an emphasis on pedestrian and transit-oriented amenities, housing that relates to the street, diversity of uses and population, and public spaces. Proponents' theories are an alternate to designs that encourage suburban sprawl (large subdivisions of large houses with no public space) and reliance on the automobile.
6. Region 1: New England United States Environmental Protection Agency November 16, 2005 press release.
7. Eminent domain in America refers to the power of a government entity, be it city, state, or federal, to acquire land for a public purpose. The Fifth Amendment of the U.S. Constitution states in part, "nor shall private property be taken for public use, without just compensation." Land has been acquired by governments not only for roads and other public works but also for economic and urban redevelopment purposes. Sometimes this land would be in turn sold or leased to private developers to build projects in accordance with development agreements. Although the land is paid for subject to appraisals and negotiation, this practice has become contentious. The controversial use of eminent domain to transfer land by the government from one private entity to another culminated in the 2005 Supreme Court case of *Kelo v. City of New London, Connecticut, et al.* The resulting 5-4 opinion maintained that economic development projects were indeed valid under the "takings clause", however, it was much criticized. Several states are considering local laws or state constitutional amendments to prevent such use.
8. Telephone interview with Norman Hotson on December 22, 2009.
9. Project for Public Spaces website, www.pps.org/info/newsletter/november2004/november2004_granville, accessed July 28, 2008.
10. The ownership patterns of the rail line were complex. The line was built by both New York Central Lines and New York City, and CSX, the successor corporation to Conrail still owned the railroad. The

land underneath the structure as well as the air rights and easements were owned by the city (street crossings) and private property owners. The Rail Banking strategy is authorized by the federal government under the 1983 National Trail Systems Act in which rail corridors that have a future potential to connect to national rail systems can be used for public purposes if an easement guarantees its future use.

11. Joel Sternfeld and Adam Gopnik, "A Walk on the Highline." *The New Yorker*, May 21, 2001.

CHAPTER 4

PUBLIC POLICY AND URBAN EVOLUTION

Abandoned and underutilized industrial sites often occupy substantially large areas near their cities' central districts, sections that the municipalities now need to renew in order to grow. Cities have various strategies at their disposal to guide the direction of this new growth through public policies without necessarily investing in direct expenditures of public funds. Local government involvement with respect to zoning issues, tax incentives, environmental cleanup, and perhaps even land ownership can facilitate development. How a city retains industry or charts a new course to influence its character is reflected in its policies. Because of this flexibility, local governments can help to establish the development climate that encourages developers (for-profit and, more recently, not-for-profit) to invest resources and to take the attendant risks.

This chapter will explore the role that government plays in determining cities' postindustrial economic and physical structure. Sometimes policies lag behind what spontaneously evolves and merely confirm what's happening; other times, a city's vision of its future leads it to take specific actions. As will be seen in the following examples and throughout this book, concerned citizens as either instigators or supporters of projects are actively addressing the voids in their neighborhoods and, by galvanizing their communities, can determine the directions of development.

The importance of art and culture in spurring redevelopment of postindustrial downtowns cannot be ignored. Art has become an economic development engine. While critical to the vitality of cities, the addition of museums and institutions and the infusion of artists' housing are not necessarily the panacea to what cities need to create jobs and a well-rounded economy. Retaining industry in a way that builds on a city's strengths and needs is just as critical as wonderful galleries and open studio days to a place's economic health.

URBAN EVOLUTION, REZONING, AND DEVELOPMENT CONTROLS

Some changes occur naturally as one use displaces another, although "naturally" doesn't necessarily mean without difficulty or acrimony. The most influential example of this phenomenon is SoHo in New York City. Today, the neighborhood's streets approach an unwalkable status, as tourists flock there from all over, wandering around clutching maps and buying t-shirts and jewelry from sidewalk vendors. Stores displaying designer clothes long dislodged the art galleries of the 1970s. The art galleries had supplanted the warehouses, dry goods firms, and marginal industries of the postwar years that, in turn, had replaced the textile manufacturers and department stores of the late 1870s through the 1890s. Previously, SoHo had been the locale of the city's vibrant red light district that, in turn, had transformed the pre–Civil War residential area.

What began during the 1960s as a small pioneering effort of a few hardy souls is now an established economic development pattern of vast impact. Although not itself a brownfield, on many levels the phenomenon of SoHo is significant to the redevelopment of brownfields and industrial sites around the world. Its influence cannot be overestimated. First, it highlights the importance that art and culture play in propelling the economic engine of postindustrial cities. This theme recurs throughout this book.[1] Art and culture create a sense of community and provide destinations, such as galleries, shows, and concerts as well as the restaurants and stores that serve them. Since the SoHo experience, artists have been given credit for being able to suss out the next best neighborhoods, both for atmospheric character and good real estate values.

Just as important, perhaps, the transformation of SoHo educated the general public to appreciate the industrial aesthetic and the value of preserving the physical fabric of cities. The rise of this quarter happened at a time when cities were often considered dirty and dangerous, worthy only of being torn down and prime targets of the wrecking ball. SoHo's emergence contributed to the expansion of the historic preservation movement. Artists promoted the legacy of everyday industrial heritage by seeing the beauty of gritty buildings as meriting saving as much as grand Beaux Arts monuments. The progression from homesteading industrial areas to vibrant neighborhoods to often overcommercialized districts still happens spontaneously. Policies and laws to encourage or control such area-wide changes are now commonplace.

The blocks that Robert Moses threatened to mow down with his proposed Lower Manhattan Expressway during the late 1950s and early 1960s were colonized by artists attracted to the lofts in the cast iron buildings that had raw, unfinished open interior spaces conducive to creating large-scale art work that was a hallmark of contemporary art and, of course, cheap rent. During the 1960s, artists upgraded these lofts through sweat equity, creating illegal live-in studios and camping out in former apparel and metal shops and warehouses. With the exception of a few bars, the neighborhood lacked the residential amenities of food stores, cleaners, or even regular sanitation services because in New York businesses are responsible for hauling their own trash. (The light manufacturing businesses still tucked away nearby gladly provided odd fittings and fabrication services useful in creating some types of art, however.) Nevertheless, a small community formed when these urban artists moved in as manufacturers moved out. Landlords turned a blind eye, preferring illegal tenants who paid minimal rent to vacant buildings that produced no income. With a wink toward London's Soho district, it quickly developed a nickname: SoHo, which stands for South of Houston Street, a major east-west thoroughfare in downtown Manhattan. Although the area was and still is zoned for manufacturing, it also contained a "collection of well preserved cast-iron structures, now unrivalled in the world...[as well as a variety of] nineteenth-century commercial architectural styles...probably as complete, well documented and geographically compact as to be found in the United States" according to the New York City Landmarks Preservation Commission's 1973 report designating SoHo as an historic district. With buildings mostly constructed between 1870 and 1890, this cobblestoned light manufacturing district sandwiched between Greenwich Village and Little Italy/Chinatown was on the verge of becoming derelict when building owners could not find tenants or buyers as manufacturing and warehousing left Manhattan. Resident artists banded together to convince the City to acknowledge that the area was turning residential, if only to address the public safety issue of fire.[2] A series of half-measures and loft rent laws were patched together

Figure 4.1
A typical SoHo street in New York City today contains a variety of styles of cast iron facades with stores on the ground floor. Today's residential lofts were once light manufacturing spaces.
Carol Berens

to allow this natural evolution of use without committing the City to forsake manufacturing and veer in a direction from which there was no return. To implement this policy, residents had to prove that they were professional artists, and laws were passed on a provisional, renewable basis.

Despite the "artist-only" requirement the city imposed on the zoning, SoHo quickly became a chic center for design stores and art galleries as many nonartists were somehow able to circumvent the professional prerequisite. Few manufacturers held on. (Every couple of years, a human-interest item appears in local newspapers about a hardy fabricator or supplier who has somehow managed to survive.) Gleaming lofts with clean white walls, high ceilings, industrial fittings, and acres of wood floors appeared in design magazines and on covers of coffee table books touting the latest in "industrial chic." Artists were soon priced out of the neighborhood and began the search for other areas that had large spaces and, moreover, were affordable.

This cycle is now a common phenomenon not only in New York but all over as cities eye the inevitable change and try to benefit from this neighborhood regeneration while implementing policies to avoid pitfalls.

Not all industrial neighborhoods have the benefit of being as architecturally cohesive or as distinguished as SoHo, however. Neighborhoods from Providence, Rhode Island, to Omaha, Nebraska, to Portland, Oregon, deal with similar issues arising from changing economics and demographics.

* * *

Even without ownership rights, the public sector plays a strong role in orchestrating change through zoning. These large swaths of urban land where for over 100 years factories produced springs, cabinets, or textiles are industrially zoned. Rezoning these areas either to acknowledge the change of use or to encourage such transformation is a step that towns and cities take that resounds as strongly as infusions of money or exercising ownership interest. Such large-scale neighborhood regeneration can be controversial, especially when class and social issues arise. It is, however, often seen as an important economic development generator, especially when such rezoning encourages more dense residential use interspersed with recreational uses, as will be seen in the examples later in this chapter.

A critical development phase with deteriorating industrial areas and sites is often the most complex and fraught with emotion—acknowledging that industry left and will not return, whether for economic, social, or physical reasons. With the hope that an erstwhile industry can be replaced by a different one, those in power often are loathe to do anything that will preclude a wished-for stroke of good luck—the chance that a new company or industry will move in and replace the lost jobs. Eliminating manufacturing districts, however, prevents the possibility of retention or creation of well-paying jobs for a city's economy.

Despite the ability of governments to create policies and debate their future, forces of change frequently control development. In transition neighborhoods, illegal conversions and occupations occur. In addition, even rumors of possible rezoning often prevent industrial development as speculators and real estate interests buy up industrial land to warehouse for potentially more profitable use in the future, making the demise of local industry a self-fulfilling prophesy.

GREENPOINT-WILLIAMSBURG REZONING

NAME: GREENPOINT-WILLIAMSBURG REZONING

LOCATION: BROOKLYN, NEW YORK

ISSUE: REZONING OF INDUSTRIAL WATERFRONT

KEY PLAYERS: CITY PLANNING DEPARTMENT, COMMUNITY GROUPS, LANDOWNERS

TIME LINE: 2003–2005

Across the East River from Manhattan, the story of the transformation of Brooklyn's waterfront encompassing Greenpoint-Williamsburg to the north and Red Hook to the south spotlight two different approaches and neighborhood reactions. Individual activism was critical to both; however, the city tried to control the former through rezoning and a major landowner spearheaded the latter. Both tried to address the reality of neighborhood change while maintaining a mixed-use character provided by its existing manufacturing base. Mayor Michael Bloomberg's 2003 announcement of an ambitious decade-long plan to add or preserve 165,000 units of housing, many of which were to be built in former manufacturing districts, contributed to the changes. How this goal is playing out in these two neighborhoods illustrates conflicting city narratives that vie for attention: New York's severe housing shortage (especially the affordable kind) and the need to attract and keep well-paying jobs to broaden its economic base. Both neighborhoods draw attention to these competing visions of the future with the overlay of public accessibility to New York's extensive waterfront.

Since the conversion of SoHo, change in New York neighborhoods appears to have accelerated, and in the late 1990s the Brooklyn areas of Greenpoint along with its southern neighbor, Williamsburg, low-rise areas with sensible rents and spectacular views of the Manhattan skyline, were "discovered." For many years they were centers of thriving immigrant[3] communities; however, the allure of rents cheaper than Manhattan yet only one subway stop from the East Village put these neighborhoods in the gentrification viewfinder. Although the waterfront was and is a mixture of warehouses and facilities for city gas, electric and sanitation services, it was mostly inaccessible to the public, highly contaminated, and rife with environmental issues. In short, it's a classic industrialized waterfront, developed at a time when harbors were valued for their economic operations and not considered a requisite urban amenity.

When the market fosters a neighborhood transition, sociology and economics trump environmental remediation concerns. Whole areas or just isolated industrial sites may be environmentally denigrated, but once the economic viability of another use can be proven, private developers search for the means to clean the sites. While a neighborhood is still in transition, many companies that caused the contamination are still in business and are legally responsible for cleanup.

In 1992, the city issued a comprehensive waterfront plan calling for the rezoning of some of the areas of Greenpoint, but took no official action for over a decade. During the intervening years, industrial use declined, real estate investors bought up land, and residents illegally occupied the warehouses and small industrial buildings, encouraged by landlords who heard rumors of a possible rezoning plan and could get higher rents from residents than from manufacturers. Hopes of rezoning and the resulting increase in land prices made manufacturing use less valuable and contributed to driving it out.

Despite this unofficial transition in neighborhood character, even in the early 2000s, this industrial area topped the list as a site suitable for waste transfer stations and other noxious uses. However, when a power plant was proposed to be built on state land—one of the few non-built-up areas directly on the river with views of Manhattan—the community coalesced to reject the plan. In 2003, the city agreed to oppose the power plant and initiate a block-by-block rezoning of the area. As a result, the power plant site will now be an eight-acre state park.

After the city-state agreement not to build the power plant in the neighborhood, over a period of two years the city met with residents and political leaders and developed a mixed-use rezoning plan that interwove residential and commercial uses with manufacturing interests. In this part of the city, there were no large swaths of single uses separated by buffers, such as in small towns or suburbs (or as envisioned by Ebenezer Howard). The realities of urban living allowed for closer proximities of uses, and indeed existing buildings and land-use patterns accommodated housing just across the street from warehouses and factories. Many industries don't want or need to be isolated in deserted low-density areas and can easily exist in residential areas and benefit from commercial uses. Concerns about noise and traffic can be addressed as use issues by restricting traffic routes and hours rather than as a zoning issue. As a result, the Greenpoint-Williamsburg rezoning preserved industrial uses in specific areas while opening some of the area for public access to the waterfront.

REZONING ISSUES

The first examples in this chapter revolve around events that occurred in New York City and may at first appear parochial. The issues raised, however, are universal and reoccur throughout the book in various locations. Although some of the points below may seem obvious, planners will lose track of them at their peril.

- Change from industrial uses to retail and residential, whether naturally occurring or planned, engenders fears, both real and imagined, about gentrification, issues which city planners must address in order for effective rezoning to be enacted.
- Even rumors of rezoning can cause industry to leave.
- Traditional American zoning that stresses separation of uses, thereby preventing active, mixed-use urban neighborhoods, can contribute to industry's leaving. Those industries that remain, however, are often small scale and artisan in nature and provide the local services and goods that can be integrated with residential use.
- Local groups will always clamor for more recreational areas and access to waterfronts.
- The goals of landowners and lessees, whether residential or industrial, are at odds with each other.

Manufacturing proponents, however, felt the existing zoning already allowed for nuanced use, but the City turned a blind eye toward illegal residential use. The type of manufacturing that filled the Greenpoint buildings was predominantly small-scale specialized fabricators, with a preponderance of woodworking companies. Almost all large-scale manufacturing or single-use buildings had been slowly disappearing. As a result, Greenpoint industry is not the mass production, lunch-bucket, factory-bell type, but consists of many individual owners and small companies. Although the number of employees is significant, their overall presence does not overwhelm and at times is not apparent. In fact, during the rezoning process, some buildings were thought by the city to be empty, but were instead fully occupied by various manufacturers.

Many of these buildings were not single-use and manufacturers rented their spaces in buildings owned by others. Short-term leases that were not easily renewed were becoming the norm. As rezoning talks progressed the rift between owners and renters became clear. Thus, the industrial base did not speak with a unified voice—the building owners were interested in the rezoning because, if their land became allowable for residential use, their low-return properties would suddenly be worth a lot more money. The manufacturers were interested in the provision of more industrially zoned areas to ease their rental squeeze.

The conflicting issues of building housing versus retaining industry as well as waterfront access all converged in Greenpoint. As will be seen in subsequent chapters, industrial neighborhoods or those in transition have little or no recreational or park space. The provision of new parks and recreation is usually on the list of resident demands during such rezonings. The call for open space and affordable housing was countered with fervent pleas to retain industrial and manufacturing districts for the city's economic health and continuing job opportunities.

URBAN EVOLUTION, REZONING, AND DEVELOPMENT CONTROLS

Figure 4.2
When a power plant was scheduled to be built on this site, the neighborhood instigated an overall rezoning of the Greenpoint area, which calls for a mix of uses and places for public waterfront access, including this site for a future park. Much work obviously still has to be done, although the allure of the water and the view draws people to the site despite the rubble.
Carol Berens

The neighborhood was traditionally affordable for both residents and manufacturers until the recent influx of artists and Manhattan-escapees who followed the trailblazers. The change in demographics plus the allure of waterfront housing not previously available in this area made the availability of future reasonably priced housing for existing residents a prime concern for community negotiators.

The final 2005 zoning agreement gave bonuses to developments that included 20 to 25 percent affordable housing and built waterfront esplanades to be managed by the city parks department. Although certain areas retained industrial zoning, it is unclear how long the owners of these sites can hold out if a lucrative offer on their land comes their way. The rezoning of the waterfront areas into open space

Figure 4.3
One of the new riverfront esplanades mandated for all new construction along the Williamsburg waterfront as a result of the zoning change from industrial to residential use.
Carol Berens

and residential uses was not as controversial as the rezoning of the upland blocks to a mixed-use designation that allows for as-of-right residential conversion.

The city maintains that it has struck a balance with preserving the neighborhood while increasing the amenities and possibilities of much needed affordable housing. The National Trust for Historic Preservation doesn't agree. In 2007, it included the Brooklyn waterfront on its annual list of most endangered historic places, noting that not enough historic buildings were protected and the working waterfront and industrial retention would be lost. If industry could not be retained, it added, buildings should be renovated and adapted for new uses.

To that end, several preservation groups have formed around issues of saving either existing buildings or whole neighborhoods. The Municipal Arts Society, a century-old organization, has several groups eyeing the waterfront and Brooklyn's industrial heritage. Its sophisticated website, complete with an interactive map, charts the borough's industrial history. How effective this group or others like it are in channeling or restricting future growth is still an open question. They raise awareness through articles and through the use of petitions and litigation. Their level of success has been greater for landmarking individual buildings rather than defining change and helping industry to return.

RED HOOK DEVELOPMENT

NAME: RED HOOK

LOCATION: BROOKLYN, NEW YORK

ISSUE: NEIGHBORHOOD TRANSFORMATION WITHOUT OVERALL REZONING

KEY PLAYERS: LOCAL LANDOWNER, GREG O'CONNELL

TIME LINE: 1990S; ONGOING

Further south from Greenpoint-Williamsburg along the Brooklyn waterfront, the Red Hook neighborhood reprised some of the same concerns of business leaders and community groups; however, the reality of the area differs. At first blush, the difference is obvious—the waterfront in Red Hook is accessible: It is not ringed with a highway and almost half the land directly on the water is vacant. Civil War–era warehouses are built right to the water's edge and are surrounded by a combination of crumbling and rebuilt piers jutting into the harbor. Whereas river views from Greenpoint-Williamsburg are often hidden behind warehouses and gas tanks, views of the Erie Basin and New York Harbor from Red Hook are unobstructed and all-encompassing. Both share the effects of the shriveling industrial base.

Once raw sugar, grain, cotton, coffee, and spices, among many other goods, were loaded and unloaded on the piers of Red Hook and stored in its warehouses. The neighborhood, always rough—the locale of Hubert Selby Jr.'s *Last Exit to Brooklyn* as well as Al Capone's gangster beginnings—was dealt several blows by the government. In 1938, one of the largest public housing projects in New York City, the Red Hook Houses, was built, originally as part of the Federal Works Program for the Brooklyn waterfront dockworkers but whose residents are now poor and unemployed. Red Hook is isolated, severed from the rest of Brooklyn first in 1946 by the Gowanus Expressway and again in 1950 by the entrance to the Brooklyn Battery Tunnel. Despite Selby's book's title, the subway stops many blocks away, further isolating the neighborhood.

The Port Authority of New York & New Jersey dealt New York's working waterfronts a death blow when it opened the container port in Newark/Elizabeth that siphoned off much of Red Hook's trade. Since its peak in the 1950s, the loss of jobs from waterfront activity was followed by a loss of 50 percent of its population; a large majority that remains lives below the poverty line. It was the end of the line, literally and metaphorically: The police department's evidence impound lot was located on a pier so that empty cars had an

Figure 4.4
Brooklyn's Red Hook waterfront is a neighborhood in transition; the new IKEA store stakes out its spot in the industrial landscape amid buildings and piers in various states of decay and rebirth.
Carol Berens

unimpeded view of the Statue of Liberty, the Verrazano Bridge, and the New York harbor.

Over the last 25 years, however, it has had its supporters, mainly from a smattering of artists and a forceful developer, Greg O'Connell, a retired policeman who had been buying property in the area for about 20 years. The city had foreclosed on many of the buildings and sold them at auction or through special housing programs. At one point there was a city-sponsored Artists' Housing program that allowed artists to purchase property. As with many nascent developments, Mr. O'Connell encouraged people to come to the forlorn area by working with artists groups, in this case, the Brooklyn Waterfront Artists Coalition and providing free space for art shows in his Beard Street Warehouse. O'Connell, who owns about one million square feet of waterfront property, claims he doesn't want an overall rezoning so that the ambiance of the rough-and-tumble area is not lost. However, he is not against redevelopment that brings a vital mix of residents, restaurants, and artists.[4]

An overall rezoning plan failed in the late 1980s, so subsequent development has been marked with rezoning fights for each new use as parts of Red Hook remain an industrial business zone. Two of the contested uses revolved around commercial use directly on the waterfront. The first involved the conversion of a warehouse into a large Fairway, a locally known food store that agreed to provide jobs for the local residents, and apartments above. The other battle revolved around the building of an IKEA store. In order to grant permission to build, the city demanded the hiring of local residents, site improvements, and enhanced bus service to the store, as well as free ferry service from the Wall Street pier on the weekends. One year after opening, the Brooklyn borough president claimed that the Red Hook store was IKEA's top-selling store in North America.

After several decades the area is trying to overcome its isolation, but whether it can strike a balance among residential, industrial, and commercial uses and maintain its distinct flavor is still unknown. With each new change, conflicts emerge. A concrete plant is now opening adjacent to IKEA's site, a development that few are pleased with despite its being located in an industrial zone. The Port Authority, after much delay, renewed a container port lease, ensuring the continuation of traditional port activities adjacent to the emerging neighborhood.

NEON MEMORIES

Over the past few decades, the transformation of production has been swift and extreme, and it's easy to forget that the products sitting on America's tables and stored in kitchen cabinets were once made by next-door neighbors in nearby factories. It's not unusual that the long battle of fighting change often comes down to the preservation of a sign, a neon reminder of a city's industrial heritage. The 120-foot-long Pepsi-Cola sign in Long Island City now towers over a new park facing Manhattan, its present location a major bargaining point in the approval of Queens West, the development partially on the site of a former PepsiCo Bottling factory. Further west across the Hudson River, the Colgate clock tells time without its building, also freestanding in a park, while the Maxwell House Coffee's "last drop," formerly atop its Hoboken, New Jersey, factory, is displayed, cupless, in the Hoboken Historical Museum. The former factory's site is now filled with condos marketed as Maxwell Place.

Victory takes many forms, as the story of the Domino Sugar Plant that sits just above the Williamsburg Bridge shows. Although New York was once the sugar refinery center of America (the Revere Sugar factory was recently demolished in Red Hook down the street from IKEA), its capacities outstripped demand and one plant closed after another. Domino Sugar outlasted most of them, and when it stopped production in 2004, its buildings and 11 acres remained zoned for manufacturing use in the Greenpoint-Williamsburg rezoning plan. No manufacturing user stepped up to buy the property that

Figure 4.5
The PepsiCo Bottling factory closed shop here in 1999; its relocated sign towers over the new park, requirements for the approval of the Queens West project in New York.
Paul Januszewski

Figure 4.6
Colgate's factory rooftop in Jersey City, New Jersey, sported a clock and a tube of toothpaste as late as 1989. Colgate left in the early 1990s and the factory was razed for a new development called Exchange Place.
Historic American Engineering Record, NJ-2-9; HAER NJ, 9-JERCI, 18-1, Gerald Weinstein, photographer, February 1989

Figure 4.7
The Colgate clock near where its former factory was on the Jersey City waterfront, now adjacent to the Goldman Sachs tower.
Ronald L. Glassman

Figure 4.8
The Domino Sugar factory in Williamsburg, Brooklyn, will be renovated with new towers added to the site, however, on all applications to the Landmark Commission, the jaunty yellow sign was affixed to the waterfront facade.
Ronald L. Glassman

> was eventually purchased by residential developers who quickly devised plans to convert the factory to apartments and build new towers around it.
>
> The building became a New York City Landmark in 2007. Although the designation excluded the sign and the building it was attached to, design proposals presented to the Landmarks Preservation Commission prominently showed the 40-foot-tall, jaunty yellow, optimistically slanted Domino Sugar sign proudly perched atop all new additions. Perhaps one day large iconic signs will be what remains as America's industrial legacy.

Retaining Industry

The debate over a workable balance of industrial space and converted industrial space is a dynamic one. Faced with an approximately 20 percent decrease in manufacturing acreage from 2002 to 2008, New York City officials believe they have taken steps to protect this use in all the boroughs by creating Industrial Business Zones, or IBZs, whose stated purpose is to remain industrial and prohibit residential use. This program is supported by funding and a new government entity to oversee the program. The Pratt Center for Community Development, a local not-for-profit community and environmental advocate, has proposed further rezoning restrictions to safeguard factories outside these protected enclaves to make rezoning, sale, or lease of properties for other uses more difficult. This is an effort to retain manufacturing jobs, which pay more than retail jobs and are a good source of employment, a bulwark against New York's becoming a two-class city. The newly created zones acknowledge that residential land is potentially more lucrative than property zoned for manufacturing purposes. In addition to restrictive zoning, financial incentives are given in the form of per-employee tax credits for companies to relocate within an IBZ.

An October 2009 study by the New York Industrial Retention Network (NYIRN), a nonprofit economic development organization established to strengthen New York City's manufacturing sector and to promote sustainable development, stated that 39 sites within these zones have been used for commercial uses rather than industrial. The report cited the inclusion of hotels, superstores, art galleries, bars, and even two bowling alleys in these zones and claimed that these nonindustrial uses drove up rents, a situation that has caused industry to leave the city.

Maintaining industry through zoning is a concern across the country, as can be seen in San Francisco's story of rezoning over 2,200 acres in the eastern neighborhoods of East SoMA, Central Waterfront, Potrero Hill, and the Mission District, which has taken over 10 years to get to a point where it could be voted on by the Board of Supervisors in 2009. Although housing and industry conflict in the West as they do in New York, the issue over what is an industrial use is complicated in San Francisco, with its proximity to Silicon Valley, where industry is not marked by the whirl of mills, but the quiet of software development. Despite this difference, the fear is that newly permitted residential use in a previously industrial district will drive out industry.

Partnership for Creative Industrial Space, a not-for-profit group based in Providence, Rhode Island, advocated for a 2008 city ordinance that requires developers who renovate mills in the Industrial Commercial Buildings District, a local historic district, to give industrial and art tenants 90 days notice. In addition, developers are encouraged to reimburse relocation costs or risk losing development aid from the city. Conflicts arose in Providence between those involved in efforts to preserve its historic mills and the existing tenants. Rhode Island's

Historic Preservation Investment Tax Program and Providence's Urban Mill Initiative were designed to save the city's historic fabric in response to the demolition of many of these buildings. While these measures were successful in refurbishing historic buildings, many businesses and individuals were displaced.

GREENPOINT MANUFACTURING AND DESIGN CENTER

NAME: GREENPOINT MANUFACTURING AND DESIGN CENTER

LOCATION: BROOKLYN, NEW YORK

ISSUE: PROVIDING AFFORDABLE AND STABLE MANUFACTURING SPACE IN BROOKLYN

KEY INNOVATION: NOT-FOR-PROFIT DEVELOPER OF MANUFACTURING SPACE IN BROOKLYN

TIME LINE: 1990S; ONGOING

Private developers, some not-for-profit, with the help of certain municipal policies are taking up the mantle of helping industry remain in cities. In the late 1980s, David Sweeney, who was then the economic development director of the North Brooklyn Development Corporation, discovered that the area had a culture of small artisan manufacturers whose clients were locally based. His pilot project was a 360,000-square-foot building at the northern tip of the Greenpoint section of Brooklyn that New York City owned as a result of nonpayment of taxes. When it was built in the mid-1800s it was a jute factory that made rope for maritime purposes; later, a garment factory. Those days were long gone and despite the few woodworkers and other small users in the building, the city was planning to tear it down. In 1991, Mr. Sweeney formed the Greenpoint Manufacturing and Design Center (GMDC), convinced the city to sell the building for $1 and give $1 million to his organization to renovate it.

Today the building and the subsequent four buildings GMDC developed are almost 100 percent rented to small, specialty manufacturers, who occupy space ranging from as little as 500 square feet to as much as 7,000 square feet and have an average of three to five employees. Most of the tenants and workers are artisans engaged in woodworking, metal fabricating, or fine arts and produce one-of-a-kind objects rather than mass-produced items. The companies range from display makers for museums or store windows, woodworkers for architectural interiors, to costume designers for theater, film, and special events. In addition to providing employment opportunities, these businesses supply vital services and products for clients—the stores, designers, and cultural institutions—that need them, and are only a subway ride away rather than across an ocean.

As a 501(c)(3) nonprofit corporation, GMDC strives to keep rents below market rate, provide five-year leases with five-year renewal clauses, and be a "benevolent landlord." The stability of what has become to be considered long-term leases has allowed these small

Figure 4.9
The Greenpoint Manufacturing and Design Center bought this rambling Brooklyn building from New York City for $1, renovated it, and now rents studios to artisan manufacturers.
Courtesy of Greenpoint Manufacturing and Design Center

manufacturers to concentrate on their business rather than to continually search for new space when their facilities are sold for housing. The owners find that working in buildings with other manufacturers has allowed for a certain amount of cross-pollination. Almost 50 percent of the employees live in Brooklyn, with the rest living in the five boroughs or nearby suburbs.

As an industrial advocate, GMDC acquired, renovated, and manages five buildings in Brooklyn totaling slightly more than 600,000 square feet. The financial landscape has changed greatly since GDMC bought its first building. Simple transactions and conventional financing are processes of the past. As a result of the changing and gentrifying city, real estate values have escalated, and even with a downturn from the real estate bubble, acquisition and construction costs have increased about 300 percent since the purchase of its first building.

Figure 4.10
Sculptor/metal smith Richard Webber in his work space in GMDC's Manhattan Avenue building. His company, Museum Productions, makes sculptures, models, and mounts for exhibits.
Courtesy of Greenpoint Manufacturing and Design Center

Figure 4.11
221 McKibbin Street in Brooklyn containing 19 manufacturing workspaces in 72,000 square feet is the latest GMDC development. The building was entered onto the National Register in order to benefit from historic tax credits.
Courtesy of Greenpoint Manufacturing and Design Center

The last building it renovated was financed with what's become the normal—though extremely complicated—cocktail of tax credit programs (New Market and Historic Preservation), grants from foundations, and public sources through the local Industrial Development Agency and economic development groups requiring much consultation with legal firms and financing consultants.

PHILADELPHIA NAVY YARD

Name: Philadelphia Navy Yard

Location: Philadelphia, Pennsylvania

Issue: Decommissioned military base, attracting industrial uses

Key Players: Federal government, City of Philadelphia through the Philadelphia Industrial Development Corporation (PIDC)

Time Line: 1990s; ongoing

The military base closings of the 1990s in America didn't spare the birthplace of the Navy in Philadelphia. Although the Navy still has a presence there, the closing meant the loss of approximately 20,000 jobs when the city of Philadelphia received over 1,000 acres of the former base. Decommissioned in 1996 and 1998, the Navy Yard was the subject of a Mayor's 1994 Commission on Defense Conversion's Community Reuse Plan that laid out a vision for the redevelopment of the site built upon a consensus of a group of citizens, public officials, and local institutions. Philadelphia was able to acquire the property through an economic development conveyance because the federal government did not sell the property to the highest bidder, as it did with some other bases.

As a result, with the exception of the little more than 200 acres retained by the Navy, the city owns most of the property of the former Navy Yard through an entity called the Philadelphia Authority for Industrial Development (PAID), which in turn contracts to the Philadelphia Industrial Development Corporation (PIDC), a not-for-profit joint venture between the City of Philadelphia and Chamber of Commerce that manages the planning development and operations of the Navy Yard. The military conducted a comprehensive environmental review of the property before the conveyance and is responsible for removing and/or remediating any contamination. The major environmental issues have revolved around asbestos and lead paint remediation.

Separated from the city by an interstate and rail lines, the Navy Yard is isolated and creates its own world. This separation has existed for over 200 years. The goal of the redevelopment is to build upon its distinctive maritime and military character while connecting to the city for the first time. In 2004 Robert A.M. Stern Architects was commissioned to develop a revised master plan that would build upon the original 1994 plan. It outlined development goals for a mixed-use community that included opening up the waterfront to public access and creating a better connection to the rest of the city.

This plan identified five major areas that would build upon the former base's strength: a new corporate center; a research park consisting of Research and Development uses especially in energy research as well as manufacturing and distribution; the historic core that retains its noteworthy buildings and mature landscape for use for offices, retail, cultural, and perhaps residential use; a new marina with a conference center and recreational areas along with a plan for a waterfront promenade; and an area that could be developed for different uses depending upon the market. In addition, on the western part of the site is the state-of-the-art Aker Philadelphia Shipyard, which constructs 2.5 ships a year and employs 1,300 workers.

The goal of the Navy Yard is to concentrate on building up its corporate and industrial base and increase employment. The city and the state provided certain public infrastructure and capital investments in order to encourage private companies to relocate or start businesses. The private joint venture of Liberty Property Trust/Synterra Partners is developing the 70-acre corporate park and providing the infrastructure for that area. To that end the city and state have instituted several tax incentive programs to encourage companies to relocate there.

Name: Urban Outfitters

Location: Philadelphia Navy Yard

Issue: Consolidating company into campus-like setting without leaving home city

Key Players: Urban Outfitters, Meyer, Scherer & Rockcastle Ltd. (architects)

Time Line: 2004; ongoing

Changing buildings from centers of production to centers of creativity was the architects Meyer, Scherer & Rockcastle's self-described goal for the transformation of five former Navy Yard buildings into Urban Outfitters, Inc. headquarters. Previously located in six office buildings scattered around Philadelphia's Rittenhouse Square, this hometown company wanted to consolidate its four brands (Urban Outfitters, Free People, Anthropologie, and Terrain) into one facility. The owner of the company, Dick Hayne, chose the waterfront campus-like setting only a little over three miles from center city, but a world away in atmosphere. The price was right: $1 in 2004. The company subsequently spent $115 million to renovate the 250,000-square-foot buildings and upgrade the infrastructure.

The five buildings were erected over a 60-year period from 1876 to 1934 and saw many wars, going back to the Spanish American War and World War I, until they were decommissioned in 1996. With each major war effort the Navy adapted the buildings quickly, focused on the practicality of its immediate needs, often without concern for the "historic" nature of the changes. Although the buildings were on the Historic Register, the renovation was complicated by the various points of time that the buildings represented. At the beginning, architectural historians wanted the architects to chose a period and stick to it; however, the architects wanted to honor the assorted eras, not erase one in favor of another. The architects were persuasive enough to convince the State Historic Properties Office and were able to obtain the 20 percent federal historic preservation tax credit. They opened up

Figure 4.12
Urban Outfitters bought five buildings, one for each of its brands, to create a campus at the Philadelphia Navy Yard.
©Lara Swimmer

the spaces and flooded the buildings with natural light. This fit into the workstyles of the designers, who often work in a collaborative fashion in open spaces.

As a result, the architects retained the traces of the complex's history. Materials are reused, graffiti kept, and the wide open spaces of the buildings' factory character maintained.

Because this project was based on "renovation through reuse," landscape architect Julie Bargmann and her firm D.I.R.T created landscaping that fits with that design approach. Rain gardens surround the buildings, and rubble from demolished buildings was used with filters to clean the water to be runoff into the Delaware River. Concrete slabs are recycled for patios.

Art as an Economic Development Engine

During the late twentieth and early twenty-first century, art became acknowledged as a major economic development engine. Culture in all its guises—from its creation to sales to enjoyment—is seen as a viable, if not a complete, alternative to replacing the factories of earlier times. Encouraging art and the people who make it has become a goal of many cities large and small. And for good reason. As outlined in its 2007 "Arts & Economic Prosperity III: The Economic Impact of Nonprofit Arts and Cultural Organizations and Their Audiences" Report, Americans for Art calculated that the economic benefit of not-for-profit arts groups alone in 2005 was in the billions of dollars, responsible for $166.2 billion in expenditures.

Proving arts enterprises not only economically viable but beneficial is an analysis peculiar to America, where the arts and culture in general are often considered luxuries reserved for the elite (whether self-appointed or not), especially when government spending is involved. In Europe, the government's role in the arts and its funding is seen as more pivotal to culture's continuance and preservation. This difference is highlighted during Congressional arguments over appropriations and projects when funding for the arts is discussed, competing with money for economic essentials such as food, housing, and maintenance of the military. Because art needs to be seen as paying its way in America, those supporting arts allocations usually cite an economic basis for their position.

In addition to the economic activity generated, art proponents maintain that art venues and events enliven neighborhoods, enrich a town's sense of community, and become important, if not central tourist attractions. Cultural institutions are sightseeing destinations not only for large metropolises but for medium-sized towns and those that are merely specks on the map. In fact, building or creating a museum is almost a clichéd solution for a town's economic woes—the economic developer's version of *Field of Dreams*. This solution has worked more often than not, at least in terms of fixing or cleaning up abandoned buildings and degraded sites. (Whether they pay back the public investment or economically replace the industry that's left is a more complicated issue.) The subject of cultural institutions as tourist destinations is a larger issue than a public policy one, and will be covered in Chapter 7.

Recognizing that art, artists, and economic development are cozy partners, in early 2010, the Ford Foundation announced its commitment of $100 million of grants to develop arts spaces nationwide over ten years. These funds will go toward the construction, maintenance and enhancement of arts facilities. Named "Supporting Diverse Art Spaces Initiative," this program will support the development of live/work spaces for artists in the anticipation that these projects will spur new businesses such as restaurants, stores, and other cultural facilities that will enliven their neighborhoods. The funds will also provide financial and management education arts groups.

On a more home-grown level involving less public investment is the conversion of industrial sites by artists themselves and the public policies that encourage or impede this development. When art and artists have trouble maintaining a presence in an area, some cities or neighborhood groups propose courses of action to retain artists and help them create a stable community. Perhaps the importance of the arts to a city and its overall community was best poetically expressed by Andrei Codrescu when he wrote that "Artists use the viable materials of an area, including its past, present, and future, to fashion a city's identity. . . . Urban planners, no matter how enlightened for forward-looking, cannot map the future without artists."[5]

Since the phenomenon of SoHo, artists have been regarded as talented bloodhounds adept at sniffing out great real estate deals. This also happened in Minneapolis, Minnesota, where many of the city's districts contain warehouses, old mills and factories as a result of the city's pivotal role in the movement of goods by river and rail. As with SoHo, during the 1970s, its warehouse district on the west side of the river was colonized by artists, a naturally occurring change when landlords sought to fill their abandoned buildings with paying tenants. Within 10 years it quickly turned into an entertainment and restaurant center, a development that priced the original settlers out. Some of the neighborhood transformation was due to gentrification; however, city policy played a part when it allowed the construction of a sports arena in the area, thereby creating a proliferation of sports bars and the introduction of a different ambiance.

As a result, when displaced artists in search of other accommodations started settling in the Northeast neighborhood, the Northeast Minneapolis Arts Association (NEMAA) commissioned a 15-year "Arts Action Plan for Northeast." This study sought to propose public policies that would encourage the arts and artists as well as maintain the historic urban fabric of this warehouse quarter. The NEMAA is, in its own words "a non-profit arts agency with the mission of promoting and supporting the quality and diversity of artistic resources based in Northeast Minneapolis to benefit the greater community."

This 2002 plan recommended certain zoning and administrative procedures to take place to encourage the arts as well as prevent the overcommercialization of the district with other uses. In the words of the plan, "Northeast Minneapolis' reason for exploring the creation of an Arts District was not the same as other communities'. In other words, the reasons for examining the feasibility of such a district was to first support the artists, and thereby the larger community. It was not to use the artists to pump more money into the Northeast Minneapolis area (although this will be a benefit)."[6]

As a result, in 2003 Minneapolis designated the Northeast Minneapolis Arts District and created an arts zoning overlay that encourages certain policies to make a working arts district viable. One of the study's conclusions was that galleries and other places for artists to sell their work were as critical as creating affordable living and working spaces. Regular arts events are scheduled during the year to bring the public to the area to look at and buy art. In addition, certain warehouse buildings mandate that artists' studios be periodically open to the public. One of the largest of the warehouses, the Northrup King Building, a complex of 10 buildings dating from 1917, when it was home to a seed company, opens its studios to the public at an event called First Thursdays throughout the year. A former grain mill, called the California Building, has been renting work-only studios to artists since the 1980s and also has monthly open studio events on the second Saturdays of the month. The buildings, while not reserved for artists, are privately owned and have remained studios.

On a more practical level, the report exhorted all city agencies to work together to foster the arts, with policies such as changing building codes to permit phased adaptation of warehouse buildings into live/work environments rather than insisting on complete conversion at one time. Although this zoning overlay was enacted, few buildings have been converted because of lack of demand. In this area, artists tend to live elsewhere, but prefer to work in studio buildings in order to be part of a community and especially to take advantage of events such as the open studios and gallery shows and enhanced sale opportunities.

Artspace

NAME: ARTSPACE

LOCATION: BASED IN MINNEAPOLIS, PROJECTS THROUGHOUT AMERICA

ISSUE: MAINTAINING AFFORDABLE LIVE/WORKSPACE FOR ARTISTS

KEY INNOVATION: NOT-FOR-PROFIT ARTIST HOUSING DEVELOPER AND CONSULTANT

TIME LINE: 1979; ONGOING

A more vigorous response to the change of Minneapolis's warehouse district on behalf of artists was the creation of Artspace in 1979. Originally started as an advocate for artists, the organization realized that it could only control the maintenance of affordable housing by developing and owning its properties. In Lowertown, an area of St. Paul, Minnesota, it converted two adjacent warehouse buildings two blocks from the riverfront, the Tilsner and Northern warehouses, into live/work artists' studios in 1990. A former backwater of the city—when the Northern Warehouse opened there were fewer than 750 people in Lowertown—is now a revived bustling area, in part because of the investment in its existing infrastructure and by bringing people into the area. More importantly from Artspace's point of view, all 118 live/work lofts developed are still occupied by artists.

From these projects and through happenstance and need, Artspace has turned into a major consultant and nonprofit developer of housing for the arts and artists throughout America. Its mission is "to create, foster, and preserve affordable space for artists and arts organizations."[7] Cities and towns, either on their own or goaded by their arts councils or vocal individuals, seek its advice on how to foster their creative community. Upon request, Artspace conducts focus groups and market studies to determine if the area can sustain a project or to advise how to enhance resources for nurturing creative elements in neighborhoods. These communities are evaluated according to five criteria.

1. The first thing Artspace looks for, and the most important aspect for the success of a project, is the commitment of the community leadership, the passionate spearhead who will stick with the project through its development vicissitudes. This theme runs through almost all the redevelopment projects presented in this book: A steadfast advocate is critical to a project's success.

2. After assessing the commitment of a locality, Artspace determines if there is indeed an artist market for such housing or arts use. While some projects do attract artists to them, the need must be there beforehand, it can't be imposed upon from the outside.

3. The localities must be capable of using the financing tools. As will be seen in succeeding chapters, redevelopment of abandoned sites is complex, and with the additional requirement of affordable housing, the financing mechanisms are complicated and are not legal or applicable in all locations.

4. Artspace then determines if there are local individuals or philanthropies who can financially contribute to fill financial gaps, should they occur.

Figure 4.13
The Northern Warehouse (left) and Tilsner Artists Cooperative in the Lowertown section of St. Paul, Minnesota, were Artspace's first development projects in 1990.
© *Artspace Projects, Inc.*

Figure 4.14
Live/workspace in the Northern Warehouse in St. Paul, Minnesota, allows residents to create their own workspaces according to their needs. The exposed structure and brick show off the building's original industrial character.
© *Artspace Projects, Inc.*

Figure 4.15
The Tilsner Artists Cooperative in St. Paul, Minnesota, provides live/work studios.
© Artspace Projects, Inc.

Figure 4.16
Traffic Zone is a joint venture between a co-op of 23 artists and Artspace in a converted 1886 warehouse located in Minneapolis's Warehouse District. The rusticated limestone building contains artists' studios, and exhibition and commercial space, including Artspace's offices, opened in 1995.
© Artspace Projects, Inc.

5. Last, but obviously not least, is the assessment of available buildings and sites in appropriate neighborhoods—if it fits in with Artspace's vision. Almost all of Artspace housing units are live/workspaces that require open floor plans so that residents can adapt the space to their needs. Large windows, which are usually the hallmark of old factory buildings, provide light for painters and others.

Today, in addition to the Minneapolis/St. Paul area, Artspace has completed 16 live/work facilities throughout America, including Buffalo, New York; Seattle, Washington; Fort Lauderdale, Florida; Portland, Oregon; and Galveston, Texas. Projects are not restricted to industrial sites and include renovation of downtown buildings such as department stores, car dealerships, and even a hospital as well as industrial warehouses.

ARTSCAPE

NAME: ARTSCAPE

LOCATION: TORONTO, CANADA

ISSUE: PREVENTING ARTISTS FROM BEING DISPLACED AND USING ARTS TO REGENERATE NEIGHBORHOODS

TIME LINE: 1986; ONGOING

The active nurturing of the art community, as well as providing affordable artist housing and studios, is not confined to the United States. In 1986, the Toronto Arts Council, concerned about what it called the "SoHo effect"—artists being driven from their homes and studios because of gentrification—created Artscape, a not-for-profit urban development organization that provides affordable work and live/workspaces for artists and rehearsal, performance, office, and storage facilities for nonprofit cultural organizations. While the group was founded to address a particular dearth of affordable space during a real estate boom, it has expanded its mission to use the arts to regenerate neighborhoods as well as to actively work to nurture the creative sectors of its city. Its real estate activities are centered in Toronto, however, it acts as an advocate and consultant throughout Canada and elsewhere. In its own words, it "has evolved from a studio provider focused on the relief of poverty to a creative urban development group that promotes wealth generation."[8]

Its six projects throughout Toronto contain approximately 300 tenants, the most recent one being the conversion of the 60,000-square-foot Wychwood Car Barns, a former abandoned streetcar repair facility, into a community center that opened in 2008. The five interconnected garages built during the early part of the twentieth century were surrounded by four acres of storage yards. After years of local debate which included a program charrette about the future of this five-acre parcel in the middle of a residential neighborhood, Artscape partnered with the city of Toronto and the Stop Community Food Centre to create the first Canadian Heritage building to receive LEED Gold certification.

Today, Artscape Wychwood Barns is a live/work artist community for families that contains studio and office space for

Figure 4.17
Artscape Toronto's Wychwood Barns project converted a streetcar repair facility into live/work artist community along with a center for environmental and arts issues surrounded by a four-acre park. Completed in the fall of 2008, this is the first Canadian Heritage building to receive LEED Gold certification.
Photo courtesy Artscape www.torontoartscape.on.ca

Figure 4.18
The farmer's market in Artscape Toronto's Wychwood Barns project.
Photo courtesy Artscape www.torontoartscape.on.ca.

individual artists as well as nonprofit arts and environmental organizations. A food production and education center hosts a farmer's market, conducts classes in gardening, and runs a commercial kitchen. The renovated buildings are surrounded by a four-acre park, which is integrated with some of the structures. The developers see it as proof that adaptive reuse of historic buildings can be combined with sustainable development. The builders diverted 90 percent of the demolition from landfills, used local and recyclable materials, and were able to harvest one acre of roof water for toilet facilities and irrigation. In keeping with its history of a public transportation facility, it is designated a transit-oriented development.

After several decades of experience, Artscape has been able to codify the development process for arts and culture-related projects into five steps, according to Tim Jones, its executive director.

1. The most important step is the shared vision that comes from the community, not imposed from above.
2. It looks for a critical mass of creative people who buy into the vision.
3. Successful projects benefit from a diversity of uses and people. Artscape's projects involve artists in all media—painters, sculptors, musicians, dancers—as well as organizations. As seen in the Wychwood Barn project and with the Distillery District project presented in Chapter 8, it attempts to integrate its projects into the surrounding area in order to shape and transform communities.
4. It looks for partnerships.
5. It looks for development capacity.

Pioneering Artist Live/Work Projects— Westbeth and Piano Craft Guild

Acknowledging the precarious balance that artists play in the life of a city—simultaneously courted only to be chased away by high rents—two early ground-breaking projects took up the daunting task of establishing artist live/workspaces to provide secure and affordable housing for this often economically marginal group. Westbeth in New York City, soon followed by the Piano Craft Guild in Boston in the late 1960s and 1970s, inaugurated this approach and pointed the way for organizations such as Artspace and Artscape. At the time of these conversions, the concept was not legal in many cities, and to implement these projects, building codes needed to be changed or adapted. These projects reflect a time when industry was starting to leave urban centers and the search for creative ideas to improve the urban fabric was strong.

Westbeth Artist Housing,[9] in the far West Village in Manhattan, occupies an imposing complex of five buildings that had until the mid-1960s been the home of Bell Telephone Laboratories. Billing itself as "The World's Largest Artists Community," Westbeth now fills a city block and is home to 384 artists[10] as well as some arts-related groups such as the Merce Cunningham Dance Foundation, and public spaces where works by resident artists are presented. "Artists" at Westbeth is broadly defined and encompasses sculptors, painters, writers, photographers, filmmakers, dancers, and more.

A pioneering project at the time of its opening in 1971, Westbeth's industrial neighborhood was still functioning as such. Adjacent to the meatpacking district, the elevated West Side Highway, the Hudson River and its working piers and pierced by an elevated railroad

Figure 4.19
Bell Laboratories building in 1934, which was converted into the Westbeth artist housing, accommodated the elevated train that ran through buildings in New York City.
Courtesy of Friends of the High Line

Figure 4.20
New York's Westbeth today shows that little has changed except the removal of the train tracks; however the opening in the building remains.
Carol Berens

(the extant parts of which are now a park called the High Line), the area was a no-man's land after dusk. The project's history is a series of firsts—in zoning, architecture, and financial structure with few precedents to lead the way. It was among the first major adaptive reuse projects to formally rehabilitate an industrial building to residential use (most existing artist lofts at that time were converted illegally), and the first time the Department of Housing and Urban Development's Federal Housing Administration (FHA) used its housing program funds for a specific professional group.[11] In addition, on a permitting level, the city as well as the FHA had to approve units without defined bedrooms and allow residential use in an industrial district.

In the mid-1960s the National Council on the Arts,[12] then a newly formed organization established to mold government arts policy in America, embraced the idea of artist housing in order to strengthen urban areas as well as support the arts. Given the expensive housing in New York City as well as its concentration of artists, representatives of the J.M. Kaplan Fund, a philanthropic organization involved in supporting the arts, searched for an appropriate building to conduct this experiment. Matching grants in 1967 and 1968 from the National Endowment for the Arts and the J.M. Kaplan Fund enabled the creation of the nonprofit Westbeth Corporation, which bought the Bell Labs building for $2.5 million. This project was ultimately funded by the Department of Housing and Urban Development's Federal Housing Administration, which issued a $12 million mortgage to the Westbeth Corporation. It is run as a not-for-profit 501(c)(3) corporation, enabling it to receive a number of abatements and subsidies during its history.

Westbeth's era was a heady time for adaptive reuse, government cooperation, and acknowledgment of the benefits that artists bring to a city. In fact, when the Board of Estimate (now, the City Council) approved the project, it stated that it "will bring important benefits to Greenwich Village, New York and to the nation, not only in an artistic sense, but in an economic sense as well."[13] As a result of a fortuitous connection from architecture school, Richard Meier was chosen to be the architect, and the project started him on his way to a prize-filled career. Interior spaces were designed to be as open as possible, so that each apartment could be subdivided by residents as needed. (Permitting issues were resolved with dotted lines representing sleeping areas to assure government agencies that the plans could meet code.)

Today, after many years of being an outpost on the far west side, the area has transformed into a chic district of bars and boutiques with Hudson River Park extending past its riverfront facade, no longer impeded by an elevated highway. The building is surrounded by multi-million-dollar apartments and artist studios, both newly built and converted.[14] Amid this gentrification, it is estimated that a quarter to a third of Westbeth's residents qualify for rent subsidies under federal and city programs. When it started, it was thought that the artist residents would move on; however, many have not been able to afford to leave, indicating that perhaps the business of art was more beneficial to the neighborhood than to the artists themselves. Westbeth has financially wobbled over time; however, it appears to be stable and its previous 40-year tax abatement has been renewed by the city for another 40 years.

One of Westbeth's immediate descendents is the Piano Craft Guild, a 1974 conversion of the 250,000-square-foot Chickering Piano Factory in Boston into 174 apartments and 30,000 square feet of commercial space. By the early 1970s, pianos were no longer being made in the 1853 building, which had become home to a few artists and light manufacturing enterprises that could not support the tax rolls and building repairs. A local planner, Robert Gelaradin, and architects Simeon Bruner and Leland Cott, donned developer hats, purchased the property, and created the live/work artists' spaces. Boosted by both a construction loan and permanent mortgage from the Massachusetts Housing Finance Agency, as well as tenant relocation help from the Boston Redevelopment Authority, the project was constructed for $10.50 a square foot, estimated at that time of double-digit inflation to be one-third the cost of a new construction in 1974. Given the economic constraints, the renovation

Figure 4.21
The interior courtyard of Westbeth, designed by Richard Meier in 1969, was an early artists live/workplace. The half-round balconies connect adjacent apartments and act as fire escapes.
Carol Berens

Figure 4.22
The bell-bottoms indicate the era of the 1974 Piano Craft Guild in the Boston, Massachusetts conversion, an early adaptive reuse of an urban factory for artists' housing. To keep costs down existing materials were kept and reused wherever possible.
Greg Heins, 1973

was bare-bones. Brick walls and wood columns were left exposed as were pipes and electrical conduits. Original wood floors were kept and patched. There was no attempt to make new materials blend in—new is new and old is old. In order to manipulate large-scale art works, extra-wide corridors and tall apartment doors were built, as were electrical outlets at ceiling height for spotlights. Some of the studios were designed for specific artists with slop sinks and moveable storage wall systems. A gallery mounted rotating exhibits of residents' work.

Although the building is massive, a large courtyard is hidden behind its facade and the building wings are only 49 feet deep, enabling apartments on both sides of the double-loaded corridor to be flooded with light. Ceiling heights ranged from 10 to 20 feet. At the time of its opening, the *AIA Journal* included it in a section highlighting adaptive reuse projects as an example of the possibility of regeneration of America's central cities. The idealism didn't last, and it is now market-rate housing with few artists remaining.

Figure 4.23
Boston's Piano Craft Guild appears more massive than it is, as its facade hides a large interior courtyard which made conversion to residential use easier.
Bruner/Cott, 2006

ARTISTS' STUDIOS–TORPEDO FACTORY ART CENTER AND LES FRIGOS

Art and individual foresight and perseverance—two major renovation storylines—converge in the establishment of the Torpedo Factory Art Center. About the same time that artists were staking claims in SoHo, Marian Van Landingham, president of the Alexandria Art League, was traipsing around the Alexandria waterfront and came upon a boarded up, sprawling building where torpedoes were made and munitions stored for the U.S. Navy from the end of World War I through 1945. After World War II its cavernous space was

Figure 4.24
The Torpedo Factory Art Center on the Alexandria, Virginia, waterfront was a white elephant in the early 1970s until Marian Van Landingham and the Alexandria Art League marshaled sweat equity to create artists' studios, a template for others around the country.
Torpedo Factory Building from the rear in 70s.

used by the Smithsonian Institution as well as Congress and the military to store documents, furniture, art, and even dinosaur bones. The city of Alexandria had bought the building from the federal government in 1969 without a specific use in mind. Considered a white elephant because its industrial look conflicted with the traditional architecture of Alexandria, the 72,000-square-foot building inspired Ms. Van Landingham, who envisioned it as the perfect place for the Art Leagues' galleries, classrooms, and artists' studios. Artists donated their time and energy to remove decades of debris, clean the building, paint their studios, and make it ready for the public. She convinced the city, which funded an ad hoc art show in 1974 to celebrate Alexandria's bicentennial, to create a more permanent facility. The Torpedo Factory Art Center was an immediate success and in the early 1980s underwent a complete renovation. Today, the Art Center hosts galleries and supports art classes as well as rents out over 84 studios to 160 artists who must work in the studios

Figure 4.25
The building known as Les Frigos in Paris was a cold food storage facility run by the railroad until the 1980s, when artists started occupying the buildings as squatters.
Carol Berens

and allow the public in during posted visiting hours. The Art Center was not only an impetus to revive Alexandria's waterfront and an inspiration for other art centers around the country, such as the Northeast Minneapolis plan and Lowell's Brush Gallery & Studios, but also the start of Ms. Van Landingham's 24-year political career in the Virginia House of Delegates.

Across the Atlantic in Paris, another white elephant languished without an obvious use. A former cold storage facility, built in 1921 and used by the railroads to transport and distribute perishables before the food market moved to Rungis from Les Halles in the late 1960s, remained empty for over 10 years before artists started creating studios in 1980. Basically a giant refrigerator, Les Frigos, as the building is fondly called, has interior walls nearly 27 inches thick. Musicians, theater people, as well all types of artists found the soundproof rooms with high ceilings fit their needs, and illegally squatted in this once desolate area of Paris. It's now an established artists' enclave in one of the newest upscale districts (it's surrounded by the Bibliothèque Nationale and the relocated Paris University, Jussieu, which recently renovated the "Grands Moulins"). Open studio days, or "portes ourvertes," are held periodically.

Figure 4.26
At Paris's Les Frigos, artists' studios are behind 27-inch-thick walls, whose insulated doors sport graffiti, which is still somewhat in vogue in Paris. The building is also used by musicians and sound artists, who take advantage of the soundproofing.
Carol Berens

Zoning and Incentives for Artists

Trying to develop a cohesive public policy to encourage artists to settle in their towns as well as not be driven out is a problem for many cities, such as Boston, Massachusetts, and Providence, Rhode Island, which have combined zoning restrictions and tax incentives or penalties in order to maintain stable artist communities. Recently the Boston Redevelopment Authority worked with various city departments to develop a program called the Artist Space Initiative, which acknowledges that "artists have helped transform marginal neighborhoods into dynamic communities." The Boston Zoning Code now makes an exception to allow artists to build live/work units in industrially zoned areas of the city, the only occupational group permitted to reside there.

Boston is actively courting projects to create artist spaces that are permanently dedicated to such use through deed restrictions. Cognizant of artists' need for nontraditional space for either working or for live/work studios, it is searching for projects to support in "buffer zones" between industrial and residential neighborhoods. In addition, to facilitate development of more artist studio space, it created design guidelines for such units. A relationship with LINC, or Leveraging Investments in Creativity, a 10-year-old organization supported by philanthropic foundations, provides support and a clearinghouse of information and services for artists.

Providence, Rhode Island, created an Artist Tax Free District in 2005 in which artists are given economic incentives to rent or purchase space within three West Side Arts neighborhoods. Artists who rent or purchase space within the defined districts and are certified eligible by the state council on the arts are entitled to sales, use, and state income tax abatements. The intent of this legislation is to offset the increased real estate values in these areas, which were driving the artists out, as well as to encourage artists to own property in the neighborhoods.

Kansas City's Crossroads area of 100 blocks is another warehouse district that has been settled since the late 1980s by artists and has made its mark as a distinctive district with specialty artisan shops and design stores as well as its First Friday's "Art Crawl" gallery openings. In 2007, an effort to prevent artists from being priced out of the area, the city initiated a tax abatement program for art-related properties, which extended to design-oriented stores.

The ever-changing city balances natural evolution and public policy. In defining and competing visions of the postindustrial city, much policy appears to be playing catch-up. Whether these policies will work in changing economic environments is only known after the fact.

Endnotes

1. Richard Florida's 2002 book, *The Rise of the Creative Class: and How It's Transforming Work, Leisure, Community and Everyday Life,* charts the importance of the creative class, which he classifies as not only artists and musicians but also high-tech workers, in giving cities an allure and economic development advantage. Whether his thesis is accurate or not, the belief in this phenomenon has taken on a life of its own. Artspace's vice president of consulting and resource development indicated that some cities have approached that organization trying to implement Florida's analysis.

2. According to the *AIA Guide to New York City*, fourth edition (Norval White & Elliot Willensky, Three Rivers Press, New York, 2000), the area was once "called Hell's Hundred Acres because of the many fires in overcrowded, untended warehouses filled with flammables." p. 98. Over some building doors one can still see the occasional "AIR" signs which stands for "Artist in Residence" to inform firefighters where people lived.

3. In Greenpoint, the predominant group was and is Polish with a recent influx of Hispanic; Williamsburg is more multiethnic, with predominant groups being Hasidic Jews, Puerto Ricans and Dominicans,

ENDNOTES

and within the past decade, young people looking for the "next affordable neighborhood."

4. Rich Calder and Tim Liddy, *The New York Post* "Red Hook's Bright Ikea," May 28, 2008.
5. Andrei Codrescu, *Architecture*, "Art: the vanguard of real estate," June, 1999, v. 88, no. 6, p. 154.
6. Northeast Minneapolis Arts Action Plan, September 2002, p. 17.
7. www.artspace.org
8. www.torontoartscape.on.ca/about/history, accessed December 6, 2009.
9. Westbeth combines the names of the streets where the building is located—West and Bethune streets.
10. The project is still so popular that the waiting list was closed to new names in 2007.
11. National Register of Historic Places Application Section 8, page 7.
12. The National Council on the Arts advises the chairman of the National Endowment for the Arts on initiatives, funding guidelines, and grants. It was started in 1964 under President Lyndon Johnson and has through its history included notable artists in all fields.
13. Board of Estimate Calendar, April 4, 1968, 34-35, as quoted in the National Register of Historic Places Application Section 8, page 15.
14. Just a few blocks south, modernist glass towers designed by Richard Meier, the architect of Westbeth, front the Hudson River.

CHAPTER 5

ENVIRONMENTAL REMEDIATION AND DEVELOPMENT

Although once the economic bedrocks of their communities, nineteenth- and twentieth-century industrial factories and plants were smelly, dirty neighbors, their districts self-proclaimed no-man's lands. Even when they didn't spew sooty smoke and noxious fumes, these places were sealed off from the life of their cities, separated from commercial and better residential areas by roads and railroad tracks. As seen in the previous chapters, these original locations shaped land-use patterns and thwarted further development or revitalization of many cities. These defunct industrial sites now occupy some of the potentially best urban sites, whether on the waterfront or in other critical locations.

Aside from being physically intimidating, industry involves harmful and toxic substances, and this self-imposed quarantine served to protect nonindustrial areas while creating, in effect, centers of toxicity. Industrial isolation also allowed contamination to continue to exist, whether through fear, ignorance, or the expense of removal. Over time, however, responses to environmental degradation have evolved, although legal developments and financial support have been slow to follow. Changing attitudes and procedures—from avoidance to treatment—have been critical to the redevelopment of industrial sites.

The debate over the design of food stamps many years ago symbolized the ambivalence of society to the existence and impact of industry. The then-paper scrips pictured a factory sporting a tall chimney. Question: Should smoke be shown coming out of the chimney or not? Smoke implied that factories were in full operation, work was to be had, the economy was on the mend. Smoke, however, was a clear sign of air pollution, obviously bad. This societal dilemma has not been fully resolved. That fewer workers were actually making their livings in smokestack industries even then was an issue to be avoided, as the factory remained, and still remains, a powerful symbol of work.

ENVIRONMENTAL REGULATION

In the late 1970s and early 1980s, America roiled with fear of the poisons in its midst. The fiasco of hazardous chemicals seeping up through the ground and into Love Canal homes and the evacuation of Times Beach, Missouri, as a result of dioxin sprayed on its dirt roads, spurred a spate of federal and state laws that mandated cleanup and assigned liabilities.

As with many hot-button political issues, one defining event usually clarifies issues, clearly demarcating a before and after. In 1963 Rachel Carson's *Silent Spring* focused the world's attention on the unintentional negative byproducts of chemicals and industrial progress. As a result, in 1963 and 1970, the Clean Air Act was passed, soon followed in 1972 by the Clean Water Act.

LOVE CANAL AND TIMES BEACH

In 1974, in a small upstate New York town around Niagara Falls, chemical ooze seeped into basements and infiltrated playfields, the result of barrels of chemicals that had been recklessly buried over decades. America responded with a flurry of major federal and state legislation to address the concerns of alarmed citizens who demanded action against the devastation by the residues of industry. Since then, industry has received a mixed reception—needed for economic survival, but the harborer of poison and toxic brews. Love Canal serves as the poster child for environmental cleanup, with direct repercussions on the redevelopment of industrial sites.

Love Canal was originally an abortive attempt at building a connector between the upper and lower Niagara River in the late 1890s by an entrepreneur named William T. Love. The unfinished canal was sold in 1920, only to be used for approximately 30 years as an industrial dumping site by both municipal governments and the Hooker Chemical Corporation. In 1953, Hooker Chemical covered the canal and sold part of it to the Board of Education, though warning that chemical wastes were buried on the land. An elementary school opened on the site in 1955, and as veterans returned from World War II, homes were built in the area to accommodate them. By 1978 there were over 1,000 residential units, both single-family houses and apartments, in an area where it has been estimated 20,000 tons of toxic waste were buried. From 1978 through 1980, several evacuations of homes in the Love Canal neighborhood closest to the dump site were ordered and federal relocation funds were provided.

The area has been the focus of extensive cleanup efforts; however, the epicenter of the contamination is and will always be a containment area secured behind a chain-linked fence. A local development office refurbished some of the outer ring houses, and 20 years after the original evacuation people began to move in. Controversy about the safety of the soil still remains.

Times Beach, Missouri's story is slightly different. It was not the crass behavior of an existing industry that created the problem, but the use in the early 1970s of waste oil contaminated with the chemical dioxin to tamp down dust on dirt roads that were subsequently paved. A devastating flood in 1982 infiltrated the toxic chemical into the soil, and the town of Times Beach was evacuated. Contaminated soil and debris from the town and other sites in eastern Missouri were burned in an onsite incinerator. Today, Route 66 State Park marks the former site of Times Beach. However, its most important marker is the role that it and Love Canal played in the framing of environmental laws in the 1980s and 1990s in America.

In direct response to the revelations at Love Canal, in December 1980 Congress enacted the Comprehensive Environmental Response, Compensation and Liability Act (CERCLA), which established a fund to help clean up toxic sites. The law established a national priority list of tainted sites scheduled to be decontaminated along with an account financed by polluting companies. These "Superfund" sites, as they became known, were often toxic dumps whose cleanup trumped any redevelopment plans.[1] Past and present owners and operators became liable for cleanup of defined hazardous substances. Hampered by underfunding and haphazard administration in its formative years, CERCLA has been amended and reauthorized over time, and although critics have decried its ineffectiveness, Congress has been deadlocked when trying to change it.

These laws made the entities that financed projects on a contaminated site—whether the contamination was known at that time or not—liable for cleanup. Many of these sites were orphans, their original owners and polluters existing, if known at all, as nostalgic names of past glory. The law actually had an unintended consequence of discouraging banks and other institutions from financing or developing these properties, which then languished because of difficulty in obtaining funding. In addition to not relieving residual liability, remediation was expected to restore the land to nearly pristine condition. Regulations meant to protect public health and the environment were actually allowing contaminated sites to remain idle, continually and sadly deteriorating.

Because of these problems, government officials and developers started reevaluating certain assumptions about levels of required decontamination. Toward the middle of the 1990s, policies that stressed site cleanup in accordance to redevelopment plans were implemented in order to address the issue of abandoned areas that were draining cities of their vitality. In effect, the objective was reframed, and the goal became reuse rather than merely cleanup. Today's environmental question is how to heal the scarred areas of towns and cities in order to create jobs and places to live and play, and the responses can be modulated to address specific uses. Remediation strategies are now targeted to specific site uses and related to the level of risk. For instance, land scheduled to be paved over as a parking lot or covered by a building will not require the same level of decontamination as a playground.

BROWNFIELDS

The concept of brownfields acknowledges that environmental remediation is just one aspect of redevelopment that affects land-use strategies, financial viability, and timing of projects; in short, their feasibility. To that end, Congress passed the Brownfield Revitalization and Environmental Restoration Act of 2000, a version of which was signed into law in January 2002. According to the U.S. Environmental Protection Agency (EPA), a "'[b]rownfield site' means real property, the expansion, redevelopment, or reuse of which many be complicated by the presence or potential presence of a hazardous substance, pollutant, or contaminant."[2] That brownfield discussions inevitably end up as a series of acronyms familiar to insiders and consultants highlights the complexity of dealing with a subject whose policies and processes differ from state to state, country to country, and year to year. In addition to federal laws and guidelines, each state has different environmental rules, regulations, and more and more, incentive programs. As with all legislation, programs are modified or eliminated as a result of their outcomes, and of course, changing political goals.

The emphasis of brownfield programs usually focuses on the proposed development. In America, the goal is to encourage the private sector to build. These programs often take the form of government grants, loans, and increasingly, tax credits or incentives. For brownfield projects the upfront costs of site investigation and market viability studies are difficult hurdles to overcome, and many brownfield programs concentrate on technical assistance and limitation of liability, as well as feasibility studies that include reuse and financial viability. The reality is that projects often turn into multiphased and multistep processes, if only to respond to the requirements of the government programs. Because of the intricate nature of the regulations, the topic will be included within project discussions, not discussed separately. In fact, all projects included in this book were built on contaminated property, some more difficult to remediate than others. The importance of their development, however, revolves around their end uses and their transformative effect on communities, not their cleanup per se.

In general, more recent environmental programs attempt to make the development of industrial sites more closely align with the phasing and process of regular development projects, with the increased costs and time of site assessment and cleanup equalized, to some extent, by government grants and incentives. As with all real estate projects, success or failure rests in how accurately the reuse planning gauges the market potential and timing for sites. Cleaning up these sites goes hand-in-hand with economic development efforts. As "smart growth" is encouraged, that is, rebuilding within existing cities and near transit nodes, almost all development projects require some form of remediation. The issue becomes more of degree and one more item on the development checklist along with economics, market studies, zoning, and architectural design.

Because of the complexities involved in reconciling legal requirements and the ever-changing financial incentives and programs, some states and localities have determined that having a "one-stop" shop to address developers' and owners' interests is the most efficient way of developing these properties. Whether this is the town planning or the environmental protection department depends upon the area's resources.

In order to take advantage of all the programs and funding sources that are available to both localities and developers, environmental consultants have been playing a larger role in implementing the ever-changing policies and advising clients. The first step in identifying a brownfield site is the analysis of both the physical site and its history, which is then put into Phase I and II environmental surveys. Although due diligence is a critical step in any development project, for sites that are known hazardous areas this review is more critical because of monetary and liability issues. If the site is contaminated, a master plan for either removing the offending chemicals or remediating them onsite is drawn up for approval and applications for various brownfield programs. Once a project has been approved and constructed, sometimes postdevelopment monitoring will be required to treat groundwater or assess ongoing vapor intrusion, if any.

As will be seen in the examples in this chapter, the remediation of brownfields with respect to land falls into three general categories: removing the contamination from the site, capping or burying it, or phytoremediating it with plants or natural cleansing actions of the land and/or water patterns. Developing brownfields, while still a challenge, can also be encouraged by certain regulations, one of which is "Brownfields Voluntary Cleanup Programs," which offers the carrot rather than the stick. These programs, which in America vary on a state-by-state basis, attempt to develop a streamlined cleanup process that also provides liability protection in order to encourage the transfer of property. The goal is to provide more certainty regarding environmental requirements to purchasers and future owners so that developers can predict costs and time lines associated with cleanup. If approved for redevelopment under these programs, projects usually are eligible for tax incentives.

MUSEUM OF GLASS

NAME: MUSEUM OF GLASS

LOCATION: TACOMA, WASHINGTON

ISSUE: SITE ASSESSMENT AND CLEANUP AGREEMENT

RESOLUTION: $200,000 BROWNFIELDS ASSESSMENT PILOT GRANT DEFINED REMEDIATION PROGRAM FOR CITY TO IMPLEMENT AND TO ALLOW MUSEUM TO BUILD NEW FACILITY

TIME LINE: 1996

Although sometimes the grant amounts appear small, they can make the difference between a municipality being able to jump start a project with the information to chart the rest of the way. An early participant in the Environmental Protection Agency's Brownfields Pilot Program was Tacoma, Washington. Starting in 1996 with a $200,000 Brownfields Assessment Pilot Grant that focused on encouraging economic growth and downtown revival, the city conducted environmental studies to determine the cleanup costs. The area was originally an industrial zone containing mill and waterfront industries which, in an all-too-familiar story, had left, leaving behind contamination and abandoned buildings. This waterfront property on the Commencement Bay was separated from downtown by an Interstate Highway.

The city, faced with a faltering economy, had decided its future required redefinition and chose to use art as its growth generator. It had a willing developer in the Museum of Glass, a private institution that would display the works of its native son, Dale Chihuly. Armed with the results of the site assessment, the City of Tacoma spent $1.3 million to clean up and convey the site to the Museum of Glass which built its privately raised $58 million facility. A pedestrian walkway, the Chihuly Bridge of Glass, links the museum to the city over the highway and was built with Federal Highway Administration funds as well as local and state contributions.

THE CAN COMPANY

NAME: THE CAN COMPANY

LOCATION: BALTIMORE, MARYLAND

ISSUE: VACANT CAN FACTORY

RESOLUTION: FIRST PROPERTY TO SUCCESSFULLY COMPLETE MARYLAND'S BROWNFIELDS VOLUNTARY CLEAN-UP PROGRAM.

TIME LINE: 1999; SECOND PHASE FINISHED IN 2005

The first project to successfully complete Maryland's Brownfields Voluntary Clean-Up Program was the Can Company in the Canton area of Baltimore. From 1895 to the late 1980s, first the Norton Tin Can and Plate Company and then the American Can Company manufactured their products at this plant until the National Can Company bought the facility, only to close it. It remained vacant for many years, despite city and private developers' efforts to find uses for the site. Unfortunately, those years of operation resulted in lead soil contamination.

The development of this site by Struever Bros. Eccles & Rouse was enabled, as are all projects of any scale, by cobbling together various programs, which in this case included the Historic Tax Credits (the work was done in accordance with the Department of Interior National Park Service standards, which included restoration of the steel sash windows) as well as brownfield tax incentives and public works grants. The 200,000-square-foot complex now contains retail and office space. In 1999 the project received the Maryland Historic Trust's Preservation Award, the Maryland Department of Planning Smart Growth Award, and the National Trust for Historic Preservation Honor Award. Not only did this project restore a vacant property, it was critical to transforming the Canton neighborhood into a mixed-use center within an existing community.

Figure 5.1
The restored Can Company in Baltimore, Maryland, was the first property to successfully complete Maryland's Brownfields Voluntary Clean-Up Program and was the winner of several smart growth and historic restoration awards.
Ron Solomon © 2009

Figure 5.2
The formerly derelict Can Company campus in the Canton district of Baltimore, Maryland, was a blight on the neighborhood until it was restored.
Ron Solomon © 2009

Figure 5.3
The completed 200,000-square-foot Can Company development contains stores and offices.
Ron Solomon © 2009

Sustainability Issues

The issue of sustainability has immensely encouraged the redevelopment of former industrial sites, especially those in urban areas. In America, the allure of developing on land outside cities contributed to growth into the suburbs and beyond. Because of the resulting sprawl, longer commuting times, and air pollution, government goals have changed and "smart growth" initiatives and projects that are near public transit are encouraged. In effect, development has now made a U-turn and is returning to the cities with their surfeit of brownfields. Hand in hand with revised regulations and incentive programs, reuse and recycling of these sites are building.

Smart Growth and LEED

Toward this end, in 1996 the EPA and several nonprofit and government organizations formed the Smart Growth Network to respond to community concerns about how to create more livable communities that also encourage economic growth. This group is part of a public awareness network educating localities about strategies toward promoting smart growth in their communities. High on its list of goals is creating walkable neighborhoods, encouraging community collaboration, developing a mix of uses, and preserving open space as well as encouraging development in existing communities.

Vermont is one state of many that have enacted Smart Growth regulations with the intent of curbing sprawl, protecting agricultural land, and reducing traffic congestion, among other environmental issues. Although many land-use decisions are made on the local level, state-wide laws in Vermont allow the state to determine the direction new town plans and zoning take. On the local level, Vermont towns are like most around the country: Volunteers on town planning and town boards face the day-to-day decisions regarding land use and economic development and health of their towns. Vermont, however, has created guidelines that towns either must or should consider about the environment and reducing sprawl. Organizations such as the not-for-profit Smart Growth Vermont provide workshops, partnerships, as well as information concerning laws that encourage healthy downtowns that concentrate growth. Projects that reuse abandoned industrial sites that are close to existing urban centers benefit from these policies.

Environmental issues have evolved, and a desire to avoid further global climate change seems to have recently eclipsed the fear of chemical contamination. Renovating industrial sites addresses both concerns simultaneously. Reusing existing buildings and developing land efficiently limits energy outlay as buildings represent a large percentage of energy use, consuming natural resources and contributing a significant percentage of carbon dioxide emissions. The U.S. Green Building Council developed the Leadership in Energy and Environmental Design (LEED) system for measuring and certifying environmentally friendly construction on both a building and community basis in order to have a unified definition of what a "green building" is. The system evaluates projects for, among other things, energy savings and emissions reduction, but above all, monitors the "stewardship of resources and sensitivity to their impacts."

Monitoring LEED ratings is not only a way to evaluate projects with respect to energy use, but also has become an effective marketing tool. The system evaluates buildings over their lifecycles and looks at costs over time. American municipalities are beginning to provide incentives in the form of various tax abatements for constructing LEED-certified buildings. The redevelopment of industrial sites, especially those located in urban areas, fulfills this mission by bringing development back into cities, limiting suburban sprawl, and thus subsequent automobile travel time with accessible public transportation. As a result, favorable LEED ratings through the reuse of existing buildings and sites is another attribute helping to renovate these industrial sites. To that end, many of these projects achieve points for brownfield redevelopment, community connectivity, and public transportation access and help toward obtaining LEED certification before design or materials are even decided upon.

Remediation and Landscape Architecture

Landscape architects are on the frontline of addressing environmental degradation and its transformation into healthy ecosystems. Many of these projects do not merely cart the contamination offsite, as is often done for many reclamation projects, but rework the land and showcase the cleanup processes that are an integral part of the project. Past site use is not obliterated but highlighted as part of the design, which exploits the changing nature of landscape design and harnesses the cleansing quality of plants to cure rather than destroy the site over time. Visitors are educated about history of the site as well as the restoration process. Just as renovated buildings often underscore their industrial past, landscape can do the same.

REMEDIATION AND LANDSCAPE ARCHITECTURE

AMD&ART

Name: AMD&ART

Location: Vintondale, Pennsylvania

Issue: Severe environmental degradation due to acid mine drainage in an underserved community

Key Players: T. Allan Comp, Bob Deason, Julie Bargmann, and Stacey Levy with the local community, AmeriCorps, and VISTA volunteers

Resolution: Environmental remediation to create a new park that integrates art works that relate to former mining community

Time Line: 1994 to 2005

Projects that reflect and embrace their area's industrial past highlight their heritage rather than obliterate it. A prime example of this type of environmental project is AMD&ART, on the site of a former coal mine that operated in the Borough of Vintondale in the heart of Appalachian southwestern Pennsylvania. The mine, which opened in 1906, closed nearly 60 years later in 1963, bequeathed a legacy of polluted land and water brought about by the acidic runoff from preregulatory coal mining and decaying mine equipment that remained. The closing of the mine created ongoing acid-mine drainage (AMD) as well as a shattered and distrustful community. The remaining population, who for generations helped fuel the advances of American industry under grueling working conditions and in poverty, were forsaken, their economy in tatters.

In 1994, T. Allan Comp, a former historian and developer, brought together a multidisciplined group of professionals composed of geologists, hydrologists, historians, artists, landscape architects, community members, and a corps of volunteers. The area has been transformed into a 35-acre park with active recreation as well as passive landscape features that recall the site's history as well as neutralize the AMD and reflect the cleansing process. The winner of numerous environmental awards culminating with the United States Environmental Protection Agency's Phoenix Award in 2005, the park is now run by the Borough of Vintondale.

While with the National Heritage Areas Program and then at the Office of Surface Mining, Mr. Comp became familiar with the social and economic devastation of Appalachia as well as passive water treatment processes. Traditionally, the process for water treatment was hidden behind fences or camouflaged by trees, which did the job, but brought no economic development benefits. Mr. Comp looked for a way to flaunt and celebrate the process and furnish the area with a reason to be proud of its roots and a new sense of place to redefine its future.

He worked quietly with individuals in the community for two years before there was even a public meeting. Inspired by large-scale "earth art" of the 1980s, he then brought together a design team composed of Bob Deason, a hydrologist; Julie Bargmann, a landscape architect; and Stacey Levy, an artist, to work with the community and AmeriCorps and VISTA volunteers. This team's job was to help shape the community's aspiration and give it "good form" and at the same time include recreation, art, education centers, and a historical presence.

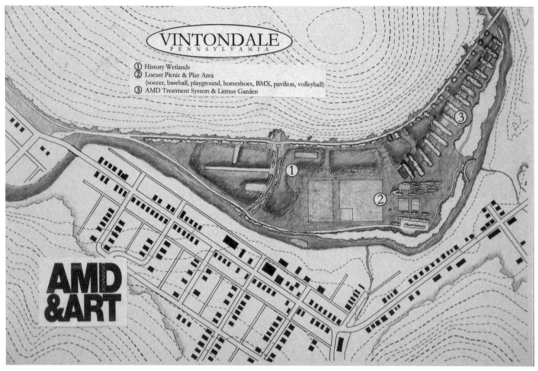

Figure 5.4
The Site Plan for AMD&ART in Vintondale in southwestern Pennsylvania, shows how a remediation project also able accommodated the recreation needs of the local community.
AMD&ART

The resulting passive water treatment system features a series of six man-made keystone-shaped interconnected ponds and spillways that flow though the site and are lined with limestone to neutralize the acid. Each pond cleans a different element, its function described on nearby signs. For example, the first pond from one of the mines is the "Acid Pool," which has high levels of aluminum and iron and whose water turns orange when reacting to the base limestone. With succeeding ponds, the water changes color from orange to blue to green to reflect the natural process as different elements and metals are removed. The last pond is aerated and is pure enough to feed an adjacent wetland that is home to cattails, migrating birds, and other aquatic life. The water then flows into Blacklick Creek. Alongside these ponds, volunteers, many from the Green Museum,[3] planted a Litmus Garden in 2001, which is composed of trees and shrubs whose colors mirror those of the water. In the fall, the trees turn from red to silver.

In addition to scientists and landscape architects, artists were brought to the site to create art that reflects the mine and its community's history, some of it culled from workshops with residents and former miners. Pictures taken from an old film clip of 1930s miners lining up as if to go to work are etched on a granite slab, the

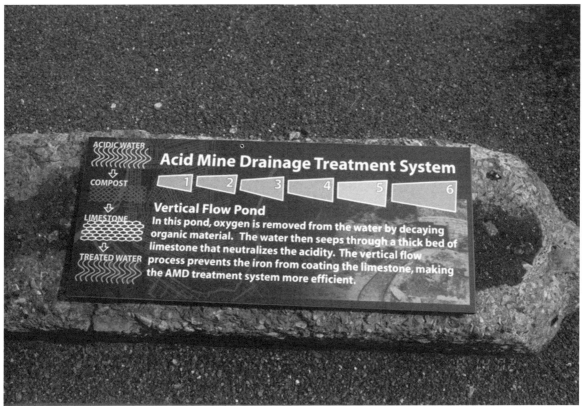

Figure 5.5
The site markers at AMD&ART explain the passive water treatment system whose filtering process consists of six man-made keystone-shaped ponds that process polluted water into clean.
T. Allan Comp

former door of a mine shaft. A mosaic of community images as well as an old map portrays the history of the town. Coal waste, called "bony," is fashioned into sculpture.

This park opened in 2005 and contains areas for ball fields and other active recreation, a pavilion for meetings and education groups, as well as the art that is interspersed in the landscape. It is bounded by the Blacklick Creek and the Ghost Town Road, an abandoned railroad bed and now a hiking and biking path connecting the area to towns that no longer exist. The Borough of Vintondale now operates the park, Mr. Comp's self-described role as "keeper of the vision," complete. The hope is that the park and its activities can be self-sustaining. A passive filtration system has the advantage of not requiring too much upkeep.

The funds for this project came from a host of sources and grants, including several targeted grants from the EPA highlighting different goals and needs, from Environmental Justice, Sustainable Development, Brownfields Job Training and Environmental Education; Pennsylvania Council on the Arts, and private foundations. The borough donated the 35 acres for the park

Figure 5.6
A clean pond in the restored landscape at AMD&ART. The water before treatment for acid runoff was a bright orange.
Photos by T. Allan Comp

and the Southern Alleghenies Conservancy will maintain the water treatment and wetlands system. Much of the labor came from volunteers from groups including AmericCorps and Vista, as well as from local environmental groups. At the time it was built, it was possible to sell wetlands credits, which the park was able to do as the water treatment was so effective.

Another proponent of this method of recalling a site's history is Julie Bargmann whose firm's name, D.I.R.T (Design Investigations Reclaiming Terrain), embodies her approach to remediation. As stated on her website, her firm's goal is to "unearth site histories as the place to start. We reuse existing materials with an artistic vengeance." She reclaims scarred sites not through the removal of toxic material but through the cleansing process as a way of honoring its past use. At Vintondale, Pennsylvania, she was a vital team member, and she was a member of the design team with William McDonough and Nelson/Byrd Landscape Architects for a master plan for remediating an existing industrial plant in the 2000 pilot project at the Ford Rouge Plant in Dearborn, Michigan. As a test program, phytoremediation is being evaluated to determine if it is an economic and beneficial way to deal with the removal of PAH compounds (polyaromatic hydrocarbons), which are byproducts of the steel-making process. In this program, the plants will break down the contaminants into compounds that can be absorbed into the roots, thereby eliminating the PAH compounds from the soil. An added benefit is the filtering of stormwater runoff and the resulting restoration of wildlife habitats.

Alumnae Valley

Name: Alumnae Valley restoration

Location: Wellesley College campus, Wellesley, Massachusetts

Issue: Remediate contamination while restoring historic sense of place

Key Players: Michael Van Valkenburgh Associates, Inc.

Resolution: New master plan to restore natural hydrology while return land to useful place in campus

Time Line: 1998 (master plan) and 2005

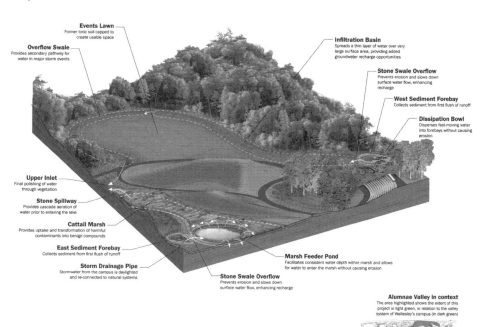

Figure 5.7
This diagram of Wellesley College's Alumnae Valley in Wellesley, Massachusetts, shows the methodology used to restore the hydrology of the site to integrate with the campus as originally intended. *Michael Van Valkenburgh Associates, Inc.*

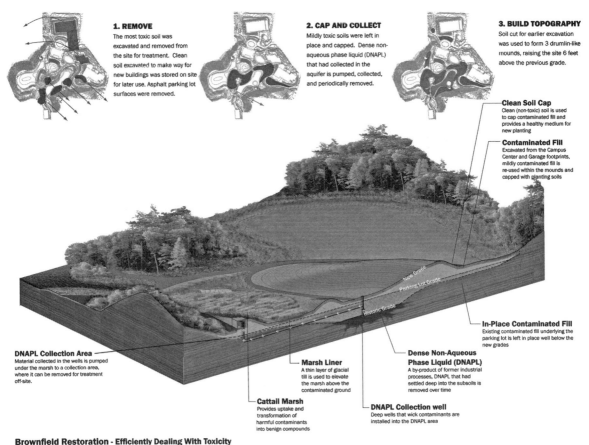

Figure 5.8
At Wellesley College's Alumnae Valley, brownfields were dealt with in three general ways: removal; capping, with deep wells to collect material to be periodically removed; and changing the topography with fill to address drainage issues as well as create visual interest.
Michael Van Valkenburgh Associates, Inc.

Wellesley College's Alumnae Valley is an interesting study in brownfield remediation as it employs all three methods of dealing with contamination while restoring the historic sense of place. Wellesley campus was originally master planned by Frederick Law Olmsted, Jr., Arthur Shurtliff, and Ralph Adams Cram in 1921 to integrate campus buildings with the landscape. In 1998, Michael Van Valkenburgh Associates, Inc. (MVVA) created a new master plan to address changes made to the original campus concept over its previous 70 years. Key among the specific projects is the reconfigured 13.5 acres which restores the hydrology and landscape of an area that was never integrated into the campus design as originally intended. First the site of a natural gas pump station and landfill, it was then covered in asphalt for a 175-car parking lot.

Because the initial pump station soil contamination had been paved over, removal of the pavement would release the contaminants.

Using a combination of soil removal, capping of contaminates, and raising the level of parts of the site restores the original hydrology with respect to the whole campus, enhances the water runoff, and connects the campus with the lake beyond. Some toxic soil was removed for treatment offsite. The byproducts of the natural gas processing which had collected in the watershed beneath the parking lot are pumped out periodically and removed for treatment. Mildly contaminated soils were kept onsite and used to modulate the topography to restore water flow and capped with clean fill.

Connecting the valley's hydrological system to the rest of the campus as well as Lake Waban beyond was an integral part of the design. The valley now acts as a wetland with basins and marshes that treat the site's runoff water. It reorients the campus and provides gathering spaces for small and large groups on the Events Lawn and an amphitheater. The man-made hills that guide the water also increase the visual interest of the site. This project won the 2006 General Design Award of Excellence from the American Society of Landscape Architects.

The issue of environmental remediation and reuse of industrial properties, like that of financing in the next chapter, is complex and is best addressed on a project-by-project basis. Broad-based generalities aren't helpful, as regulation and enforcement vary according to location and changes in the law. The concept of brownfields, which focuses on the reuse of properties, and the increasing importance of smart growth combined with LEED certification are only positive steps in the redevelopment of industrial sites.

ENDNOTES

1. In fact, the City of Niagara Falls where Love Canal, the poster child of environmental contamination, is located did little to rethink its original development, but pushed government entities to clean and restore as much of the area as possible. Today, although the area was delisted by the EPA in 2004 after 21 years and an estimated $400 million, a fenced-in contaminated area remains capped and sealed; however, several blocks from this center, the residential subdivision of small houses has been repopulated and a local development corporation has built some infill houses. The area changed its name to Black Creek Village.
2. U.S. Environmental Protection Agency website (http://epa.gov/brownfields/glossary.htm).
3. Green museum is a web-based museum of environmental art (www.greenmusuem.org).

CHAPTER 6

DEVELOPMENT FINANCING PROGRAMS

Development financing, as with environmental regulation, is a project-by-project subject that doesn't easily lend itself to simple overviews. There are, of course, instances of simple redevelopments of these industrial sites done within the private sector by private developers for private users with comparatively standard financing. These projects, such as Toronto's Distillery District and Philadelphia's Piazza at Schmidts, both discussed in other chapters, stand out because they are so rare. Projects, even apparently simple ones, now require a mixture of intricate financing mechanisms and government support more than before. The positive aspect of this complex story is that there are programs that, while not specifically focused on previous industrial sites, are applicable to their redevelopment. Seldom can a project be accomplished today with just one financing source or program, requiring developers, who can be the end users or not-for-profit organizations, to, in their collective words, "cobble together a cocktail of funding sources."

Discussions of financing are complicated by ever-shifting borrowing, environmental, and tax laws, which not only change over the years, but in America also vary from state to state, making generalizations difficult. Pertinent issues concerning a lender's liability because of previous use or pollution were addressed by brownfield provisions and discussed in the previous chapter. Many projects in this book take advantage of the gamut of tax credits and incentives, and grants from governments as well as foundations, in addition to standard financing. These credits, however, need purchasers, and in times of reduced profits, companies do not need the writeoffs, so markets for selling these tax credits can dry up.

In America, by far the most commonly used and valuable mechanism for developing industrial properties is the Rehabilitation Tax Credit program. This financing device is adaptable to historic structures as well as non-historic buildings erected before 1936. In addition, industrial redevelopment can also be eligible for the New Markets Tax Credits, a federal program designed to encourage development in defined low-income communities and in conjunction with historic tax credits. As many abandoned industrial facilities are located in now underserved areas and were built at the beginning of the last century, these programs have proved to be helpful instruments for redevelopment.

In America, other financing programs are available through state and local governments, such as block grants and façade improvement initiatives, all of which are better understood through the project examples below. In addition, certain residential programs can avail themselves of low-income tax credits. Whether providing tax credits, loans, or grants, there is no question that government at all levels plays a critical role in financing these projects, which often pose difficult development problems either because of site conditions or decades of inactivity. When standard government programs don't cover expenses for important projects, legislative allocations are quite common, as is foundation support, especially for projects developed by not-for-profits.

European large-scale public projects have different mechanisms for funds, many of which are government grants or government-initiated projects; however, as seen in the story of the National Waterfront Museum in Swansea, Wales, (Chapter 7) the process is no less stressful nor convoluted.

Tax Credit Programs

Historic Tax Credits

Buildings that are listed on the National Register of Historic Places, can qualify for the Historic Tax Credits, a federal program outlined in Section 47 of Internal Revenue Code to encourage preservation and adaptive reuse of certified historic structures. These credits qualify owners to receive a 20 percent reduction on a dollar-for-dollar basis of federal income tax, calculated as a percentage of approved and qualified rehabilitation expenditures. These credits can be syndicated, making them powerful financial instruments. The projects must be commercial, income-producing ventures for at least five years, thereby precluding condominium conversions.

If a property is not on the National Register, the owner can prove its eligibility and apply for listing. Some states have their own tax credit program; however, their existence and scope vary from state to state. Although it is a federal program, applications are first administered on the state level and then by the National Park Service. Its three steps are:

1. Confirmation that the building or site is on the National Register or is eligible to be on it. If the latter, applications are made through the State Historic Properties Office.

2. Application for the proposed rehabilitation to make certain that the work meets the program's requirements in terms of scope and time schedule. Most important, the work proposed must be done in accordance with the Secretary of the Interior's Standards for Historic Rehabilitation.

3. Documentation that completed work has been done as approved in item 2 above.

Credits are only available to building owners after projects are completed and tax forms are filed. Some developers who cannot use the tax deduction syndicate the credits as a way of receiving cash in lieu of reducing taxes. Because this is a tax-based program, applicants must be for-profit, tax-paying entities. As a result, nonprofits often join forces with for-profit developers or entities established to provide this service in order to access these funds. Although the tax benefit is great, complying with historical preservation standards can interfere with development plans, as the requirements are quite rigorous and apply to both the interior and exterior of the building. The additional approval steps can translate into more time and money for the project.

Rehabilitation Tax Credits

Rehabilitation tax credits are similar in principle to the Historic Tax Credits; however, structures do not have to be eligible for the National Register of Historic Places nor does the rehabilitation have to be according to the Secretary of the Interior's Standards for Historic Rehabilitation. The structure, however, has to have been built before 1936, and three of four original walls need to remain. The tax credit is 10 percent. This program is also quite helpful for the redevelopment of industrial sites, as many such buildings and complexes can meet this threshold.

NEW MARKETS TAX CREDITS

The New Markets Tax Credits program was designed to bring investment into communities that have limited access to equity markets. They can be used in concert with other tax credit programs such as Historic Tax Credits. To be eligible, a nonresidential project has to be located in a defined low-income community. A community development entity provides equity or loans to qualified businesses and obtains the qualified tax credits (up to 39 percent) spun off by the project. These tax credits are then transferred to the bank or investment partner that has provided equity to the community development entity. The total amount of credits is capped on a yearly basis and community development groups compete against each other to receive annual allocations.

AMERICAN BREWERY—OFFICE CONVERSION

NAME: AMERICAN BREWERY BUILDING

LOCATION: BALTIMORE, MARYLAND

FORMER USE: BREWERY, VACANT FOR 30 YEARS

PROJECT: RENOVATION INTO HEADQUARTERS FOR HUMANIM, A BALTIMORE-BASED SOCIAL SERVICE GROUP

DEVELOPER: AMERICAN BREWERY, LLC (JOINT VENTURE OF HUMANIM; THE CONTRACTOR, STREUVER BROS., ECCLES & ROUSE; AND THE PROJECT MANAGER, GOTHAM DEVELOPMENT)

FINANCIAL SNAPSHOT: NUMEROUS SOURCES INCLUDING:
- FEDERAL HISTORIC TAX CREDITS
- NEW MARKET TAX CREDITS
- STATE AND CITY LOANS AND GRANTS, INCLUDING BROWNFIELDS REVITALIZATION INCENTIVE
- NATIONAL TRUST LOAN FUND
- PRIVATE FOUNDATION AND INDIVIDUAL DONATIONS: THE HARRY AND JEANNETTE WEINBERG FOUNDATION, KRESGE FOUNDATION, MARYLAND HISTORIC TRUST, FRANCE-MERRICK FOUNDATION, AMONG OTHERS

TIME LINE: RFP FROM CITY: 2005; MOVE-IN: MAY 2009

The redevelopment of the American Brewery building in the severely run-down section of East Baltimore, Maryland, demonstrates how all these programs and incentives in the hands of a willing and determined buyer, a savvy developer, and the right team were knit together to create a successful project. Located in the heart of a crime-ridden and destitute area accurately headlined in the *Baltimore Sun's* 2006 two-part series, "A Neighborhood Abandoned," the building had remained vacant for 30 years, towering over the nearby boarded-up two-story row houses. The American Brewery building stood empty through several failed development schemes. Then the Columbia, Maryland–based

Figure 6.1
American Brewery (before). The 1887 John F. Wiessner Brewery recalls an era when beer was king in Baltimore, Maryland. It fell on hard times and was vacant for over 30 years before Humanim, a not-for-profit social service organization turned developer, cobbled together numerous sources of funding to create its headquarters.
© Cho Benn Holback + Associates

social services organization, Humanim, Inc., chose it as its new headquarters site for its offices and outreach programs, inspired by both the building and the neighborhood, ripe for the services it offers. The group provides job training and clinical support for children and adults with developmental and behavioral disabilities and expects to employ 250 people, many from the community.

Humanim moved in May 2009, and while it's too soon to calculate the transformative effect on the neighborhood, the renovation has already won numerous awards. The project is the recipient of the American Institute of Architect's (AIA) Maryland 2009 Public Building of the Year Award as well as the AIA Baltimore Chapter, Trostel Award for Historic Preservation and Good Design = Good Business Award. In its citation, the jury commented that "the highly-detailed historic building façade and interiors, which are intrinsically eccentric, were not covered, but used in a contemporary way."[1] In addition, the Urban Land Institute honored Humanim as developer with a Baltimore 2009 WaveMaker Award.

John Frederick Wiessner, a German immigrant, built his eponymous brewery in 1887 in what can only be described as an exuberant and idiosyncratic style. Described as "a monument to the development of brewing" in its 1973 National Register listing, the American Brewery building was sited on top of a hill at what was then the northern boundary of Baltimore. German beer making during the turn-of-the-century Baltimore was a thriving local industry until its demise as a result of anti-German attitudes during World War I, only to be followed a few years later by Prohibition. In the early 1930s, the

TAX CREDIT PROGRAMS

Figure 6.2
The American Brewery (before) in Baltimore, Maryland, building stands heads and shoulders above the neighborhood buildings, half of which were either razed or are boarded up.
© Cho Benn Holback + Associates

building was used for the manufacture of malt syrup, and at the end of Prohibition beer production, albeit for a national not a local market, resumed. The new operators renamed their facility the American Brewery; however, they—as well as the surrounding neighborhood—were less successful than their predecessors. In 1973, operations shut down and the building was abandoned, sharing the fate of adjacent deserted structures. It was deeded to the city of Baltimore in 1977.

To redevelop the building, financial and market issues dwarfed physical ones despite the years of neglect and the deterioration of the building. The hurdle of finding a tenant who enhanced the neighborhood had been overcome when representatives from Humanim, searching for a new headquarters in an area that needed its services, discovered the building when riding around the area. They contacted a local developer, Streuver Bros., Eccles & Rouse, who had much experience renovating historic structures and agreed to mentor Humanim for this project. Project costs ballooned to $25 million, a high amount for any developer to confront.

Because the property was owned by the city, regulations required that it issue a Request for Proposals in order to dispose of it. The 2005 RFP asked proposers not only to submit a price but also to show that it would benefit the struggling community. There were two other bidders; however, Humanim, as a social service provider who would help members seeking work as well as hire from within the community, won the bid. The entire brewery property, including a warehouse, was included in the RFP and the land was conveyed subject to a Land Disposition Agreement, which obligated the purchasers to produce its proposed project.[2]

Before it started building, Humanim conducted many community focus groups in order to become part of the neighborhood, to assess the programs and outreach needed, and to gain support of a population that often is suspicious of outsiders. In addition to providing employment and social services, it supported the community by hiring local security companies during construction and after opening, hiring local caterers and other service providers. Its design reflects the openness it wanted to present with an open plan interior with glass partitions and no private offices.

The building's architectural attributes as well as its location in an impoverished area made it eligible for many programs that enabled the project to go forward. Humanim, a nonprofit entity and therefore tax-exempt, was able to turn the project's considerable Historic and New Market Tax Credits into cash by forming a for-profit development corporation, American Brewery LLC, with the contractor, Streuver Bros., Eccles & Rouse, and the project manager, Gotham Development. These credits were then syndicated to tax-paying entities. The National Trust Community Investment Corporation, a for-profit subsidiary of the not-for-profit National Trust for Historic Preservation, is one such investor and acted in that capacity for the American Brewery project. Funds came from all possible sources, including donations from foundations that Humanim, as a nonprofit, was able to seek. In addition, Humanim, with Streuver guiding it, became the developer and was able to charge a developer fee, which it collected to reinvest in its programs.

The Baltimore-based architect chosen, Cho Benn Holback + Associates, had much experience converting former industrial buildings, many of which were historic, and worked with the state historic preservation office that scrutinized the design, especially details and materials. With the American Brewery building, for example, some of the beer-making apparatus, such as the grain chute, were required to be kept. On this particular project, the front facade of the building remained the same; however, the interior was altered, as was the rear elevation. This design flexibility was necessary because Humanim required open offices and spaces in order to make the community and their clients welcome.

All in all, the Humanim renovation benefited from approximately $11 million in tax credits, a little less than 50 percent of the cost of the project. The remainder of the funds came from a combination of donations of nearly $4.4 million, loans from the National Trust Loan Fund, and grants from the city. In total, financing came from numerous sources. Aside from being a difficult juggling act, financing from such a multitude of sources creates its own problems. In this case, lack of clarity about who was subordinate to whom became a critical question and almost prevented the closing.

This project was one in which the financial issues overshadowed the environmental ones. Aside from lead paint and decade's worth of pigeon droppings, the cleanup work dealt mostly with the effects of years of exposure to the elements. There was some arsenic, lead, and mercury found in the soil, which was removed from the site after the LLC applied for a Voluntary Cleanup Program permit and received a grant under the State of Maryland's Brownfields Revitalization Incentive Program.

Lessons Learned
- Create community support—both on a government and community level
- Bring together a strong, experienced development team
- Be flexible and creative in looking for financing sources
- Expect to face adversity and be determined to work through it—strong advocates are invaluable

The story of the reuse of the American Brewery Building is a small-scale exemplar of the arc of industrial redevelopment that shows how difficult, yet possible, such projects are. Originally built on the outskirts of its city and representing the pinnacle of its industry, the brewery bore the brunt of social and demographic changes. Left to deteriorate for decades, it was at one time slated to be demolished, considered an impediment to future development. A determined and willing buyer with a use that worked with the neighborhood had the tenacity to figure out how to create the project it needed. This project and others like it, however, would not be feasible without the financial instruments of tax credits and support of government and a wide array of philanthropic groups, foundations, and individual donors.

WASHINGTON MILLS BUILDING NO. 1—RESIDENTIAL CONVERSION

NAME: WASHINGTON MILLS BUILDING NO. 1

LOCATION: LAWRENCE, MASSACHUSETTS

FORMER USE: WOOLEN TEXTILE MILL

PROJECT: RESIDENTIAL CONVERSION WITH LIVE/WORKSPACES

DEVELOPER: ARCHITECTURAL HERITAGE FOUNDATION/BANC OF AMERICA, CDC

FINANCIAL SNAPSHOT:
- FEDERAL AND STATE HISTORIC TAX CREDITS
- MASSACHUSETTS HOUSING PARTNERSHIP
- MASSACHUSETTS DEPARTMENT OF HOUSING AND COMMUNITY DEVELOPMENT
- MASSDEVELOPMENT (STATE'S FINANCE AND DEVELOPMENT AUTHORITY)

TIME LINE: CONSTRUCTION START: 2006; MOVE-IN 2008

Several miles northeast from Lowell along the Merrimack River, is Lawrence, Massachusetts, a former mill town that has not experienced its neighbor's achievements in the renovation and revitalization of its abandoned buildings. Although its history and role in America's rise in textile manufacture is similar, it did not attract recent development like its neighbor nor spark the imagination of an artist community. The city refrained from encouraging residential use in its mill district in hopes of attracting industry for its fine stock of industrial buildings; however, industry continued to leave, not arrive. Then in 2003, in an effort to revive its downtown, Lawrence approved a zoning overlay to encourage residential use in the former industrial area of the city. This overlay was part of a coordinated "Gateway" effort that addressed environmental remediation issues as well as economic development efforts to revive what had become one of the poorest communities in America, just 35 miles from Boston.

The Boston-based Architectural Heritage Foundation (AHF) is a not-for-profit firm that specializes in the renovation of historic properties, both as an owner and as a consultant. For the Washington Mills Building No. 1, AHF became a 50-50 partner with Banc of America, CDC and bought the building to develop into housing. Construction started in 2006 and the building opened 17 months later. Today the building is home to 155 residential live/work units one-half mile from Lawrence's intermodal transit center. The goal of this project was not merely the renovation of the 240,000-square-foot former mill, but the start of the transformation of this downtrodden town. Only 10 percent of the apartments were reserved as affordable units, a low number in order to encourage market rate housing in the downtown area. The project was given a National Preservation Honor Award by the National Trust for Historic Preservation in 2008 for, in the words of the award, "not only the quality of its recent renovation but also for the impact of its rebirth on the city of Lawrence."

Built in 1886, the Washington Mills Building No. 1 was the home of the American Woolen Company that produced worsted yarns and fabrics for menswear and employed 6,500 workers in its heyday. The financing for this $43 million project came from a multitude of sources. In addition to receiving Federal and State Historic Rehabilitation Tax Credits, the developers received state economic development and housing grants, as well as donations from private foundations. Bank of America provided the construction loan and mortgage. As a not-for-profit organization, AHF can, in its words, "leverage funds inaccessible to for-profit developers, such as non-profit targeted public funds, grants and charitable contributions." Because of this, it was able to receive a multimillion dollar grant from the Commonwealth of Massachusetts that filled the gap because the state historic tax credit allocation had been met for the year it was to start construction.

It is important to note that tax credit policies vary from state to state. First, not all states have their own tax credit program—some states do not collect income tax, so the incentive is useless, and others do not provide such programs. In addition, state tax credits are often worth less than their face value because of tax policies. In addition, state tax liability is much lower than federal tax rates, and many owners are unable to use the credit, which can be greater than the tax bill. Massachusetts does allow for a direct transfer of credit. In addition, many states require, as does the federal policy, that properties taking advantage of tax credits must be income-producing for at least five years. Therefore, as in this case, the project was required to be rental housing.

TAX CREDIT PROGRAMS

Figure 6.3
The red brick Washington Mills Building No. 1 in Lawrence, Massachusetts, before its renovation sits next to the canal that fed it power in its heyday as a woolen mill.
Kara Cicchetti, Architectural Heritage Foundation

Lessons Learned

- Create a project that aligns with, and if possible, furthers government initiatives
- Not-for-profit development groups can be strong components in a development team—
- Work with financing sources that are familiar with historic and industrial projects

The renovation of the Washington Mills Building No. 1 shows that as evocative as old mill buildings are, the conversion to other uses does not always happen spontaneously. It is important to work with the local community: In this case the city of Lawrence developed a zoning overlay to control development in order to build upon its "smart growth" initiatives and encourage people to move into its downtown. With its life/workspaces the renovation was envisioned as a project that would entice artists to move in; however, that has not happened. The project is almost completely rented, and its residents are nonartists, either young professionals or others who are relocating from elsewhere in the region.

Conservation Easements

Federal Historic Preservation Tax Incentive Program

Historic properties can benefit from the Federal Historic Preservation Tax Incentive Program through which owners of eligible historic properties guarantee not to change the exterior appearance of their properties. The owners give an easement to the facade or other aspects of the building to a qualified charitable or government organization. In return, owners claim a tax deduction. This historic preservation easement protects the exterior from change without approval from the entity who owns the easement; however, it does not preclude interior changes. The easement is written into the deed and does not prohibit resale; however, it binds future owners.

Austin, Nichols & Co.— Residential Conversion

NAME: AUSTIN, NICHOLS & CO. WAREHOUSE

LOCATION: WILLIAMSBURG WATERFRONT, BROOKLYN, NEW YORK

FORMER USE: WAREHOUSE

PROJECT: CONVERSION TO RENTAL APARTMENTS

DEVELOPER: PRIVATE INVESTMENT GROUP

KEY PLAYERS: TRUST FOR ARCHITECTURAL EASEMENTS

In 2006, when a development group bought the Austin, Nichols & Co. warehouse on the Brooklyn waterfront in the Williamsburg section of the borough, the New York City Council had recently denied the building landmark designation, overriding the Preservation Commission's recommendation. This 1915 Cass Gilbert-designed warehouse was built to serve as the distribution point for what was then the world's largest wholesale grocery business. Goods were once unloaded from barges at the river into the building and up large elevators or onto trains that passed through the building on a rail line that extended to Long Island. The 179-foot by 440-foot reinforced concrete building occupies an entire city block, and its "Egyptian Revival style" buttresses its commanding presence on the Brooklyn waterfront. According to the Preservation Commission's report, this pioneering building was built by Horace Havemeyer, whose family had controlled most of the Williamsburg waterfront, having established the Sugar Refineries Company, often called the "Sugar Trust."[3]

Figure 6.4
The 1915 Cass Gilbert-designed Austin, Nichols & Co. Warehouse on the Brooklyn, New York, waterfront sports little ornament and clearly expresses its utilitarian purpose. The long-gone electric sign further publicized the building from the river, modestly proclaiming, "Sunbeam Pure Foods—The World's Best."
Collection of The New-York Historical Society

The owners, with permits in hand, were about to demolish the structure and build a high-rise apartment building on the site when they were approached by a representative from the Trust for Architectural Easements, who showed them that, with the right mix of tax credit financing, restoring the building would be economically feasible. Not only did saving the building become as economically feasible as destroying and building anew, it gave the developers a project that stood out from the competition of new housing being built around it as a result of the rezoning described in Chapter 4.

The numbers worked, and the owners applied for and received a listing on the State and National Registers, entitling them to a host of

Figure 6.5
The opening for the train that ran through Brooklyn's Austin, Nichols & Co. Warehouse is on the right of this view of the building from the city side.
Collection of The New-York Historical Society

tax credits and benefits. In addition to the tax credits described above, with this building, the Trust for Architectural Easements's deed language prohibits destruction of the warehouse, prevents use of the development rights (i.e., selling air rights), and preserves the building's height and bulk in perpetuity.

Conservation easements are stronger development restrictions than those imposed by tax credits, which are generally effective for five years on a sliding scale. (As with the Washington Mills No. 1 building, use of tax credits preclude the sale of units as condominiums and the housing was required to be rental and income producing.) Benefiting from this program can be a complicated process: The value of the easement is determined by an independent appraiser, and a building must be on the National Register

Figure 6.6
The new penthouses can be seen peeking over the coved cornice of the Austin, Nichols & Co. Warehouse in Brooklyn—the square footage (i.e., floor area) carved out for the courtyard was allowed to be transferred to the roof.
Carol Berens

or be a contributing building within an historic district.

In order to adapt this massive building for residential use, courtyards were carved into the center of the building, in effect separating the building into four zones. That work had to be done in accordance with the Secretary of the Interior's standards meant that all the changes had to be approved at both the federal and state levels: Paint colors as well as interior changes are reviewed by the historic preservation offices. To compensate for square footage subtracted from the building by the courtyards, rooftop penthouses were allowed. Although the windows look small from the outside, they are correctly sized when seeing them from the interior rooms.

This project shows how a private development entity can take advantage of the tax-based programs that have evolved to save an important part of the city's industrial patrimony. The development team was guided, in part, by the not-for-profit Trust for Architectural Easements, a group that understood the historic development process and was adept at seeking and acquiring approvals.

Figure 6.7
The interior courtyard details recall Austin, Nichols & Co. Warehouse's industrial past. The walls alternate solids and voids to add visual interest to the large area (under construction).
Carol Berens

Tax Increment Financing for Brownfields

Tax increment financing (TIF) is a public financing method that uses future gains in taxes to finance current improvements that will create those gains. In other words, projects can borrow against future state and local (often including school) taxes to pay for costs related to developing sites within certain areas or under certain conditions, such as brownfield remediation. The underlying theory behind this state-run initiative is that by bringing fallow property back on the market, the value of surrounding real estate will increase and in turn encourage future investment, both effects that will generate increased tax revenues.

Although policies vary from state to state, there are two broad-based ways TIF is distributed: on a specific property-by-property basis or by creating a TIF district that includes the property to be developed as well as surrounding area as a way of providing amenities to the area. When a TIF district is formed, its base tax amount is determined and frozen. All subsequent increases in tax revenue, the "tax increment," go directly to the TIF district to pay off the bonds and/or loans that are issued to finance the project. Debt payment is generally structured on a 20- to 30-year basis, after which the TIF structure is retired and property becomes fully assessed with all the tax going to the local entities. If, however, the TIF project fails to produce the tax increment necessary to repay the bonds or loans, the local government, the guarantor of the debt, is liable for the amounts due.

According to the Council of Development Financing Agencies, 49 states have TIF-enabling legislation, which is one of the most widely used forms for development finance today. However, some limit municipalities from creating districts for public infrastructure such as roads and sewers and exclude brownfields or the preliminary cleanup costs associated with them. Brownfields projects that use TIF are usually quite large redevelopments and are typified by Atlantic Station in Atlanta, a conversion of a steel mill into a mixed-use mini-city development in its Roswell section.

As with environmental issues, the issues these projects present are specific and complex and are best understood in the context of their stories. Several of the developments with respect to tax credits have made the redevelopment of industrial sites possible, as many of these sites fit within the financing guidelines. This has not only helped private developers but also the not-for-profit sector, which has become quite active in pursuing its goals by developing on its own.

Endnotes

1. American Institute of Architects Maryland Chapter website, www.aiabalt.com/displaycommon.cfm?an=1&subarticlenbr=29, accessed November 12, 2009.
2. For financing and legal reasons, the property and the LDA were subsequently subdivided and discussions are starting about future development that would complement Humanim's programs.
3. New York City Landmarks Preservation Commission report, September 20, 2005, Designation List 386, LP-2163.

SECTION 3

PROJECT TYPES

CHAPTER 7

CULTURAL PROJECTS

As seen in Chapter 4, the powerful economic development partners of art and tourism often work together to rescue abandoned industrial buildings and sites and infuse life into moribund areas. Museums now operate in former mills, factories, and industrial wastelands in North Adams, Massachusetts; Tacoma, Washington; Minneapolis, Minnesota; and Swansea, Wales—just a few of the many cultural venues around the world that have pinned their hopes on being the key to their local and regional economic development renewal. In most cases, the reason for the support given to the institution being established, while considered important in and of itself, often rests upon the cachet the museum or cultural center will bring to the city as a destination as well as the ancillary uses that are expected to arise as a result. The cities' hope that the crowds these places attract will entice other uses and business to the area.

Both large and small cities use their adaptive reuse projects to maintain a neighborhoods' sense of history in hopes of attracting visitors who will not only come for the exhibits, but remain to eat, shop, and perhaps stay overnight. These projects create a focus of activity, sources of employment, and retail opportunities as well as remind visitors and residents of past achievements and success. Other cities opt to erase the past and create fresh symbols in order to change their image, superimposing striking concert halls or museums on urban wastelands, a phenomenon epitomized by Sydney's Opera House, Cleveland's Rock and Roll Hall of Fame and Museum, and of course, Bilbao's Guggenheim Museum of Art.

Merging the world of the culture and economic development, high-profile museums and cultural centers lure visitors to once run-down former industrial areas with attention-getting buildings. Because of the large areas and huge infrastructure investment required, these projects are almost always government-initiated, with the costs and efforts justified by projected job generation and the economic benefit gained through increased tourism and newly burnished image.

ARCHITECTURE AS ADVERTISING

One of the instantly recognizable modern-day examples of "look-at-me architecture" is the Sydney Opera House in Australia. Built during the 1950s and 1960s and opened in 1973, stories of its torturous design problems, construction history, and cost overruns sometimes overshadowed the building itself. It does, however, symbolize its city. Located on the site of a former railroad depot on Bennelong Point overlooking the

Sydney Harbor, the building got its start as the subject of a government-sponsored design competition won by Danish architect Jorn Utzoøn. City officials searching for a way to stand out look toward Sydney Opera House's white nesting shells roof floating over the water and imagine they can conjure up an image as individual and as compelling for itself.

Bilbao, Spain, followed suit. As recounted in Chapter 8, that city embarked upon redeveloping a riverside industrial wasteland crisscrossed with railroad tracks. It cleaned and sold the sites in addition to investing in the city's infrastructure, especially its transportation facilities and waterfront public space. In 1991, early in their redevelopment program, city leaders lured the Guggenheim Museum, which in turn hired Frank O. Gehry and Associates to create a signature building after an invitation-only competition. In order to attract such an esteemed institution to what was a former outpost, the Basque government paid 100 percent of the development cost, which included funds to supply art for the collection as well as annual maintenance. Now Bilbao is a must-see detour on the tourist map, and the sightseeing euros it has attracted have repaid the city's gamble several times over. How well the museum integrates with the rest of the city continues to be debated among architects and city planners. In this instance, the Guggenheim is a franchise, an American institution that has created a toehold on a foreign land with little representation of local artists or connection with the local culture. No one can deny, however, that a city few had previously heard of is now known by cultural tourists around the globe.

These large government-sponsored projects have made competitions and public bidding for developers and architects commonplace and expected. This relatively recent use of international architectural competitions has encouraged the concept as buildings as billboard—advertisement for a city. This has either made or reinforced architectural reputations, often worldwide. Gehry had been a practicing architect for several decades with many awards under his belt before Bilbao, but after that project he became the subject of films, one-man museum shows, and even an episode on *The Simpsons*.

Many of these large-scale, from-the-ground-up redevelopments are located on a harbor, for decades a traditional no-man's land to all but longshoremen, its insalubrious uses deliberately separated from a city's downtown by tenements, warehouses, and highways. New, glittery, and (hopefully) successful, these developments often come at a cost to a city's urban sense. Investing large amounts of public money to attract large attention-getting institutions is a speculative venture, one mainly suitable for a city whose image needs redefining and spirit needs lifting. As eye-catching as they are, these projects can create a second center for a city, refocusing activity and energy from its traditional center to the edges. Reclaiming land at its periphery with a building out of scale or character with its core is a city's way of moving to the suburbs within its borders. The following projects illustrate other means of integrating cultural institutions within the existing urban fabric.

Museums of Industry

As the number of operational factories dwindles, the allure of recounting the industrial story becomes more compelling. From tiny mill museums dotting the countryside and riverfronts of England and New England to the more traditional museums such as the Charles River Museum of Industry in Waltham, Massachusetts, these centers animate the memory of our industrial past. Through interactive exhibits children in towns and cities in America and Europe are taught how their forbearers made their livings, and visitors are reminded of the area's renown, a bitter-sweet retrospective of former accomplishments. Rather than manufacturing goods for use, these museums manufacture goods as part of demonstrations, showcasing the products and processes that are never returning to their place of origin.

Routes of Industrial Heritage

Museum: European Route of Industrial Heritage

Location: Web-based tourist network of important industrial sites throughout Europe

Former Uses: Ten themed routes: textiles, mining, iron and steel production, energy, manufacturing, water management, service and leisure, transport and communications, industrial landscapes, and housing and architecture

The European Route of Industrial Heritage (ERIH) is a tourist network of important industrial sites that leads through Great Britain, the Netherlands, Belgium, Luxemburg, France, and Germany. The Route recognizes that northwestern Europe was the "cradle of the Industrial Revolution," and was established to, in its words, "protect Europe's industrial heritage sites and use their preservation as a motor for the development of regions that are often suffering from economic decline."[1] In addition to guiding travelers through regions and important industrial sites, the Route creates a virtual library to facilitate research among organizations and academic institutions involved with preserving and disseminating information about these sites.

Ten themed routes encompass areas that made their reputations from textiles, mining, iron and steel production, energy, transport, and industrial landscapes. In addition, regional routes guide visitors to sites within a defined area. This route system contains Anchor Points (which will be noted in the following descriptions), and major industrial monuments within each itinerary. In addition to highlighting specific buildings or factories, web-based information highlights points of local interest surrounding sites or in the area to encourage tourism.

NATIONAL PARKS SERVICE NATIONAL HERITAGE CORRIDORS

The closest system in America is the National Parks Service's National Heritage Corridors, which highlight different regional interests, some of which are based upon past industrial history. For instance, the Blackstone River Valley National Heritage Corridor runs from Worcester, Massachusetts, to Providence, Rhode Island, and marks the birth of the American Industrial Revolution and the importance of the Blackstone Canal with six visitor centers. Highlights include the Slater Mill in Pawtucket, Rhode Island; Knowlton Hat Factory in Upton, Massachusetts; and The Museum of Work and Culture in Woonsocket, Rhode Island. The latter, located in the former Barnai Worsted Company and Lincoln Textile Company textile mill, charts the immigration of French Canadians to this area as the rising textile industry searched for new workers. Although the Blackstone Falls powered many textile factories in the 1700s and 1800s, many of the mills have been converted to housing and the surrounding areas are parks.

CROWN AND EAGLE MILL

The Crown and Eagle Mill in North Uxbridge, Massachusetts, is within the Blackstone River Valley National Heritage Corridor. The Blackstone River Valley lays claim to being among the first industrialized areas in America. The structures were built as two cotton mills around 1823–1827 of local granite. They were

Figure 7.1
The National Parks Service's National Heritage Corridors are loosely defined routes, some of which are based on previous industrial history. The former cotton Crown and Eagle Mills in the Blackstone River National Heritage Corridor in North Uxbridge, Massachusetts, were burned in 1975; however its granite walls remained.
Bruner/Cott, 1982

Figure 7.2
The Crown and Eagle Mills buildings in North Uxbridge, Massachusetts, were rebuilt by the architects, Bruner/Cott & Associates, using what materials could be salvaged as well as restoring the landscape, especially the canals that made this one of the first industrialized areas in America.
Nick Wheeler, 1984

> vandalized and burnt in the mid-1970s and since have been renovated and converted as senior housing. Legend has it that the mills' builder, Roger Rogerson, named the first mill after his English homeland and the second one after his adopted one. These mills were once part of a village, complete with company store, worker homes, and mansion.
>
> The restoration retained what was possible of the stone structure and new infill was inserted in the middle. The canals, which were the original reason for the location of the mills, were restored. The site is on the National Register of Historic Places.

The National Parks Service's Heritage Areas is another program that may or may not include industrial sites depending upon the area. Heritage Areas are designated by the United States Congress and link towns within a region that have a cohesive story to tell and contain historic and scenic resources. The Essex (based in Salem, Massachusetts), the MotorCities (Detroit, Michigan), and Rivers of Steel (Homestead, Pennsylvania) National Heritage Areas, among others, contain some industrial museums and sites.

Mill Museums

As the first industrial buildings, mills have long and tangled histories with their places: Upon arrival, they were responsible for creating and defining their cities as successful entities; upon leaving, they removed the economic base they helped establish. Whether forsaken for being inefficient, outmoded, or prohibitively expensive when their products became obsolete or were more economically produced elsewhere, their empty hulks remain and litter the riverbanks that delivered energy or blight the centers of towns that grew up around them.

Converting raw material into manufactured products, mills were the laboratories of changing industrial methods and are the precursors of the modern factory. This early history of manufacturing and urban development can be experienced by going to mill museums, many of which offer interactive exhibits and workshops where visitors learn traditional handiwork and participate in methods of manufacture and production. Museums that tell stories in their original buildings have successful track records of appealing to tourists across America and Europe. Many institutions supplement exhibits with workshops that teach traditional ways of making goods, thereby supporting local crafts and becoming centers of activity which, in turn, encourage memberships and establish a community. The historic nature of these buildings along with their unadorned but striking architecture allows these mills to be self-referential museums, but also adds a level of complexity to the renovation with respect to historical accuracy and additional costs to comply with state or national regulations.

Exhibits often spotlight the sociological aspect of manufacturing by recounting the struggles of the labor movement and stories of the myriad waves of immigrants who worked and settled in the area. In addition to showing mechanical processes and highlighting architectural features, the best of them show how the industry transformed their towns and regions, physically as well as demographically. When the mill museum building was at the zenith of its production, it was just one of many; now, as the sole survivor, it represents them all.

Audax Textile Museum

Museum: Audax Textile Museum

Location: Tilburg, The Netherlands

Former Use: Woolen Textile Mill

Date: 2008

Major Goals: Increase the museum's public presence and create knowledge center for the field of textile design; combine facilities of textile museum with regional archives; explore textile manufacture today including unusual and new applications of fabric of all kinds

Key Players: Municipality of Tilburg/Audax Textielmuseum/ cepezed

Although textile manufacture started the Industrial Revolution in England and its expansion fostered regional specialties in Europe and economic independence in America, it has all but vanished from these places of origin, leaving mill buildings in its wake. Whether of stone, wood, or brick, these simple but imposing buildings aesthetically define their towns or at least sections of it, while their abandonment not only removed the machines but changed the nature of what once filled the daily lives of the residents. As a result, even in the immediate neighborhood of these mills there are few people who know how textiles used to be made or are produced today. Thus, the focus of these museums is often the loom room, where demonstrations of the manufacturing process as well as the daily lives and experience of mill workers are portrayed.

Until the 1960s when foreign competition drove the textile industry from Europe, Tilburg was the woolen textile capital of the Netherlands. At first, woolen cloth was manufactured in sheep herders' homes, but as the nineteenth century progressed, weaving became more mechanized and relocated to mills. By the late 1880s, Tilburg's woolen mills numbered in the mid-hundreds. The industry continued as a mainstay of the city's economy, bolstered by the need for warm military uniforms during World War II. The Audax Textile Museum, located in the former facility of the woolen fabrics manufacturer Mommers & Co., tells the story of the weavers and the place that mills had in the town. Not wallowing in the past, the center explores textile manufacture today, including unusual and new applications of fabric of all kinds.

The 2008 renovation and expansion as a result of the museum's merger with the Tilburg Regional Archives created a new, highly visible entrance as well as reorganized the circulation with the existing buildings. The Delft-based architectural firm, cepezed, designed the large, modern steel and glass structure to contrast with the traditional massive brick buildings of the existing mill. This entrance responds to the museum's desire to visually mark its place in the city, open itself up to the neighborhood, and invite the public in. The museum and archives are now accessed from the glass wing, which affords presentation space, a café, and from the top floor, a panoramic view of the mill complex and surrounding area.

Now an Anchor Point on the European Route of Industrial Heritage, the museum's permanent and temporary exhibitions present an array of

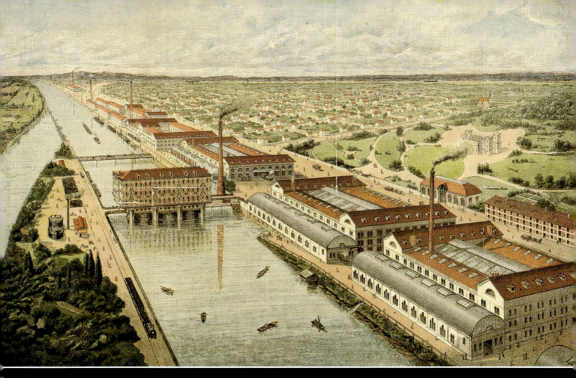

Figure C-1
Bird's eye panorama of Noisiel, France, in 1890 showing the relationship between the housing and factory, with its famous mill straddling the Marne River.
Collection Nestlé déposée en mairie de Noisiel. © Nestlé France et mairie de Noisiel

Figure C-2
The mill at Noisiel today. The 1872 Menier Chocolate factory in Noisiel, France, harnessed the power of the Marne River and was one of the most structurally advanced buildings of its time as well as one of the most ornate.
Nestlé France S.A.S

Figure C-3
The pipes, ducts, and elevators of the Centre Pompidou in Paris are color coded according to the services they carry.

◀ Figure C-4
This overhead view of Granville Island in Vancouver, Canada, shows the conversion of industrial buildings into the public market with a view of False Creek.
Granville Island

▼ Figure C-5
The master plan for the Philadelphia Navy Yard is divided into five sections including the working shipyard at the west, the adjacent historic core which contains Urban Outfitters, a corporate center to its north, a potential research park and space for future development as yet unplanned. The Navy Yard hopes to provide sites for industry to expand and relocate.
Philadephia Industrial Development Corp.

Figure C-6
The design at Urban Outfitters headquarters at the Philadelphia Navy Yard retained the industrial traces of its wide range of history. The building is right on the harbor with ships at the back door.
© Lara Swimmer

Figure C-7
The Piazza at Schmitds in Philadelphia is a privately developed gathering space designed with the Piazza Navona in mind. Small shops are at the ground level of the new apartment buildings and activities such as movies and sports events are projected on the screen on the restored warehouse.
Peter Kubilus

Figure C-8
New York's newest park, the High Line, transformed from an abandoned elevated railroad, affords wonderful vistas of the Hudson River and the city.
Iwan Baan © 2009

▲ Figure C-9
The waterfront promenade was required by Baltimore, Maryland, for the Tide Point renovation.
Design Collective

▲ Figure C-10
The Can Company in Baltimore, Maryland, transformed a vacant factory into offices and retail under a Brownfields Voluntary Clean-Up Program.
Ron Solomon © 2009

Alumnae Valley Landscape Renewal Aerial Diagram
Wellesley College, Wellesley Massachusetts

1. West Sediment Forebay
2. Infiltration Basin
3. Overflow Swale
4. Upper Inlet
5. Lower Inlet
6. Boat Ramp
7. Stone Spillway
8. Cattail Marsh
9. Marsh Feeder Pond
10. East Sediment Forebay
11. DNAPL Collection Area
12. Physical Plant Service Area
13. Campus Center Loading Dock
14. Parking Facility Access
15. Visitor Parking

▲ Figure C-11
This diagram shows how the landscape of Alumnae Valley, Wellesley College, Wellesley, Massachusetts, was changed to address contamination as well as to restore the hydrology of the site.
Michael Van Valkenburgh Associates, Inc.

▶ Figure C-12
The 2007 renovation of the Washington Building No. 1, a former woolen mill in Lawrence, Massachusetts, was done according to historic standards in order to benefit from both federal and state historic tax credits. The goal was to attract residents to the downtown area with live/workspaces.
Porter Gifford

Figure C-13
View from the river of the Mill City Museum in Minneapolis, Minnesota, which has kept the silos and its proud sign. *Architecture & Interior Design: Meyer, Scherer & Rockcastle, Ltd. (MS&R); Photography: Assassi Productions*

Figure C-14
The National Waterfront Museum in Swansea is approached from the town through a park. The building gently reflects the curves of the old rail tracks that used to bring coal and goods to the waterfront for shipping. *Photo: Rob Watkins/www.robwatkins.co.uk*

Figure C-15
Gallery design at MASS MoCA in North Adams, Massachusetts contrasts original details and rough finishes with new art in soaring spaces.
Robert Polidori, 1999

Figure C-16
The Museum of Contemporary Art Detroit (MOCAD) is a decorated shed, the newest cultural institution in Detroit, Michigan that only mounts special shows and has no permanent collection.
Zago Architecture

Figure C-17
Panorama of Baltimore's Inner Harbor: The Power Plant's pier is connected to the Baltimore National Aquarium, seen on the right.
© Kevin Weber Photography

Figure C-18
Jo Coenan planned KNSM Island (right) with its large-scale housing blocks as the first island to be developed. West 8's Borneo Island (left) and Sporenburg (middle) are composed of a sea of dense low-rise housing with several large buildings placed at an angle to give direction to the area and provide vistas from the apartments.
West 8 Urban Design & Landscape Architecture

▲ Figure C-19
Panorama looking toward Amsterdam shows the contrast of MVRDV's Silodam with the existing nineteenth- and twentieth-century warehouses that were built on a dam protecting the harbor. They've since been converted into housing.
© Brian Rose

▶ Figure C-20
Container City 2 (eastern elevation) on Trinity Wharf is part of the London Docklands development that's rented to artists, designed by Nicholas Lacey.
Teresa Lundquist

▲ Figure C-21
Montreal's Redpath Lofts, converted from an abandoned sugar refinery by the Groupe Cardinal Hardy, are reflected in the Lachine Canal, transitioning from its former industrial use to being Montreal's recreational waterway.
© Denis Farley, Developper Groupe Gueymard, architect Cardinal Hardy

◀ Figure C-22
As an early renovation project, the revitalization of the Vieux-Port of Montreal recalled its industrial past and was critical to enhancing the public waterfront of the St. Lawrence River.
© Denis Farley, Developper Société du Vieux-Port de Montréal, architect Cardinal Hardy

Figure C-23
The Distillery District project in Toronto is a large-scale conversion of the historic former Gooderham and Worts distillery into an arts and entertainment destination.
Photo courtesy of Artscape, www.torontoartscape.on.ca

Figure C-24
Canal St. Martin, formerly used to bring goods into the central city, is now part of the park network that threads through eastern Paris.
Phillipe Besnard

Figure C-25
At the Landscape Park Duisburg Nord in Germany, the former open wastewater canal is being used to clean the site. It is fed by rainwater and channeled by a 10-foot-diameter underground main and sealed by a layer of clay.
© *Latz + Partners*

Figure C-26
The Seattle Olympic Sculpture Park was built by the Seattle Art Museum to accommodate its outdoor sculpture collection.
© *Lara Swimmer*

Figure 7.3
Audax Textile Museum in Tilburg, the Netherlands, was designed by cepezed, a Delft-based architectural firm. The new entrance connects to the old mill buildings, while exhibits such as the large-scale textile sculpture showcase new uses for traditional material.
© Fas Keuzenkamp. Audax Textile Museum in Tilburg designed by cepezed.

historical artifacts from a medieval dye book to contemporary art. Its displays range from steam-driven equipment to computer-run machines as well as multimedia presentations. In addition, textiles are used as construction materials, showing off new technical advances of this traditional yet endlessly adaptable material. The exterior of the new archives building, an enclosed box supported by steel columns atop an existing brick building, is clad with a water-inhibiting PVC polyester fabric, while stretched textile serves as ceiling and wall systems. On the front façade, announcements of museum events are composed from a grid of LED lights incorporated in the textile wall system.

Figure 7.4
The interior display in the Audax Textile Museum produces textiles as an exhibit within a refurbished mill building showcasing the exposed structure and skylights.
© Fas Keuzenkamp. Audax Textile Museum in Tilburg designed by cepezed.

Mill City Museum

MUSEUM: MINNEAPOLIS MILL CITY MUSEUM

LOCATION: MINNEAPOLIS, MINNESOTA

FORMER USE: FLOUR MILL

DATES: OPENED 2003

MAJOR GOALS: MUSEUM RECOUNTING HISTORY OF FLOUR MILLING, RIVERFRONT REVIVAL

KEY PLAYERS: MILL CITY MUSEUM; CITY OF MINNEAPOLIS; MEYER, SCHERER & ROCKCASTLE, LTD.

The Gold Medal Flour neon sign proudly announces the Mill City Museum at the center of the Mill District on the west bank of the Mississippi River overlooking the Mill Ruins Park. Once part of America's thriving flour milling district, the museum's building has survived several fires, and since its opening in 2003, is the center of the revived riverfront industrial district. The museum recalls the time when grain would arrive by rail from the northern plains, be milled in one of many mills powered by the Saint Anthony Falls in the Mississippi River, and then be loaded into rail cars and shipped east. From the late 1880s to just after World War I, Minneapolis called itself the "Flour Milling Capital of the World." In the early twentieth century, its "Flour Trust," consisting of three corporations now known as General Mills, Pillsbury Flour Mills Company, and Standard Milling Company, controlled approximately 97 percent of the nation's flour supply. These mills produced an average of 16 million barrels of flour annually. The industry attracted an influx of workers to toil in its mills as well as the ironworks, bag fabricators, and barrel makers and other industries that supported its goods. In the early part of the twentieth century Minneapolis saw its population increase 350 percent.

The milling industry's long slow demise began in the 1930s, when milling was no longer dependent upon water power. It was abetted by a change in the tax law that made it cheaper to ship grain rather than flour, and the Depression sealed its fate.

One of the largest of these mills was the Washburn A Mill,[2] which had been constructed in 1878 and rebuilt several times after being damaged by fires before being shuttered for good in 1965. Six years later this home to General Mills and Betty Crocker was added to the National Register of Historic Places and became a National Historic Landmark in 1983. Soon after closing, a private entity bought the property; however, development proved elusive. In 1980, the city of Minneapolis bought the property, intent on preserving the building and using it to connect the city to its riverfront. The city began consulting with the Minneapolis Historical Society and Thomas Meyer, a local architect who had written his thesis on the history of Saint Anthony Falls, about how to reinvent the riverfront, which at this time was a derelict no-man's-land. Desolate mills lined the riverbanks, and on the city side of the mills—railroad tracks that once enabled Minneapolis's flour to be shipped around the world—had been ripped up. In their place was either vacant land or, many years later starting in the early 1990s, the hesitant beginnings of newly built loft-type housing.[3]

During initial discussions about revival of the waterfront in 1991, a fire of unknown origin ravaged the mill again; however, this tragedy turned into a defining moment. The fire burned, in the words of Mr. Meyer, "an atrium" in the massive complex, making it easier to see the possibilities of reuse. Bolstered by a forceful local Historical Society and working with Mr. Meyer's firm, Meyer, Scherer & Rockcastle, Ltd. (MS&R), the city stabilized the building and removed the resulting asbestos- and PCB-contaminated debris. It is worth noting that throughout the decades-long redevelopment process, the city's community development agency was active and involved in promoting the reinvention of the riverfront and the role that the museum would play in this renewal. Among other actions, it was able to engage elected officials to financially support their efforts.

The fire rekindled conversion efforts: The museum started fundraising while the architectural and business plans were being developed. The building was on the National Register of Historic Places and a National Historic Landmark;

Figure 7.5
The Mill City Museum in Minneapolis, Minnesota, spurred a riverfront revival, including residential loft conversions and the development of the waterfront. The North Star Blankets sign stands atop the 1864 North Star Woolen Mill that was one of the few textile factories along the Mississippi in Minneapolis. It closed in 1949.
Architecture & Interior Design:Meyer, Scherer & Rockcastle, Ltd. (MS&R); Photography: Assassi Productions

however, its being a ruin posed problems for the State Historic Properties Office, who denied the project's application for Historic Tax Credits. This was a financial blow as only the 10 percent credit was allowed. Even fire-ravaged, the 142,000-square-foot structure was too big for the museum alone. A public-private partnership was created to add an office condominium that occupied 62,000 square feet or approximately 44 percent of the building and, more importantly, provided needed capital for the construction. These offices on the upper floors above the museum were quickly sold, two of them to MS&R.

The rest of the funds were raised through the sale of a façade easement to a local preservation group. The city donated the building to the Minneapolis Historical Society, which relied heavily on donations and appropriations from various levels of government—state, county, and city.

The museum opened in 2003 as the lynchpin in the redevelopment of the west side of the Minneapolis. Today, the museum is surrounded by housing, both newly built and converted from

Figure 7.6
View from above of the Mill City Museum's atrium that had been ravaged by fire and is now an outdoor gathering space for the museum.
Architecture & Interior Design: Meyer, Scherer & Rockcastle, Ltd. (MS&R);
Photography: Assassi Productions

Figure 7.7
The route of milling flour can be observed from the spectator platforms of the freight elevator of the Mill City Museum in Minneapolis.
Architecture & Interior Design: Meyer, Scherer & Rockcastle, Ltd. (MS&R); Photography: Assassi Productions

warehouses as well as the recently relocated Guthrie Theater, designed by Jean Nouvel. The museum was the first major project on the riverfront—when plans were being formed for the old mill building, surrounding development had been so spotty that there was no community with which to negotiate or have public discussions.

The building not only animates the river bank which is now called the Mill Ruins Park, but its several entries on three levels—from the city side, river side, and the rail corridor—link riverfront and downtown. The museum tells the story of grain farming, millings, and food product development, as well as labor and immigrant experiences. The exposed ruins keep history palpably alive. The "atrium" created by the 1991 fire is now the Ruin Courtyard. A 30-seat theater is in a freight elevator that tells the gravity-based story of the flour mill. From the top observation deck are views of the Mississippi River and surrounding area. Mill artifacts are preserved and incorporated into exhibits, and pictures of the milling mechanisms that extended through the height of the building are drawn on the courtyard façade windows.

Figure 7.8
The artifacts of the old mill were kept whenever possible to become part of the exhibitions of the Minneapolis Mill City Museum.
Architecture & Interior Design: Meyer, Scherer & Rockcastle, Ltd. (MS&R);
Photography: Assassi Productions

CULTURAL PROJECTS

Sloss Furnaces National Historic Landmark

MUSEUM: SLOSS FURNACES NATIONAL HISTORIC LANDMARK

LOCATION: BIRMINGHAM, ALABAMA

FORMER USE: IRON AND STEEL MILL

DATES: 1977

MAJOR GOALS: PRESERVE PART OF THE CITY'S INDUSTRIAL HERITAGE

KEY PLAYERS: LOCAL PRESERVATION ACTIVISTS, CITY OF BIRMINGHAM

Figure 7.9
Birmingham, Alabama, could be seen from Sloss Furnace in the early 1900s.
Courtesy of Sloss Furnaces National Historic Landmark

Figure 7.10
Birmingham, Alabama, can still be seen from the top of Sloss Furnace.
Historic American Engineering Record, AL-3-133; Jet Lowe, photographer, Spring 1994

Heavy industry did not require the waterfront for energy or transport but instead relied on natural resources and good train connections. Iron ore (which was needed to create different forms of iron, steel, and other manufactured goods) was mined from the Jones Valley, which was also rich in deposits of coal, white limestone, dolomite, and clay. Colonel James Withers Sloss persuaded the L&N Railroad to run through this valley, which permitted the transportation of goods through what was to become an extensive rail network. The minerals and railroad combined to bring into being both the city of Birmingham, Alabama, and the Sloss Furnaces. After the Civil War, the south's prodigious production of pig iron was instrumental in helping the region regain confidence and establish an economic base. The Sloss Furnace Company, which operated from 1882 to 1971, became the second largest pig iron company in the Birmingham area and by World War I was among the largest producers of the product in the world. World War II and the subsequent economic boom only expanded the market for iron and steel.

By the 1960s and 1970s, however, changing construction needs and environmental

Figure 7.11
Metal casting workshops and exhibitions are done at Sloss Furnace.
Courtesy of Sloss Furnaces National Historic Landmark

regulations soon made the production of pig iron obsolete. In early 1970, Sloss's blast furnaces were shut down and the property given to the Alabama State Fair Authority to be developed into a museum. It was an era of destruction, however, and preservation at that time was considered infeasible. Concurrent with discussions of Sloss's destruction in 1969, Birmingham's railroad hub, a sprawling two-block domed landmark built in 1909 as Terminal Station, was demolished and replaced by ahighway.

That act prodded local preservationists, who coalesced and organized parades and rallies to save the blast furnaces that had made Birmingham the center of industry in southeastern America.

In 1976, a survey of the facility was done by the Historic American Engineering Record (HAER), the Department of the Interior, and the city of Birmingham. Consequently, the city of Birmingham gained control of the site, and in 1977 city voters passed a $3.3 million bond to

Figure 7.12
Sloss Furnace offers metal working studios.
Courtesy of Sloss Furnaces National Historic Landmark

preserve the plant and create a museum for the city. Today, two 400-ton blast furnaces and 40 factory-related buildings comprise its collection. The historic structures were stabilized and parts are used as an active cultural center in Birmingham, hosting community events, festivals, and spectaculars as well as maintaining a program in metal arts. Sloss Furnaces became a National Historic Landmark in 1981 and remains the only preserved twentieth-century blast furnace in the United States.

The metal arts program takes place in old factory buildings and hosts educational programs and workshops and supports artist studios. A casting shed is now a foundry and fabrication shop that can cast iron, melt bronze and aluminum, and mold various materials. This heavy iron and steel center that forged rails, beams, and machinery is now used to create metal sculpture and teach visitors what made the area economically prominent.

Museums That Tell the Industrial Story

National Waterfront Museum

MUSEUM: NATIONAL WATERFRONT MUSEUM

LOCATION: SWANSEA, WALES

FORMER USE: WAREHOUSE, WORKING PORT

DATES: OPENED IN 2005

MAJOR GOALS: TOURIST DESTINATION TO TELL THE INDUSTRIAL MARITIME STORY

KEY PLAYERS: NATIONAL WATERFRONT MUSEUM, CITY AND COUNTY OF SWANSEA, WALES, AND HERITAGE LOTTERY

The National Waterfront Museum in Swansea got its new start when it was kicked out of its Cardiff Bay home because it didn't fit with the city's major redevelopment plans. As with many such events in life, what first appeared to be bad news turned into a piece of good luck. Faced with relocation, the museum sold its existing property for £7.5 million and for £3 million bought a storage facility large enough to hold its entire collection in one place. For the first time, curators could get an overview of what they had. The museum then started searching for what would end up being its £33 million new home and an Anchor Point on the European Route of Industrial Heritage.

The museum issued a call for proposals to Welsh cities for site options that would fulfill its criteria for a waterfront location so that it could tell the maritime story of receiving coal for export, have storage facilities for goods and, of course, possess a working harbor. In addition, the proposing town had to demonstrate it could draw 200,000 tourists a year. The search committee analyzed the submitted responses on a weighted matrix and Swansea, which already had a small waterfront museum in an existing building, won the bid. The resulting project is a partnership between the City and County of Swansea and the Welsh National Museum.

The project was funded by an "amazing cocktail" of funding sources as described by the owner's representative, Richard Bevins. The project got its start by receiving a pledge of £11 million from the United Kingdom Heritage Lottery Fund, the largest grant ever given to a project in Wales. In order to collect, however, it had to confirm that the museum had a working budget and sources of money to finish the project. With the help of a consultant, it pieced together grants (there were no loans) from the European Union as a "deprived area of Europe," the Welsh Development Agency, the Welsh Assembly Government, the London Building-in-kind, fundraising, the proceeds from its Cardiff building sale as well as the donation of buildings and land from Swansea.

In choosing the architects, although there were interviews in which past work was reviewed, the selection was based upon chemistry of the team—people with whom the museum believed it could work. This was felt to be the best way to keep the project on time and budget, and to ensure good communications. The architects chosen, London-based Wilkinson

MUSEUMS OF INDUSTRY

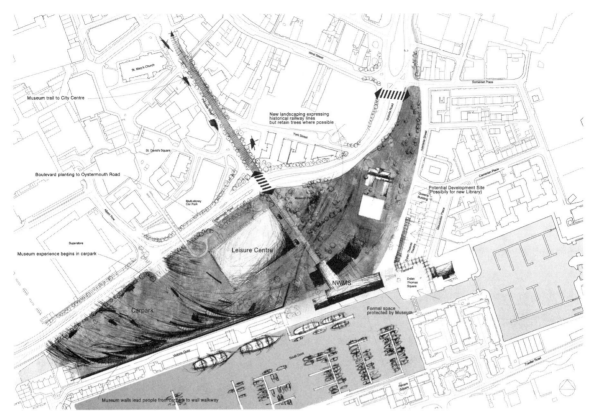

Figure 7.13
The site plan for the National Waterfront Museum in Swansea, Wales, shows how the museum and marina, which contains historic ships, are connected to the town center. The public enters the museum through the park.
Wilkinson Eyre Architects

Eyre Architects, were given several mandates. First, the facility was to be designed as a destination, not just a museum. In addition, it was to be sympathetic to the existing building and site, which had been used as an active shipping port. The new part was to reflect the story of the Welsh industrial maritime.

The site, as part of a working waterfront, had contained extensive railroad siding that contaminated the soil, which had to be removed. The existing warehouse was refurbished and a large canopy now extends over the waterfront promenade overlooking the port that contains historic ships. The new building subtly curves to reflect the path of the original railroad tracks, some of which remain in the landscaping. There are two distinct facades: a glass one that faces the town to welcome visitors and is lit at night like a sign, and one of slate, a native stone, which faces the water and can withstand the sea winds.

Figure 7.14
The new building by Wilkinson Eyre Architects has two distinct facades—an undulating glass and metal façade that faces the town (shown) and, on the other side, an enclosed slate to combat seaside location.
Hélène Binet photographer/Wilkinson Eyre Architects

Figure 7.15
A new canopy links the existing refurbished warehouse building to the marina and working harbor that contains historic ships.
Hélène Binet photographer/Wilkinson Eyre Architects

The result is a museum that now draws a broad demographic of about 250,000 tourists a year. The fear was that if the museum were static and told the maritime story in a traditional way, it would only attract older men. The displays, however, focus on the impact of industry on society and the life of the city; in effect, they are more about the people, working conditions, housing, and the Welsh experience than the industrial process. Virtual reality exhibits allow visitors to experience the life of a coal miner, participate in worker strife, and learn about the interconnection between the raw materials and global trade. The museum's annual budget includes funds for regularly changing displays to encourage repeat visitors.

Although a fair amount of maintenance money is funded by the government, both from

Swansea and Wales (no admission is charged), about £500,000 annually needs to be raised by the museum. Its business plan incorporated commercial components into the complex such as restaurants, a sailing store, as well as parking and a café. In addition, the ground floor to the original warehouse building is designed to have flexible spaces. Display cases are on tracks and can be moved about to create open spaces for events—from corporate meetings and presentations to weddings.

From the start the project was envisioned as one to regenerate the town and the site is connected to the town through a park and open space that leads from the town to the museum and then to the waterfront. This space is actively programmed with carnivals and festivals during all four seasons. The project has received awards from the Royal Institute for British Architects, the Civic Trust, and the UK Regeneration Award as the best design-led regeneration project.

CHARLES RIVER MUSEUM

MUSEUM: CHARLES RIVER MUSEUM OF INDUSTRY & INNOVATION

LOCATION: WALTHAM, MASSACHUSETTS

FORMER USE: FIRST MECHANIZED TEXTILE MILL; FOUNDED BY FRANCIS CABOT LOWELL

DATE: 1980

MAJOR GOALS: MEMORIALIZE THE START OF THE INDUSTRIAL REVOLUTION IN AMERICA

The Boston Manufacturing Company is credited as being the first capitalized corporation as well as the first major industrial corporation in America. Founded in Waltham, Massachusetts in 1813 by Francis Cabot Lowell along with a group of investors, it represents the integration of mechanized production from raw material to a finished product under one roof and under single management. Looms powered by the 12-foot waterfall of the Charles River transformed cotton threads into finished fabric. The mill was so successful that others were built adjacent to it, and a few years later, the power from the falls proved insufficient for the mill and the textile center moved to Lowell (see Chapter 1; Figure 1-2). Although much of the textile production had moved, manufacturing continued in the building.

The building was designated a National Historic Landmark in 1977, when it was deserted and almost torn down. With the help of a $10 million urban revitalization grant, Waltham created the Charles River Museum of Industry & Innovation in the steam-powered engine and boiler rooms and opened in 1980. The museum's exhibits not only recount the important place that Waltham and Lowell have in the development of industrial progress in America but also show other inventions and artifacts from industry that made this area important such as watch making and automobile manufacture. The museum's exhibits are geared to children and demonstrate actual machinery in operation. To connect to the next generation of entrepreneurs, it also hosts monthly Mass Innovation Nights, when inventors can showcase their wares to the general public and manufacturers. The remainder of the old mill has been converted into loft apartments.

Adaptive Reuse

Some museums and cultural centers are created in old industrial buildings because the large, open raw spaces of old factories and warehouses lend themselves to the exhibition of contemporary art. What goes on in the building generally does not relate to the former use, although its design often extols it. Often created as economic development projects rather than historic renovation ones, these places have a spotty record of reviving their towns.

MASS MoCA

Museum: MASS MoCA

Location: North Adams, Massachusetts

Former Use: Electric factory

Dates: From 1985 onward

Major Goals: Economically revive and redefine industrial town

Key Players: Thomas Krens, North Adams officials

Nestled in the hills of the Berkshires on the slopes of Mount Greylock in northwestern Massachusetts, North Adams remained an industrial town from the late 1700s until the mid-1980s as its neighbors to the south developed into a cultural and tourist center for New Yorkers and Bostonians. The building that is the present-day sprawling Massachusetts Museum of Contemporary Art, or MASS MoCA as it's known, reflects its site's long history that started as a small mill facility that took advantage of a powerful water supply to saw wood and manufacture various products. As the Civil War commenced, Arnold Print Works began its 80-year run printing cloth and building 25 of the 26 buildings that exist today. When it closed in 1942, the Sprague Electric Company bought the site to convert to an electronics plant, fueled by orders driven by World War II. Throughout these times, North Adams had become a magnet for immigrants and workers, and Sprague employees comprised approximately 25 percent of the town's population.

In 1985, Sprague shut down its North Adams facility, depriving the town of its major employer and leaving at its center a vacant and rambling 13-acre factory, approximately one-third of its downtown business district. This was a low blow to the town as it contributed to already high levels of local unemployment and left the area without a viable economic base. Over the years, major transportation routes had changed and North Adams was not as accessible by road, rail, or air, precluding another industry's taking Sprague's spot. Developers were courted and ideas bandied about from ski resort to casino gambling, but nothing took root, nor did any of the economics work.

Several miles to the west was Williamstown, home to the Sterling and Francine Clark Art Institute as well as Williams College. Soon after Sprague's closing, the then-director of the Williams Museum of Art, Thomas Krens, needed a large exhibition space for the contemporary art that did not fit in the existing galleries at Williams. The art director was searching not

Figure 7.16
The existing Sprague factory sprawled over 13 acres, almost one-third of the business district of North Adams, Massachusetts, when the company left and plans were being made to turn it into MASS MoCA.
MASS MoCA, 1997

only for larger space but for more "adventurous" galleries, in which art would not be restricted to white-walled enclosed rooms. The undefined, even gritty rooms of the Sprague factory, sparked the imagination of the artists, who were intrigued with adapting this space for contemporary art. A concerted effort by local officials and businesses to adapt the building for arts uses and to help turn the economy of North Adams around began. They pinned their hope not only on the proximity to the cultural venues of Williamstown, but also the anticipation that North Adams could entice visitors to Tanglewood and Jacob's Pillow in the southern Berkshires.

For the next 13 years plans for MASS MoCA evolved, and today it is one of the largest contemporary arts centers in America and is on the National Historic Register. Its 750,000 square feet now contain 10 galleries, two theaters, rehearsal and support spaces with multimedia capability, as well as outdoor cinema and other performance spaces. The transformation proceeded in fits and starts, encouraged by a $35 million bond issued by the Commonwealth of Massachusetts and a petition in support of a museum signed by 10,000 people from the community. The buildings were donated by the American Annuity Group.

In 1988, as a result of a master plan competition, a joint venture consisting of Frank O. Gehry, Robert Venturi, Skidmore, Owings & Merrill, and Bruner/Cott & Associates was chosen to define an approach for converting the complex of buildings for arts uses and to assess that feasibility. Their proposal vowed a "non-interference" with the existing structure and architectural features. Economic and political changes delayed the progression of the vacant factory to cultural center, with the fate of the institution hanging in the balance. Through the tenacity of the directors and cultural leaders, it was able to limp along until the financial wherewithal was attained.

It wasn't until 1995 that the project received matching funds from the Commonwealth for the renovation (the rest came from private and institutional donations). In the interim, a phased project was developed and plans for the museum evolved from a series of static galleries to a multidisciplinary center for the visual, performing, and media arts. Accommodation for installation art, video sculpture, happenings, and large-scale sound and landscape environmental art forced the designers to rethink the physical galleries.

Finished in 1999, the renovation by Simeon Bruner of Bruner/Cott & Associates, upholds much of the rawness associated with a factory building by retaining exposed bricks, structural elements, ducts, and pipes. Some of this roughness was a result of frugality as the budget for construction was low, however, philosophically, the industrial nature of the space came to be seen as an asset, something to be kept, not sanitized. The goal, as Mr. Bruner wrote, "was to make the art more approachable and less sacred. The spaces are finished like a studio, but scaled like a museum."[4] The contrast between the old facility and the new art, some of it shown as it was being made or in progess, became the design intent. Connections and bridges between the buildings have been kept, but two buildings were demolished to facilitate circulation and create outdoor courtyard space. The design won the 2000 AIA National Honor Award for Architecture.

As interesting and exciting as this renovation is, however, it does not answer the question of whether art can replace industry in what is, for all intents and purposes, an isolated community. North Adams was and is at root a working-class town and many of the residents lack the skills to transition from an industrial economy to a service one. Many of the service jobs that were created as a result of the museum do not pay as well as the factory jobs that were lost. The town now attracts tourists as a result of the museum, empty storefronts now are galleries, and a nascent arts community has arisen, but it is an economy that works more for the newcomers than for the original locals. Unemployment was reduced when the museum opened; however, the statistics may be skewed because those who left cannot be counted.

While North Adams is not the new SoHo, some spinoff development to capitalize on art and culture has occurred. About one mile from MASS MoCA is the Eclipse Mill Artist Lofts, a condominium live/work building established in 2005. A converted textile mill located in an industrial area, the building now houses 40 artists, including painters, writers, textile artists, and potters, as well as a ground floor bookstore and two art galleries. The deed restriction requires

Figure 7.17
MASS MoCA in North Adams, renovated from a rambling 25-building former electronics factory, still retains its raw industrial details. The Hoosic River runs through the property.
Bruner/Cott & Associates, 1997

Figure 7.18
At MASS MoCA in North Adams, Massachusetts, a steel structure was inserted within the courtyard created between the buildings and is used as performance and gallery space.
Robert Polidori, 1999

that residents use the space primarily for their work, as residential use must be accessory or secondary. The building had entered into a slow decline and contained only a few light manufacturing companies when the city of North Adams took possession and, with an urban renewal grant, installed new windows to make it habitable. In addition to the galleries, artists are encouraged to participate in the artistic life of North Adams, such as opening their studios during the annual North Adams Open Studios weekend in October.

THE TEMPORARY CONTEMPORARY

Raw industrial space and contemporary art seem to be made for each other. The high ceilings, exposed systems, and unfinished surfaces complement the experimental nature of the art being exhibited. Several years before MASS MoCA was a reality and when the Los Angeles Museum of Contemporary Art, or MOCA, was building a new Isozaki-designed facility downtown, a warehouse outside Little Tokyo was converted by Frank O. Gehry and Associates into what were supposed to be provisional galleries. The high volumes and flowing spaces of this then-outpost, called the Temporary Contemporary, was so popular it became a beloved fixture and became The Geffen Contemporary at MOCA. It is now one of three MOCA branches, which together have one of the largest permanent collections of such art in America. It recently has fallen on hard times because of financial reasons, not because of the need for different, more adaptable space.

Figure 7.19
Los Angeles's Geffen Contemporary at MOCA was meant to be temporary when it was converted in the early 1980s from a warehouse, but proved too popular to close.
Carol Berens

ADAPTIVE REUSE

Dia:Beacon

Museum: Dia:Beacon

Location: Beacon, New York

Former Use: Nabisco box printing factory

Dates: Opened 2003

Major Goals: Accommodate permanent collection of Dia Art Foundation; revive upstate town

Key Players: Michael Govan, former director of Dia Art Foundation; Leonard Riggio, former Dia Art Foundation chairman

Figure 7.20
The Judd Gallery at Dia:Beacon in upstate New York showcases the original industrial building elements such as the roof trusses, clerestories, and large, open spaces that complement contemporary art.
David Joseph

Built in 1929 as Nabisco's box printing factory in Beacon, New York, to produce the packaging for its biscuits and cookies among other products, the brick and steel structure's more than 34,000 square feet of skylights suffuse the space with a soft natural light. The building, located along the Hudson River in a small industrial town about 90 minutes north of Grand Central Station, overlooks the Hudson River. During its operational days, which ended in 1991, the cartons were shipped by rail (part of which is now the High Line park) to Nabisco's bakeries on the west side of Manhattan in what is now Chelsea Market, a mixed-use building housing a food market and offices.

The design, by OpenOffice[5] arts + architecture collaborative (Alan Koch, Lyn Rice, Galia Solomonoff, Linda Taalman, partners-in-charge)

Figure 7.21
The landscaping at Dia: Beacon in upstate New York was designed by Robert Irwin with plants whose colors reflect the seasons. The trees at the entrance have grown to almost obscure the entrance to the museum.
Judith Bing

is an exercise in restraint, one in which the original building's structure is a backdrop for the art, most of which is postwar. The integrity of the industrial building's construction and finishes remains intact. Because the building was used for graphics and printing, the quality of light is the most striking characteristic of the space. Dia and the designers opted not to add electric lighting in the galleries with skylights or perimeter windows, and as a result, opening hours in the winter are reduced to accommodate shorter days. The large scale of the pieces in Dia Art Foundation's permanent collection ranges from the sculptures by Richard Serra, Donald Judd, and Louise Bourgeois through light works by Dan Flavin to paintings by Agnes Martin and Andy Warhol and is quite at home within the 240,000 square feet of gallery space. The master plan and landscaping were designed by Robert Irwin.

The $50 million project was financed mostly through foundation funds and individuals ($30 million from Leonard Riggio) and philanthropic donations as well as government grants. International Paper Company, the previous owner, had a $2 million price tag on the property, but it agreed to donate it provided that Dia paid for the approximately $1 million environmental cleanup. There were great hopes that the relocation of this arts institution would help transform this economically struggling part of the state. Although some artists in search of cheaper live/workspaces have moved in, change has come slowly and tentatively. The retail area in downtown Beacon has yet to be able to expand in response to the tourists who come to see the art. An environmental group, Scenic Hudson, has been working with Dia to refurbish the waterfront in the area and has acquired property along the river.

Museum of Contemporary Art Detroit (MOCAD)

Museum: Museum of Contemporary Art Detroit

Location: Detroit, Michigan

Former Use: Automobile distributor

Dates: 2006

Major Goals: Create a new institution for contemporary art

Key Players: Local arts patrons

Another museum that adopted the "leaving things as we've found them" school of renovation is the Museum of Contemporary Art Detroit, or MOCAD, as it calls itself. Located in an abandoned car dealership building on Woodward Avenue, MOCAD's conversion is a "decorated shed." Its one-story standalone building's facade is covered with a Barry McGee artwork of blown-up graffiti lettering with a mechanized hooded sculpture appearing to be painting the sign. The interior has been left as it was found with peeling paint, existing partitions, and floors.

The raw space is particularly suited, not only to the museum's budget but to its mission which is self-described as being "responsive to the cultural content of our time, fuelling crucial dialogue, collaboration, and public engagement."

Although not technically an industrial site, its city is the poster child for industrial abandonment and its aesthetic embraces the industrial. The 22,000-square-foot building was bought by the Richard and Jane Manoogian Foundation when it was originally envisioned as an extension of the Detroit Institute of Art that could mount more contemporary works such as the Geffen Contemporary does in Los Angeles or the Queens-based P.S./1 does for New York's Museum of Modern Art. When those plans fell through because of budget considerations, MOCAD forged on alone with a plan to not have a permanent collection, but rather to rely on traveling exhibitions and special programs and become an active cultural center. The architect Andrew Zago has been quoted as saying that "Even in the long term, our goal is to keep the character of an industrial space."[6] The museum opened in 2006, and it directly opposes those urban development plans that pin their hopes on a brand new building. This is not a place that wants to be sanitized.

Figure 7.22
Museum of Contemporary Art Detroit (MOCAD) took over a vacant automobile dealership and left much of the industrial elements in place.
Zago Architecture

Figure 7.23
Little was done to the interior of the Museum of Contemporary Art Detroit. All exhibits are temporary—the museum does not have a permanent collection. Sometimes it's difficult to tell what is part of the building and what is part of the exhibit.
Zago Architecture

The transformation of industrial buildings to cultural centers has elicited much commentary about this phenomenon being the metaphor of the postindustrial age—the change from a production society to a consumer one. Instead of manufacturing goods these places now make entertainment. Despite this image, art and industry do work well together by not only telling the industrial story or exhibiting paintings and sculpture, but also by giving new life to abandoned buildings and neighborhoods.

As shown in this chapter, a town or city does not need the architectural clout of Sydney's Opera House or Bilboa's Guggenheim Museum in order to become a local or regional draw. These other institutions, especially those that restore their historic buildings or relate to the local culture resonate strongly. In addition, many of these smaller institutions represent the concerted efforts of local activists who have identified a void and created an institution, sometimes from scratch—whether a contemporary art or mill museum—and revived their industrial sites and economically bolstered their communities.

ENDNOTES

1. www.erih.net/topmenu/about-erih.html (accessed October 1, 2009).
2. Buffalo, with its easy access to the east coast and exporting ports, quickly superseded Minneapolis in the distribution of grain. The form and construction of the round grain elevators that rise from the Buffalo River and are a potent symbol of that city were developed in Minneapolis. Many of the Minneapolis companies established a foothold in Buffalo. The Frontier Elevator shown in Chapter 2 (Figure 2-10) was originally a Washburn Crosby elevator and is now owned by General Mills.
3. The warehouse district in Minneapolis had made loft living attractive in the 1970s and 1980s; this area, like SoHo in New York, became commercialized and is now an entertainment district. The new lofts mimic the warehouses in style, however are further east of the warehouse district.
4. Simeon Bruner, *MASS MoCA From Mill to Museum,* p. 113.
5. The firm no longer exists. Other project participants are Ove Arup (MEP), Ross Dalland (structural), Jeffrey Shrimpton (historic preservation), and Robert Irwin (landscape).
6. Rebecca Mazzei, *The Detroit Metro Times,* October 11, 2006. Accessed November 29, 2009 (www.metrotimes.com/editorial/story.asp?id=9717).

CHAPTER 8

RESIDENTIAL, COMMERCIAL, AND MIXED-USE DEVELOPMENTS

Not every place can or wants to be a cultural mecca. Projects that provide new housing opportunities, allow companies to stay in the area with updated office space, and redefine retail experiences for residents as well as tourists may better respond to the needs of the community and be more economically viable. Their range is wide—from the redevelopment of a simple mill building to the creation of new sections in formerly uninhabitable areas of older cities.

Whether large or small, these ventures can change the character of entire neighborhoods or create them anew from the once-busy docks and empty swaths of land. The best of them are transformative, not only for their own cities but also as inspirations for others. The early projects were truly pioneering efforts whose importance turned out to be not only the redevelopment of their specific site but also a reaffirmation of the role of the city itself.

As discussed in earlier chapters, the waterfront experienced industry's first settlements, as well as its first abandonments when transportation and port requirements bypassed traditional harbors. As a result, many of these projects involve waterfront development—an advantage because the elemental draw of water eases the marketing of these projects but also a disadvantage because of the complexity and expense of the redevelopment. In addition, waterfront development changes the focus of a city, sometimes creating conflicts between the old parts and the new.

Pioneering Projects

Ghirardelli Square

NAME: GHIRARDELLI SQUARE

LOCATION: SAN FRANCISCO, CALIFORNIA

FORMER USE: CHOCOLATE FACTORY

PROJECT: MIXED-USE RETAIL, "FESTIVAL MARKETPLACE"

DEVELOPER: WILLIAM MATSON ROTH

KEY PLAYERS: DEVELOPER, ARCHITECTS WURSTER, BERNARDI & EMMONS AND LAWRENCE HALPRIN

TIME LINE: 1962; ONGOING CHANGES AND EXPANSIONS

In America, retail uses anchored some of the early developer conversions that began life as

Figure 8.1
San Francisco's Ghirardelli Square transformed a chocolate factory into a "festival marketplace" reaffirming its urban role with a courtyard designed by Lawrence Halprin.
William W. Wurster/WBE Collection, (1976-2) Environmental Design Archives, University of California, Berkeley

historic preservation projects. One of the first was San Francisco's Ghirardelli Square, a 1960s transformation of a chocolate factory into a "festival marketplace" and now a well-loved fixture on the tourist agenda. Its history reinforces the individual visionary or advocate model of development. In 1962, the Ghirardelli Chocolate Company moved across the San Francisco Bay and put its square block of rambling buildings up for sale. William Matson Roth bought the complex to prevent it from being destroyed for high-rise housing, bucking the standard teardown approach of that time. The architectural firm of Wurster, Bernardi & Emmons teamed up with landscape architect Lawrence Halprin to restore the main factory buildings and transform them into a series of specialty stores surrounding a courtyard square. The complex has matured and is famous for shopping, entertainment, and of course, stellar views of the harbor. Its extraordinary location looking over the San Francisco Bay is still topped by a 15-foot-high neon "Ghirardelli" sign, a nod to its past. The square was included in the National Register of Historic Places in 1982. The complex has been sold several times since its original conversion and recently completed additional renovation that included the construction of a hotel.

Ghirardelli Square set a precedent for the historic preservation of factories located in the heart of cities as well as the successful interpretation of an urban mall, which marked the start of the postwar transformation of cities from a production to consumption economy. As with later marketplaces, such as Rouse's Faneuil Hall in Boston and Harborplace in Baltimore, it showcased an shopping center as a destination and demonstrated that maintaining a city's historical fabric could be economically viable. At a time when urban flight was assumed inevitable, it was effective in changing the image as well as the reality of a city, especially the gritty, industrial part, from one of danger and dirt to one of safety and fun. It was an important step in making cities acceptable destinations that could protect tourists and locals from urban dangers, imagined or real. In this case, single-entity ownership enabled control over development in order to pursue a definite vision of the makeover.[1]

BALTIMORE INNER HARBOR

NAME: BALTIMORE INNER HARBOR

LOCATION: BALTIMORE, MARYLAND

FORMER USE: SCARRED URBAN WATERFRONT

PROJECT: REVIVED URBAN WATERFRONT

KEY PLAYERS: BALTIMORE CITY GOVERNMENT, PRIVATE GROUPS, ROUSE DEVELOPMENT

TIME LINE: MID-1950S; ONGOING

In America, one of the first extensive urban industrial redevelopments was the redefinition of Baltimore's Inner Harbor. Initiated as a last-ditch effort to resuscitate a dying city, it expanded into a large-scale development linking downtown to the harbor with commercial and cultural development. Inner Harbor was a long-range project composed of many stages and many players that started in the mid-1950s. Through all the twists and turns over the decades, different financing and development schemes were used to harness the power of government with the flexibility of the private sector. Originally envisioned as a downtown rescue plan with no focus on the waterfront, because of happenstance, as well as the flexibility of government entities and the business community, its result has become a standard bearer of waterfront redevelopment.

Baltimore's post-war decline was early and swift. In 1954, faced with an abandoned, deteriorating harbor and a troubled retail center, a group of business leaders formed the Committee for Downtown and privately raised money to hire David Wallace of the Philadelphia planning firm Wallace McHarg Roberts & Todd to prepare a master plan for downtown. Before the master plan was could be completed, however, it was decided that the economic situation in Baltimore was too ominous, and a smaller project that could be more immediately acted upon was chosen.

A 22-acre downtown site was identified for an office building project that could be done relatively quickly. Charles Center, as it became known, was ultimately a 2-million-square-foot project that was built as a public/private partnership. The city issued a $25 million bond and enacted an urban renewal plan for the area, allowing for the exercise of eminent domain. The project was managed, not by government, but by members of the business group. The first

Figure 8.2
Historic aerial photo of the Baltimore Inner Harbor during its shipping days that shows how close the city was to the piers.
Cambridge Seven Associates

development, chosen through a competition in 1959, was One Charles Center designed by Ludwig Mies van der Rohe, completed in 1962. (It should be noted that "quickly" in development and government terms was about eight years.) Success begat success and several more office buildings, a hotel, theater, and retail facilities were being built or planned by 1963.

While the development of Charles Center progressed apace so did the deterioration of the Inner Harbor, with nearly all its piers and buildings ruined, its shipping industry nonexistent. Atypical for an American city, Baltimore's harbor is adjacent to downtown and access to it was unimpeded by major highways or buildings, many of which had been torn down by this time. While this location opened up great opportunities, this polluted waterfront was not hidden, but in full view at Baltimore's front door. The city's great potential was also its great shame. In 1963, the mayor commissioned a master plan from Wallace McHarg Roberts & Todd for the reuse of the area around the harbor as a way of bolstering the downtown.

The resulting 30-year plan ambitiously encompassed 240 acres around the three sides of the harbor and envisioned a tripartite approach: public access to the water, housing on the eastern and western sides of the harbor, and office sites facing the harbor. Most of the existing buildings around the harbor were to be torn down to achieve, as Wallace's vision statement declared, the "best use of water and open land in post-war U.S. urban renewal."[2] The business community and elected officials together created the 1964 master plan, which was backed by a voter-approved $2 million bond. The group that created Charles Center formed a private corporation and entered into a contract with the city. (This is the ancestor of the present-day Baltimore Development Corporation.) This group was charged with the complex task of managing the project on city-owned property with city funds providing the cost of operation. The project entailed the acquisition of property in the project area, relocation of businesses as well as environmental cleanup, with the expectation that this public investment in infrastructure would attract private commercial investment.

As a high priority was given to design, a design review board composed of deans of architecture schools was formed. I.M. Pei, Edward Durrell Stone, and The Architects Collaborative are just some of the well-known architects selected to design the new structures. Expanding upon the success of Charles Center, office building construction continued along with development of public space around the harbor. A wide brick promenade that made access to the water's edge easy was made possible when the redevelopment corporation persuaded the federal government not to build a highway between the downtown and harbor, as was being done throughout America at this time.[3] In addition, the public space was actively programmed with events such as fairs and ethnic festivals in order to attract residents. Ferry service, connecting nearby landmarks, such as Fort McHenry, was started.

Through thoughtful design and active programming, the waterfront became an attraction before the cultural and retail centers were built. The 1964, Inner Harbor Master Plan outlined redevelopment that would strengthen the local economy and urban infrastructure of Baltimore, not create a tourist attraction, which Baltimore had never been. Credit for this transformation is given to the arrival of the Tall Ships during the 1976 Bicentennial celebration. Crowds gathered at the waterfront for that event, which was so successful that efforts were made afterward to create activities that would attract and retain tourists in the area. As a result, the convention center (1979), Rouse's Harborplace, a "festival

Figure 8.3
The pier on which the Baltimore National Aquarium was to be built, showing how close the downtown is to the harbor.
© Cambridge Seven Associates

marketplace" (1980), the National Aquarium, and a hotel (both 1981) were built, made possible through city bonds as well as federal grants.

Development continued and continues today. Projects—both renovation and new construction on reclaimed land—line the harbor, although their growth has not been without conflict. While some believe that Inner Harbor had become too commercial (and sued to prevent Harborplace from being built on land originally scheduled for development but had become an informal park in the interim because of lack of developer interest), a high level of activity and interest points are needed to keep tourists occupied and entice locals to return. As will be seen throughout descriptions of all types of projects, diversity of uses is critical to their success.

Baltimore is now home to many museums, including a children's museum and a Museum of Industry, in addition to its world-famous aquarium. At Inner Harbor government and the business community worked together to pool public funds from all sources in order to attract private investment. Development has now expanded beyond the original area further out into the outer harbor and into old industrial neighborhoods, many of which are mixed-use projects renovated from factories whose buildings still line the waterfront.

Figure 8.4
The Baltimore National Aquarium sits at the edge of the pier, an advertisement for the revived Baltimore downtown.
Cambridge Seven Associates/Thomas Stiltz

WATERFRONT HIGHWAYS

The urban waterfront has become a redevelopment subspecialty of its own and a common place for large-scale projects. The multi-laned highways that ring major cities in America have paired with derelict industry to bar people from easy access. Several cities, however, have removed these highways specifically to open up their civic landscape to what many believe is their best feature. Portland, Oregon, was among the first to do so when in 1974 it removed Harbor Drive, a four-lane limited-access highway and replaced it with a park four years later. Starting in 1968, a Downtown Waterfront Plan recommended doing just that; however, traffic engineers wanted to widen the road instead, a plan that met with public outcry and organized opposition. The governor, the mayor, and county officials gambled that the predicted traffic jams would not happen and sided with the park proponents to create one of Portland's most notable attractions, Tom McCall Waterfront Park, now named for the governor who helped tear down Harbor Drive. This act not only

Figure 8.5
The highway separated Pittsburgh, Pennsylvania, from the Allegheny River before the pedestrian and bike path was installed.
Michael Van Valkenburgh Associates, Inc.

PIONEERING PROJECTS

Figure 8.6
Long ramps descend from the suspension bridges that span the Allegheny River in Pittsburgh, Pennsylvania, and allow access to a waterfront park.
Annie O'Neill

initiated Portland's reputation as a pedestrian-friendly city, but it spurred development in the surrounding the area.

In San Francisco, nature did what activists couldn't—demolished the Embarcadero Freeway, which blocked the city from its fabled waterfront. After the 1989 Loma Prieta earthquake damaged the freeway, the elevated highway was not rebuilt, replaced instead with an on-grade boulevard, park, and bike trail.

When tearing down a riverside highway was infeasible and impractical, Pittsburgh tried to make the best out of a difficult situation. The landscape architect Michael Van Valkenburgh Associates devised a two-tier system and squeezed a pedestrian and bike path between the highway and the river which also flooded onto the shores periodically. The upper, street area is a promenade that overlooks the river, while long, ADA-compliant ramps form a suspension bridge that connects the two parts of the city and brings people to the river level. The ramps, with their heavily landscaped slopes, help attenuate the road noise, creating a waterfront retreat once reserved for parking. Because the Army Corps of Engineers would not allow filling in the river, the pathway was cantilevered over the river beyond the existing seawall.

The park land is owned by the city; however, a not-for-profit group, the Pittsburgh Cultural Trust, was the client and financially contributed to the project through donated funds. The many levels of government involved (in addition to the city and the Army Corps, the state owned the highway and the county owned the bridges) translated into a project that took ten years to complete.

LARGE-SCALE REDEVELOPMENT

AMSTERDAM

NAME: EASTERN HARBOR DISTRICT, AMSTERDAM HARBOR, THE NETHERLANDS

FORMER USE: SHIPPING DEPOT

PROJECT: EXPAND RESIDENTIAL AND CULTURAL USES AFTER SHIPPING LEFT THE HARBOR

DEVELOPER: CITY OF AMSTERDAM, HOUSING ASSOCIATIONS

TIME LINE: 1980S; ONGOING

The transformation of Amsterdam's south bank of the IJ River is extensive and complex.[4] The project is multiphased and ongoing and has

LARGE-SCALE REDEVELOPMENT

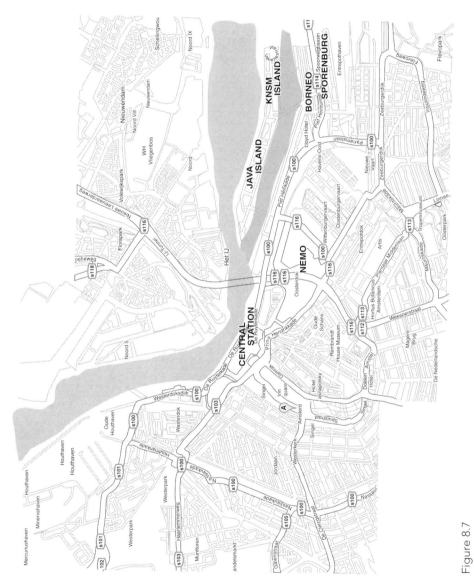

Figure 8.7
A diagrammatic map of the Amsterdam harbor shows the area that was abandoned as a port and redeveloped over the past 30 years.

already created new residential and cultural sections of the city. The Eastern Harbor District consists of man-made islands and peninsulas built during the late 1800s to form the Amsterdam harbor. Some of their names evoke their history: KNSM is named after the Royal Dutch Shipping Company; Java and Borneo Islands, recall former colonies; and Sporenburg ("rail city" in Dutch) reflects its use as a rail depot. The focus of large-scale redevelopment over the past two decades, the Eastern Docklands are now known for meticulous planning combined with adventurous architectural design.

Amsterdam, a city founded on water, paradoxically had turned away from its harbor when new urban development moved south or outside city limits. The 1898 railroad station visually blocked the harbor from the old center city, and its location prevented the harbor from expanding to accommodate large ships. During the mid-1970s, several decades after Baltimore became a port city without port activity,

Figure 8.8
Borneo and Sporenburg around the time the shipping companies were leaving, showing that the land was previously devoted to railroad sidings and the shipping industry.
West 8 Urban Design & Landscape Architecture

Amsterdam found itself in a similar situation when harbor activities were transferred from the Eastern Docklands to Amsterdam's deeper western ports or other cities such as Rotterdam. Further abandonment occurred as airplane travel supplanted cruise ships. Squatters replaced the shipping industry, and on the Eastern Docklands, artists and the homeless mingled.

The confluence of these events spurred concerted efforts at both the national and city levels to relieve a severe housing shortage and bring the middle class that had flocked to the more-affordable suburbs back to the city as well as to integrate the forsaken land with the city center. In addition, many of its corporations relocated to the southern part of the city in search of space to grow as expansion near the river was difficult. Confronted with deteriorating vacant property across from its center city and a population fleeing to the suburbs for better housing, in the late 1970s Amsterdam scheduled the area of the Eastern Docklands for redevelopment and transferred the land from the port of Amsterdam to the city of Amsterdam. The result is a high-density, mixed-use residential and cultural neighborhood built more or less from scratch, physically connected to the old city by bridges and tunnels.

The Dutch Character

Commentary about how Amsterdam accomplished what it did often revolves around the Dutch character and its historical adaptation to closely packed living conditions in a country two-thirds of which is under sea level. The Netherlands is known for its numerous polders, low-lying or drained marsh lands that are separated from surrounding bodies of water by dikes and drainage canals and require constant maintenance to prevent flooding. In the Netherlands, polders have water boards that are independent of government and manage water levels and conduct long-term planning. As a result, the Dutch are said to get their practicality and capacity for cooperation and consensus-building from working together on these boards.

Planning in the Netherlands, a small, compact country with a relatively large population, reflects a comfort with dense development and strict government control. Development in Amsterdam and other Dutch cities is more understandable in light of how issues concerning land ownership, housing, and consensus-building are addressed. In the Netherlands, municipalities own land, a mechanism used to control development and create revenue. In 1896, the metropolitan council of Amsterdam voted to purchase property through a municipal corporation which issues ground leases so that municipal investment in infrastructure and planning would benefit public coffers rather than individual owners. As a result, Amsterdam now owns most of the land within its boundaries. The ground lease terms are long—from 49 to 99 years. The cost of ground leases is adjusted over time according to a system established by the municipality or its urban districts.[5]

The city's land ownership provides Amsterdam with a great deal of control over housing, a large percentage of which is rental and categorized as "social housing." In 1901, responding to abysmal slum conditions and widespread poverty, religious organizations and unions were permitted to form not-for-profit housing associations and received government loans, subsidies, and tax rebates to build and operate housing.[6] These associations grew in power and influence, especially during the postwar rebuilding efforts. In some neighborhoods, 75 percent of housing units were social housing, a high percentage even when compared to the rest of the Netherlands. A wide range of income groups reside in this housing, not only the poor. Despite being ostensibly private and independent, housing associations played a definite public role, responsible for carrying out the job of supplying affordable housing in Amsterdam and operating under the aegis of government. Seven-year waiting lists and claims that the housing associations created a closed system were common. By the end of the twentieth century, however, housing production stagnated and housing variety became limited, characterized by a preponderance of affordable, small apartments and a dearth of quality housing for the middle class within the city.

In order to find affordable housing, people left the center of Amsterdam and moved to outlying areas and suburbs resulting in urban sprawl and exacerbated traffic problems. In the mid-1990s, endeavoring to increase the quality of center-city housing and bring a wider range of income groups back into the City as well as to discourage sprawl, Amsterdam restructured its housing sector. In 1995, after nearly 100 years, the subsidy system ended and the associations were given a one-time cash injection (17 billion euros in one year) and became independent of the state. Many associations merged and are producing new housing; social housing is operated through a revolving fund. Although the influence of the associations has been greatly reduced, they are still powerful forces, responsible for the construction about 80 percent of new housing in Amsterdam, which is now a mixture of both social rental housing and privately owned or market rate housing, as well as single-family houses—the income from the latter supports the former. The state still provides financial assistance with respect to planning, land, and infrastructure investment.[7]

In order to make the Eastern Harbor habitable, the State agreed to pay the city of Amsterdam to clean up and remove the extensive contamination caused by a century of port activities. The state would also build the transportation infrastructure to the islands, provided that the city create housing for 15,000 people in the district (an average of 100 units per hectare, or about 40 units per acre). In return, the state required Amsterdam to report annually on its progress on an agreed-upon schedule of built and/or approved units; the city was obligated to return the money if the schedule was not met.

An agreement on an approach was passed by the Amsterdam City Council in June 1985.[8] It called for six different neighborhoods to be built over a period of time to attract different economic and social groups. Each district would have different planners, who would control the overall approach and guidelines; however, actual buildings would be designed by a diverse group of architects. This approach was intended to imbue the new parts of the city with a sense of authenticity and individuality and to avoid the feeling of an undifferentiated housing project. Even though all the neighborhoods are relatively new, they don't appear to be hatched at the same time by the same designer. Rather, each district grew more organically, although, it can feel a bit like an architectural museum, with each building screaming to be recognized.

It was envisioned as being almost all residential. An agreement was signed with a shopping mall developer in which it agreed to build its facility only if no other stores would compete with it in the district. As a result, no other stores were allowed within the residential areas.

Working with the city and development groups, each planner had a different approach to housing and, thus, a different master plan. In 1990, Jo Coenen tackled the first island, KNSM, and chose to build large housing blocks presenting a wall-like facade along the waterfront. Other architects as well as Coenen designed these buildings: Hans Kollhoff with Christian Rapp; Bruno Albert; Wiel Arets Architects, and Diener & Diener Architects. Some of the old harbor warehouses were saved and converted into housing.

Java Island, by Sjoerd Soeters, was cleared of all existing buildings and divided into five sectors separated by four narrow canals. A variety of bridges accommodate bicycles, pedestrians, or cars and connect the sectors. Apartment buildings, designed by a variety of architects, line the perimeter of the sectors with large parks in their centers. Some of the apartments have small balconies facing the waterfront. The area facing south was traffic-free and building heights were limited to seven stories, while on the north the buildings were 10 stories. The canal-facing houses are more varied, although several designs are repeated.

The project details are too extensive to go into detail for all areas; however, two interesting examples highlight the process and the results of the redevelopment.

BORNEO AND SPORENBURG

The municipal planning process for the development of Borneo and Sporenburg islands, the third extension of the Eastern Harbor District, illustrates the time and effort invested in planning development in Amsterdam. Six teams were given funds and one year to create proposals, after which three finalists were chosen and provided with more time and money to refine their ideas. At the end of this process, a winner was selected.[9] The winner of the competition developed a plan that provided the legal basis and specifications of the development. This plan defined building parcels, heights, and typologies, and also included a "quality book" that outlined materials and colors. Based on this agreement, the city solicited developers who would carry out the projects and abide by the guidelines. The Borneo and Sporenburg developments reflected a change in housing policy, with 70 percent of the housing to be market rate, and the remainder being social housing.

Working against the penalty date established by the build-out schedule and loathe to return money to the state, the city had to begin planning Borneo and Sporenburg before there was a market for new housing. The area was originally programmed to be apartments in large building blocks. Because the apartments on Java Island weren't selling, there was scant interest from the builder/development community in investing in the same type of housing that was attracting few buyers in an adjacent area. The developers believed the market demanded low-rise, single-family houses. Since a goal of this development was to lure people out of the suburbs and into the city in an attempt to forestall sprawl, the competition guidelines stressed a preference for single-family houses over apartment buildings.

Adriaan Geuze and his firm West 8 Urban Design & Landscape Architecture, one of the competitors for the planning of Borneo and

Figure 8.9
Java Island in the Amsterdam Harbor was cleared of all existing buildings and divided into five sectors separated by canals, connected by fanciful bridges.
Carol Berens

Sporenburg, explored whether a scheme of low-rise, high-density could meet these requirements. Much to their surprise, they discovered that the density could be achieved with interlocking, single-family buildings combined with several large-scale apartment buildings. Referencing the European tradition of a protected city with indirect links to the harbor, which can be harsh and wind-swept, they developed a design that differed substantially from the adjacent islands' housing blocks open to the waterfront. Their aesthetic philosophy was based on the images in Vermeer paintings—the interior space bathed in light from the building opening.

They won the role of master planner for Borneo and Sporenburg in 1993, and between 1996 and 2000 when it was built, was responsible for the urban design for this area. This included the bridges and public spaces as well as the architectural supervision of the buildings designed by other architects. The ground rules were quite strict: The density was to be 100 units per hectare, individual houses were to have front doors on the street, parking for one car per unit was to be provided, and the two peninsulas were to be developed simultaneously with the narrow basin between them treated as a "water plaza." In addition, a mix of housing types—single-family homes as well as apartments—was considered essential to provide the more flexible housing options needed to compete with the suburbs and to provide

Figure 8.10
Model of Amsterdam's Borneo and Sporenburg islands showing the high-density, low-rise housing with large apartment buildings the designer calls the "meteors that hit the sea of low rise."
West 8 Urban Design & Landscape Architecture

Figure 8.11
Aerial photograph of Borneo and Sporenburg. The individually designed townhouses are on the interior canal. The red bridges were designed by West 8.
West 8 Urban Design & Landscape Architecture

the requisite diversity of residents in terms of income level, age, family size, and special needs.

This plan for the island looked afresh at how to create housing for the modern city. West 8's plan achieved the density by having a mix of low-rise, high-density, single-family houses interspersed with three large apartment buildings that are sited on the diagonal and loom over the low houses, have views of the harbor and city, and are in turn themselves landmarks for the rest of the city. He's been quoted as saying these buildings were "meteors that hit the sea of low rise."

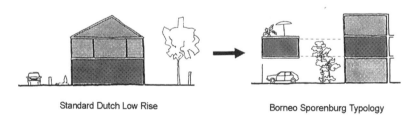

Figure 8.12
Sketch of how open space is accommodated within the Borneo house enclosure to create private open space within the structure rather than in front or rear yards in order to accommodate the required high density.
West 8 Urban Design & Landscape Architecture

LARGE-SCALE REDEVELOPMENT

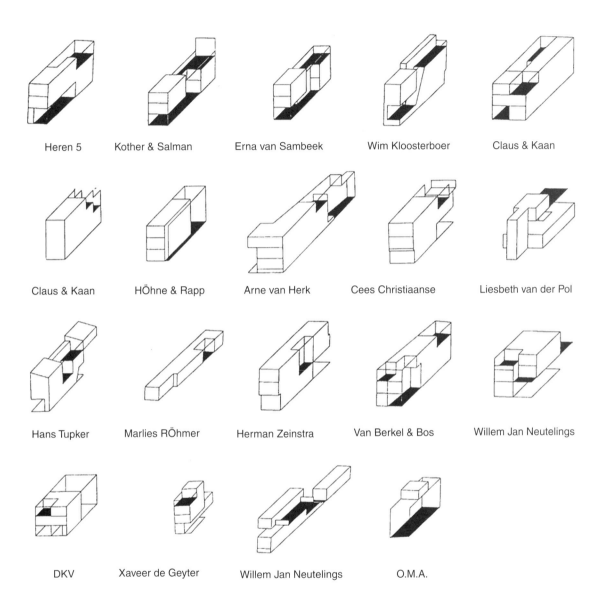

Figure 8.13
Schematic design of interlocking housing types indicating the various open space configurations within the buildings. Houses on Borneo and Sporenburg were designed by various architects within design guidelines.
West 8 Urban Design & Landscape Architecture

The resulting scheme is experimental and innovative—turning the house inside out in order to achieve the required density in a low-rise context. The single-family houses are cheek-by-jowl and are built back-to-back as front and rear yards have been eliminated. Roads are in the center of the peninsula with housing on the perimeter, many on the water's edge. Public space is minimal. Instead, with the exception of a large diagonal swath of a park, open space is contained within the houses. This is achieved by requiring each house to have between 30 to 50 percent of its structure to have voids for light from patios and roof gardens. Twenty architects were responsible for the series of interlocking homes, many of which are designed with open plans so that residents can control the interior design. Harking back to the canal design of old Amsterdam, the water between the peninsulas, as Geuze says, substitutes "blue for green"—that is, it replaces front yards, with the housing abutting the water. West 8 designed the red bridges that span the water between the two islands.

Most of the housing was done by four groups of developers, the largest of which was New Deal, which was itself a combination of four housing associations and three builders. West 8 gave these builders a list of approximately 100 "preapproved" architects. (Builders could

Figure 8.14
Close-up of the townhouses along the canal in Borneo and Sporenburg where individuals could design their own homes according to guidelines, an unusual opportunity in Amsterdam.
West 8 Urban Design & Landscape Architecture

LARGE-SCALE REDEVELOPMENT

propose other architects for consideration. At the end of the project, approximately 140 architects were involved, with New Deal using about 30 architects.) Mr. Geuze worked within the City Planning office part-time in order to supervise the builders' work and approve proposed building plans to ensure compliance with the approved plan. Plans were submitted at four major stages: the initial proposal, preliminary design, design development, and the building permit application. A "Beauty Committee" had final sign-off authority on the plans.

This area is most famously known for the 60 lots that were reserved for individual owners who were chosen by lottery. Owners, who were obligated to occupy the house, hired their own architect. Waterfront facades had to have a double-height living space, differ in terms of plane and materials from its neighbors, and create an overall pleasing pattern.

The development has been considered quite successful, especially with respect to the introduction of single-family houses and variety of design in dense Amsterdam. The absence of public

Figure 8.15
On the terrace of Silodam in Amsterdam, a housing project that looks like a barge laden with containers going out to sea; one has a close relationship with the water. The masonry buildings seen in the background are existing warehouses that have been converted into housing.
Carol Berens

space, however, is not for everyone and it has been criticized for being too "private." Most of the parcels have been built out; however, controversy has swirled around the last of the large buildings called "The Fountainhead." Originally designed by Steven Holl and scheduled to offer very expensive apartments for sale, it was not constructed because there was no market for it. Locals also considered it too massive. Consequently, KCAP Architects & Planners have redesigned the 20-story, U-shaped building, which contains three towers and is built half in the water and half on land; it also contains a primary school. The area has been vacant for so long that the residents of the neighboring buildings have grown accustomed to the open space.

SILODAM

Two warehouses (or silos)—one from the nineteenth century and the other from the twentieth—were built on a dam that protects Amsterdam from the harbor. A competition was held for new housing, the proceeds from which would help pay for the renovation of the existing structures. The new housing was required to have parking as well as a mix of social housing, and of

Figure 8.16
Amsterdam's Silodam is built in the water on pilings.
Carol Berens

LARGE-SCALE REDEVELOPMENT

course, protection from the water through dikes and pilings.

Silodam, by the Rotterdam-based firm of MVRDV, takes the opposite approach from West 8's sheltering design. The building unabashedly juts into the harbor, fully exposed to the sun and wind and looks like a floating barge of shipping containers going out to sea. The building, containing a mix of offices, work studios, and apartments, is built on pilings in the water, not on the existing dam, and is divided into four parts to achieve a variety of spaces. The building is divided into "neighborhoods" composed of 8 to 12 apartments clustered around a corridor, garden, and public space. Built between 1995 and 2003, it contains 165 residences, some with double-height spaces, some with views of the harbor, others look toward center city. The 10-story-high building is about 400 feet long and 65 feet wide and is visually broken down into sections by changes in colors and materials.

Although the Eastern Harbor District was originally envisioned to be a solely residential area, with the build-up of development, other uses were needed and, in the 1990s, a city planning memorandum added the goal of the Eastern Docklands becoming a "complete city" to encourage multiple and intensive land uses. As a result, along the South Bank of Oosterdokseiland, public buildings such as a new library, concert hall, and museum have been built.

Figure 8.17
The Nemo Science Museum by Renzo Piano (1997), which juts out into Amsterdam's IJ, is just one of the public buildings that have been constructed along the IJ.
Carol Berens

The Role of Single-Purpose Entities or Development Corporations

One of the persistent hurdles to redeveloping industrial land is the patchy ownership patterns that industry leaves behind. For the redevelopment of one factory, albeit large, land ownership may be simple—one or two entities, who hopefully are in agreement, control it. But when a project is part of an industrial zone, parcels are owned by different corporations—both existing and defunct—sometimes interspersed with smaller, individual owners. A coherent plan requires single ownership or an overriding authority or organization. Often a government entity or agency that has the power to grant tax incentives or even acquire or control the land through eminent domain will take over this role.

The establishment of a not-for-profit corporation that works in concert with government is a common mechanism for either accomplishing specific projects or being the entity through which development is done. With almost all large-scale projects, these corporations can harness the power of government-raised funds through legislative action or bond issuance and act independently and more quickly than government. The results are not always easy, as these corporations can be accused of being too powerful and unaccountable to the public. They do provide, however, project management expertise and link the community, government, and the private sector developers.

London Docklands

Name: London Docklands

Location: Eastern section of London, England

Former Use: Waterfront industries, docks, warehouses

Project: New mixed-use center of London including riverfront restoration and business center

Developer: London Docklands Development Corporation in conjunction with private developers

Time Line: 1980s; ongoing

The London Docklands Development Corporation (LDDC), created in 1981 to regenerate the eastern section of London, was an urban development corporation responsible for one of the largest real estate development projects in Europe. Tidal docks created in the early 1800s from marshland became the heart of the Port of London for almost two centuries. During that time, the fate of the area reflected the vicissitudes of London economic life, being both the setting for Jack the Ripper's crimes and Charles Dickens's novels as well as a bustling harbor. As with all historical ports, its booming trade was supported by ancillary services such as ship building and repair, warehousing, and food processing. Despite suffering from heavy bombing during World War II, it recovered and went on to handle over 60 million tons of cargo in the early 1960s, its historical peak. In what has become an all-too-familiar story, changes in transportation and containerized shipping brought about a swift and

THE ROLE OF SINGLE-PURPOSE ENTITIES OR DEVELOPMENT CORPORATIONS

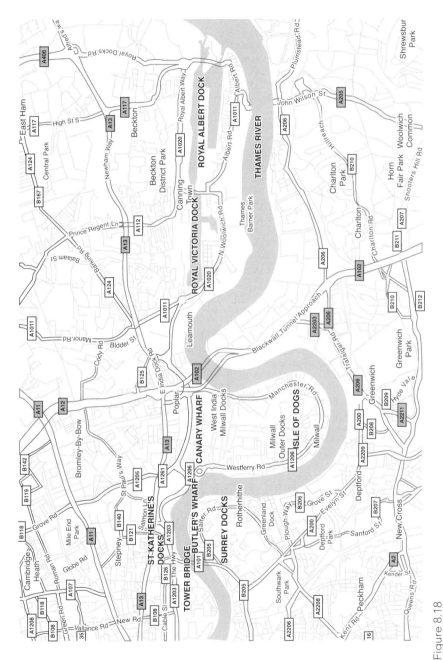

Figure 8.18
Map of London Docklands, the extensive redevelopment area as a result of the shipping industry's move to Tilbury.

brutal decline. The Port of London Authority closed the East India and then the St. Katharine Docks near the Tower Bridge in 1967 and 1968, respectively.

By the mid-1970s, most shipping activity had moved to container docks at Tilbury, leaving behind vast areas of marshland and vacant buildings. Some felt warehouse-type industrial development would be easier to achieve if the land were vacant, and many warehouses were either destroyed by fire or demolished intentionally. The docklands area spread over three boroughs and covered 8½ square miles, which was defined as the London Docklands Urban Development Area. The LDDC was created to present a unified vision of redevelopment, although some felt it was the Thatcher government's way of overriding "left-leaning" local governments. The rationale for needing a powerful organization was outlined in a Regeneration Research Report published in 1997.[10] While specifically addressing issues facing the dying London docks, it is applicable to situations faced by cities around the world and a good outline of conditions that spur both local and federal governments to create such development entities to provide external intervention. Specifically, the report stated that:

- The area experienced catastrophic job losses over a short period of time, resulting in severe unemployment among workers who did not have the skills needed in the growth areas of the London economy.
- The existing pattern of land ownership prevented market-sensitive development. A high proportion of land was held by public bodies such as the Port of London Authority, the Greater London Council, British Gas Corporation, the Dockland boroughs, and British Rail, which had neither the will nor the capital to make it available for redevelopment. In addition, much of the land had restrictions on its use. Relatively little land was in private hands.
- Costs of development and land reclamation were high and uncertain, making the area unappealing to investors.
- Local infrastructure was poor, especially the links between the Docklands and the rest of London.
- The market alone was unlikely to provide the environmental improvements, infrastructure, and amenities that were essential if the Docklands were to become an attractive place in which to live and work.

Armed with the ability to buy land as well as channel government tax incentives, the LDDC developed several plans and attracted several developers, many of whom failed and whose names have receded into the memories of those involved in 1980s real estate. The government provided a grant to the LDDC, which also received income from land sales and development proceeds. The LDDC was responsible for providing or upgrading infrastructure within its area. The relationship between the LDDC and the local boroughs was fraught because the LDDC was responsible for development, but other public services such as housing and education, remained with the boroughs.

Concurrent with the establishment of LDDC was the 1982 designation of the Isle of Dogs—part of the docklands area—as an enterprise zone, giving businesses that settled there 10-year property tax exemptions and other tax breaks. These benefits enticed the newspaper business to move there, a move that was also used to change union and labor practices. (Serious riots followed.)

THE ROLE OF SINGLE-PURPOSE ENTITIES OR DEVELOPMENT CORPORATIONS

One of the first large-scale developments of the LDDC is Canary Wharf, built on the site of the West India Docks on the Isle of Dogs, which has taken over 20 years to develop and has ridden several economic crests and valleys. The original master plan, created by the American firm of Skidmore Owings and Merrill (SOM), was emblematic of the corporate times and called for all new office buildings, most of which were designed by American firms. Olympia & York, a Canadian firm, entered into a master development agreement with LDDC to build 12.2 million square feet of office space in 1987. The first building, One Canada Square, was designed by Cesar Pelli and was completed in 1991 and is 50 stories tall. It was the United Kingdom's tallest building and, because the area is marshland, had to be constructed on a floating platform supported by piles.

The plan faltered when Olympia & York declared bankruptcy in 1992 just after the first building was completed, only to be picked up by other developers during the subsequent improved building cycle in the mid-1990s, a

Figure 8.19
London's Thames River Walk improvements include a riverside promenade. Typical warehouse conversion to residential use along the Thames River near St. Katharine's Dock. These warehouses were built close to the river to cut down on theft.
Carol Berens

process that has continued through the 2000s. The area has become a center for the financial industry, effectively establishing a second focus for this industry in London. Almost all the major banking corporations have built on Canary Wharf, with Citigroup, HSBC, and Barclays adding their own towers. The critical element in integrating this formerly isolated area into the urban fabric of London was the connection of the public transportation system with the newly built Docklands Light Railway in 1987, which reused existing rail lines. It was soon followed by the extension of the Jubilee Line, which opened for Millennium celebrations.

The LDDC closed shop in 1998,[11] a process that had begun in 1994. Control of planning and development returned to local boroughs. Although it was and remains controversial, it leveraged public investment into a postindustrial vision of a major city, effectively moving the focus

Figure 8.20
St. Katharine's Dock, designed by Thomas Telford in 1828, was never successful as it could not accommodate large cargo ships. One of the first docks to close, its charming setting is now the backdrop for restaurants, boutiques, and housing and part of the pedestrian-friendly Thames River Walk.
Carol Berens

Figure 8.21
The wrought iron bridges spanning Shad Thames near Butlers Wharf across from St. Katharine's were typical of the waterfront warehouses and were used to transfer tea, spices, and other food stuffs by wheel barrows from the riverside warehouses to those farther inland.
Carol Berens

Figure 8.22
The soaring entrance in the Tate Modern is in the former turbine hall of a converted power station, one of the riverfront cultural centers of London.
Carol Berens

of the city to the east. The addition of residential uses as well as some cultural ones, such as the Laban Center in Greenwich, has broadened the appeal of the area. Today, over 100,000 people work within the urban development area. Another government report estimated that at its closing, public sector investment neared £3,900 million, almost half of which was for transportation infrastructure.[12]

Although the London Docklands is known for its new business center and high-rise office buildings, one of the more interesting ancillary developments has been the sensitive renovation of the banks of the Thames River, including some of the smaller docks and warehouses, many of which have been renovated into upscale housing. New Thames River crossings have been built as well as new cultural institutions such as the Tate Modern, which transformed a former power station, and the Design Museum, which is in a riverside warehouse.

Olympics

One obvious use of the single-purpose entity is the local Olympic development corporation that is formed to prepare the chosen city for the one-time event. Not all Olympic cities build new facilities or use former industrial sites; most notably Los Angeles in 1984 reused existing stadiums and venues. However, cities often vie for this event in order to improve their infrastructure, something which Barcelona did and which London is now doing. Only a separate corporation with powers to spend money and hire the right people to do the work can produce the required facilities within the time constraints.

London is preparing for the 2012 Olympics with several separate agencies with mandates to run the games as well as design and build for them. The 500-acre site is a former industrial area northeast of the London Docklands called the Lower Lea Valley. The Olympic Delivery Authority (ODA) is charged with developing and building the new venues and infrastructure for the games in a way that will allow them to be used for the whole city after 2012. It was established in 2006 and is the local planning agency for the Olympic Park. To implement its job, it can buy, sell, and own land as well as contract out to designers and contractors to build the venues as well as the transportation to them.

To win the 2012 Olympics, London presented the regenerative nature of its Olympics program, most of which will be located in a poor, forgotten area suffering from the effects of industrial abandonment. As described on its website, the long-term plan for the area is for it to "be transformed into one of the largest urban parks created in Europe for more than 150 years." The River Lea will be restored and widened in order to create a wetland habitat. The sports venues will be converted for use by sports clubs and the athletes' housing will become new housing, in effect a new neighborhood. The area will benefit from improved transportation as the Dockland Light Railway will be extended.

London will not be the first city to convert an Olympics venue into parklands as Sydney's Olympic Authority did the same thing after its 2000 Olympic games. Originally called the

> Millennium Parklands, but now the Parklands at Sydney Olympic Park in Homebush Bay, the site was severely degraded and was located over former landfills containing asbestos, industrial hydrocarbons, acid sulfate soils, and petroleum waste. A majority of the waste was buried under clay-capped mounds creating changes in the topography.

Bilbao Ría 2000

Location: Bilbao, Spain

Former Use: Shipping and rail

Project: Regeneration of the waterfront

Developer: Bilbao Ría 2000, a nonprofit, publicly owned corporation

Key Players: Various public authorities such as the State-owned Land Management Company (SEPES), the Bilbao Port Authority, the rail companies, the Basque Government, and the Government Councils of Bilbao, Bizkaia, and Barakaldo

Time Line: 1992; ongoing

Bilbao, Spain, is perhaps best known around the world as the home of the Frank O. Gehry–designed Guggenheim Museum. However, that architectural billboard is the tourist face of a major renovation of a former industrial center. Founded during medieval times on the Nervíon River, Bilbao was a trading port that developed into an industrial city based on iron and steel production and shipbuilding as well as mining. Bilbao developed on both sides of the river. Industrial divestment struck Bilbao as hard as other major cities, leaving it with vast swaths of abandoned land from harbor activities that had moved to the outer bay. It was left with an inaccessible waterfront, threaded by railroad tracks or unused shipyards.

Because much of its land was devoted to the harbor, like London it was also controlled by the port authority. Bilbao Ría 2000, a nonprofit, publicly owned corporation, was started in 1992 to regenerate industrial areas in metropolitan Bilbao. It is a cooperative effort by various public authorities, and its shareholders consist of the state-owned Land Management Company (SEPES), the Bilbao Port Authority, the rail companies ADIF and FEVE, the Basque government, and the government councils of Bilbao, Bizkaia, and Barakaldo. These entities lease or otherwise transfer land belonging to them in Bilbao and surrounding areas to Bilbao Ría 2000 to be the entity that develops the properties in accordance with master plans for various areas. The developed land is then sold and the proceeds go toward the redevelopment of other areas. In addition, it receives European Union subsidies.

Critical to Bilbao Ría's mandate has been the upgrading of the city's infrastructure, cleaning the industrial pollutants from the river and land, and providing waterfront access. Rail yards have been either moved or buried to provide public open space on the river, space for new housing, and an extended subway system. A list of projects was created by a who's who of internationally known architects: Foster and Partners designed the subway system complete with Slinky-like metal and glass entrances; Santiago Calatrava, an airport terminal; Ricardo Legoretta, a hotel; and Robert A.M. Stern a shopping mall.

Foss Waterway Development Authority, Tacoma, Washington

LOCATION: TACOMA, WASHINGTON

FORMER USE: PULP MILLS AND SHIPPING

PROJECT: WATERFRONT REDEVELOPMENT AND MIXED-USE COMMUNITY

DEVELOPER: FOSS WATERWAY DEVELOPMENT AUTHORITY AND PRIVATE DEVELOPERS

TIME LINE: 1996; ONGOING

Tacoma, Washington, once an industrial powerhouse thanks to its timber trade, pulp mills, and shipping, felt the brunt of deindustrialization and was left with a harbor on the Thea Foss Waterway that was designated a Superfund site. In 1991, Tacoma bought 27 acres along the west side of the Waterway for $6.8 million and entered into agreements with various federal, state, and local regulatory agencies to clean up the site. Criteria for cleanup depended upon the intended reuse of the site, and ranged from capping the ground with clean soil, to sealing the site to complete excavation. Five years later the Foss Waterway Development Authority was formed and charged with creating a master plan for the waterfront and then selling developed sites to private investors and developers. Meetings with the community indicated that an accessible public waterfront was needed and wanted. Not only would this be considered a valuable amenity for residents, it was seen as an attraction for developers. The Authority's goal is to develop a master-planned mixed-use community that will contain 15 development sites for residential, office, and retail uses along the 1.5 miles of shoreline. An esplanade is planned to run the full length of the waterfront.

This single authority manages, leases, or sells the city-owned property. Combined with streamlined building policies, the Authority works with developers to coordinate city regulatory agencies to expedite approval processes and ensure that its master plan is implemented. One of its first projects was the Museum of Glass: International Center for Contemporary Art which was designed by Arthur Erickson on the southern end of the waterway. The 55,000-square-foot museum is topped by a distinctive cone that towers over the skyline. The Waterway is separated from downtown by an interstate highway, a condition shared by many waterfronts. In this instance, the Chihuly Bridge of Glass, a 500-foot pedestrian bridge with a permanent glass exhibit designed by Dale Chihuly, a Tacoma native, spans the highway to connect the museum to downtown.

Other development has taken place along the Thea Foss, including the conversion of the early-twentieth-century Albers cereal mill building into loft apartments, marinas, and other residential buildings. Only half of the sites have been developed as of this writing.

La Société du Vieux-Port de Montréal/Old Port of Montreal Corporation; and Canada Lands Company

NAME: LA SOCIÉTÉ DU VIEUX-PORT DE MONTRÉAL/OLD PORT OF MONTREAL CORPORATION; AND CANADA LANDS COMPANY

LOCATION: MONTREAL, CANADA

FORMER USE: INDUSTRIAL WATERFRONT OF ST. LAWRENCE RIVER AND LACHINE CANAL

PROJECT: VIEUX-PORT DE MONTRÉAL AND CANADA POST SITE

TIME LINE: 1981 AND 2007

Figure 8.23
Aerial view of Montreal's Vieux Port on the St. Lawrence River before industry left.
© Ville de Montréal

THE ROLE OF SINGLE-PURPOSE ENTITIES OR DEVELOPMENT CORPORATIONS

Figure 8.24
In one of the first redevelopments of Montreal's Vieux Port on the St. Lawrence River, the industrial structures remain to connect the new public space to its history.
© Denis Farley, Developper Société du Vieux-Port de Montréal, architect Cardinal Hardy

Canada also makes use of the single-entity development corporation and in Montreal two such corporations have been active in the redevelopment of the waterfront of the St. Lawrence River and the Lachine Canal: La Société du Vieux-Port de Montréal/Old Port of Montreal Corporation and Canada Lands Company. The former was created in 1981 by the Canadian government to develop and manage recreational, cultural, and tourist destinations for the Port of Montreal, and the latter manages, develops, or sells land the government of Canada determines it no longer needs. Both report to the federal government.

As discussed in the first chapter, the Lachine Canal transformed Montreal from a small town into an industrial center. Built for lake transport, it opened Montreal to trade from the Great Lakes and the Atlantic Ocean by allowing sea traffic to bypass the Lachine Rapids in the St. Lawrence River. The Lachine Canal went into quick, steep decline with the advent of container and deep sea shipping, which diverted shipping to the east's deep water ports and the St. Lawrence Seaway, which opened in 1960. Montreal's waterfront became derelict as industry left the area. In response, La Société du Vieux-Port de Montréal was established to facilitate public access to the waterfront. One of its first major projects was the redefinition of the waterfront of the St. Lawrence River where the eastern part of the Lachine Canal meets the river.

In 1992, in celebration of the 350th birthday of the founding of Montreal, a 1.62-mile promenade along the St. Lawrence River opened the waterfront to the public for the first time. After a proposed development approach that attempted to erase signs of Montreal's industrial heritage was rejected, the design now aesthetically builds upon the city's history, using existing silos, locks, and piers and other items that recall Montreal's importance as a port city. As a result, there are now public marinas, the Montreal Science Centre, and revived piers that cater to waterborne recreation and tourist attractions. La Société du Vieux-Port de Montréal/Old Port of Montreal Corporation is responsible for the design, landscaping, and programming of activities as well as ongoing maintenance. One of the Corporation's mandates is to encourage programs and designs that reinforce the historic urban environment. Its major focus is the public park along the river, which has become the impetus for further development of industrial sites in Montreal along the canal.

Redpath Lofts

A little more than 10 years after the opening of the Old Port of Montreal as a park, the former Redpath Sugar refinery was converted into residential lofts, signaling a revival of the areas on the border of the Lachine Canal. Erected in 1908 on the foundations of an existing factory, the refinery saw additions in 1912 and 1925 as this complex of buildings became one of the largest industrial agglomerations in Montreal. When the Redpath factory closed in 1980 and production consolidated in its Toronto factory, no other industry filled these multistory buildings, which were partially demolished. The city ended up owning it and subsequently sold it to a private developer. The three-phased project to convert the building into residential lofts and commercial spaces was completed in 2006.

The design goal as described by the architects Groupe Cardinal Hardy was to retain the industrial character of the building, still a hulking presence on the Lachine Canal. The public face of the building remains industrial in proportion, window treatment, and materials. An interior courtyard, with its promenades, metal balconies/exterior corridors, and individual entries, is more residential in scale and details. Stores on the ground floor animate the canal-side promenade and bike path as well as the interior courtyard, which the public can access. The large courtyard is a combination of hard-paved surfaces and lawn. The complex is surrounded by water on two sides with a marina located in a canal inlet.

Figure 8.25
Side marina at the Redpath Lofts in Montreal, Canada—a loft conversion from a sugar factory.
© CHA, Developper Groupe Gueymar, architect Cardinal Hardy

Figure 8.26
Interior courtyard façade of the Redpath Lofts in Montreal, Canada. The steel structure superimposed as terraces and entries to the apartments echoes the industrial character of the building.
© *Denis Farley, Developper Groupe Gueymar, architect Cardinal Hardy*

THE ROLE OF SINGLE-PURPOSE ENTITIES OR DEVELOPMENT CORPORATIONS

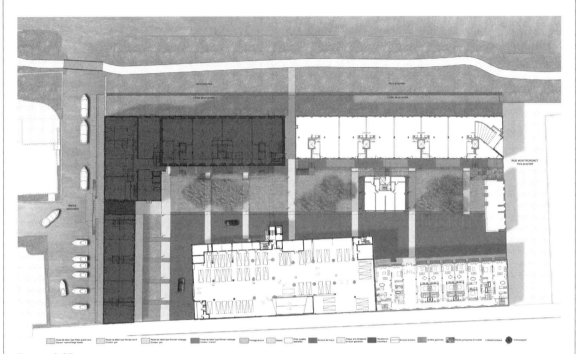

Figure 8.27
The site plan for Montreal's Redpath Lofts shows the courtyard open to the public at several places. The ground floor contains stores, and a bike/pedestrian path borders the Lachine Canal, which is beginning to see redevelopment.
© CHA, Developper Groupe Gueymar, architect Cardinal Hardy

Across the Lachine Canal from the Redpath Lofts, the former site of Canada Post's warehouse and distribution center was declared excess by the federal government in 2003, and in 2007 Canada Lands acquired it in order to dispose of its 23.7 acres (9.8 hectares). The area, called Griffentown, has witnessed the rise and fall of industrial Montreal. IOnce a populous area economically benefiting from the Lachine Canal, it saw its neighborhood shrink with the opening of the St. Lawrence Seaway. Soon after, in 1963, the city rezoned this area as solely industrial and filled in the four canal inlets, or *bassins*. The remaining inhabitants moved out. Canada Post's warehouse was built in 1978 only to be abandoned 25 years later.

In its role of developer, Canada Land issued a Request for Proposals for the preparation of a master plan and zoning change. The Montreal firm of Cardinal Hardy won the competition for the plan, which will transform this section of the Lachine Canal harbor front into a mixed-use (office, commercial, and residential) development and continue the opening up of Montreal's waterfront to the public. Developing the plan from first presentation through public consultation through approvals took nine months, with the master plan and new zoning approved in the fall of 2009. The demolition and site preparation are the next steps. One of the key elements in the new plan is the opening up of the *bassins* that were filled in during the 1960s.

Figure 8.28
Model of Canada Land proposed redevelopment across from the Redpath Lofts on the Lachine Canal in Montreal shows the reinstitution of inlets to enhance the new residential buildings.

© Denis Farley, Developer Société du Canada, architect Cardinal Hardy in collaboration with l'Oeuf

Self-Contained Projects

Not all mixed-use projects are large, government-generated conversions. Some are the dreams or grand plans of private developers who envision these projects as good real estate opportunities. These regenerative developments, although often more self-contained than government urban development plans, are usually the pioneers in transitional neighborhoods and instigate the blossoming of the surrounding area.

The Distillery District

Name: The Distillery District

Location: Toronto, Canada

Former Use: Gooderham & Worts Distillery

Project: Mixed-use development, artistic and entertainment center

Developer: Cityscape Development Corporation

Key Players: Artscape Toronto and developer

Time Line: 2001; ongoing

The Distillery District in Toronto, Canada, is a good example of the self-contained project type of development. The former Gooderham & Worts Distillery is a conglomeration of over 40 buildings on 13 acres whose historic core of Victorian-era industrial architecture is being developed into an artistic and entertainment center. Once fenced off from the city, the site's sensitive development and savvy marketing plan has made it one of the top tourist sites in Toronto. The addition of both new and proposed housing is creating a new Toronto neighborhood.

The distillery, started around 1830 by James Worts and William Gooderham, brothers-in-law, not only built facilities to make its spirits and whiskey, it also built a modest community complete with church and worker cottages. Throughout the 1880s, descendents of the founders enlarged the business, eventually becoming one of the richest families in Ontario, continuing to expand on the factory site while venturing into railroads, life insurance, and philanthropy. At one point Gooderham & Worts was the largest distillery in Canada. In 1926 it merged with Hiram Walker and over time was consumed by subsequent companies. Production ceased at this distillery in 1990.

The entire distillation process was self-contained on this site, with the district roughly divided into eight areas by function. The Stone Distillery Building, the oldest surviving building, was constructed in 1859 and was originally adjacent to the waterfront for ease of transport by ship. (Lake fill and a highway separate the site from Lake Ontario today.) The limestone building, with three-foot-thick walls at its base, was devoted to milling, fermenting, and distilling. Other areas contained facilities for barrel making, malt production, aging, and bottling. Because the manufacture of spirits is volatile, buildings were separated by streets to prevent the spread of fire, and a pump house was constructed adjacent to a warehouse and positioned over a 400,000-gallon water reservoir. The Distillery District was designated a Canadian Heritage Site in 1988.

During the mid-1990s, Allied Domecq, the last distiller and owner of the site, searched for ways to develop the property, and looking for the best economic return, proposed a plan with new buildings constructed in the middle of the site. Local preservationists objected and insisted that nothing be changed on the site. After prolonged controversy, a master development plan was agreed upon that specified the preservation of the heritage buildings and allowed fairly dense new housing provided that mandated affordable units be built first. As a result, new buildings were erected at the perimeter of the site; however, the heritage buildings languished untouched and without an intended use. In December 2001, Cityscape Development Corporation and Wallace Studios purchased the property for 12 million Canadian dollars from Allied Domecq with a novel plan for marketing and developing the site: It proposed to work on the historic center first.

The original development plan with the city set forth a rigid approach to renovating the heritage buildings that the architects felt did not allow for flexibility for eventual use; however ineffective, it remained in force. The developer engaged the Toronto-based E.R.A. Architects, Inc., to coordinate the refurbishment of heritage buildings for themselves as well as with future tenants and their architects and the city. The team negotiated with the city to renovate the structures on a building-by-building basis rather than all at one time, as originally required. Michael McClelland, and E.R.A. Architects, Inc., principal architect, mentioned in a speech that rather than renovating the buildings, their intent was to do as little as possible in order to retain the sense of age and character. This method was not only cheaper, but it was also "heritage friendly."

As with many industrial sites that grew organically over time according to need, the buildings represent a wide range of styles and eras. In the case of the distillery, many of the buildings were created for processes, machinery, and storage, not people—some ceiling heights were low, stairs and exits didn't meet present-day codes. In one warehouse, the racks for the barrels where whiskey was aged were the structural elements holding up the roof. The buildings have been or are being stabilized with minimal intervention and by reusing material as much as possible—a careful balance of accurate refurbishment combined with an adaptation to modern life and use as well as safety requirements.

The development includes close coordination with Canadian heritage and city regulators, who established a core group to respond expeditiously in addressing code and heritage issues. This was set up before the purchase was complete, as it was an "as-is" or nonconditional sale. The property is now a destination, a pedestrian-only artist and entertainment center. It is highly programmed with festivals, live music, restaurants and clubs, and other special events, and actively marketed as a location for film and television productions.

Retail chains were banned and only entrepreneurial or independent retailers, such as small-scale boutiques and galleries are allowed in an attempt to prevent it from becoming an overly commercial theme park. Critical to its rapid success, Cityscape rented two buildings, the Case Goods Warehouse and the Cannery, to Artscape, a Toronto-based not-for-profit artist support group, to provide artists and performers with affordable, below-market-rent studio spaces for 20 years. Artscape specializes in what it calls "creative place-making" and enters into partnerships to support artists and stabilize communities. By renting out these spaces to an established arts support group, the developer ensured an authentic creative atmosphere while assuring the artists they would not get priced out by gentrification. These artists brought instant vitality to the site, and within months there was a waiting list of 200 groups for the spaces.

Although the site is located within the city, its history as an industrial site made it a self-contained, fenced-off parcel for over 175 years, with few linkages or means of transportation to the center. Further segregating it are two adjacent large provincial-owned vacant parcels, preventing connection to the city. As the development has grown, more bus routes and other connections to Toronto have evolved, and a train stop will soon be constructed. It still needs more

Figure 8.29
The Distillery District project in Toronto, Canada, is transforming the former Victorian industrial enclave of the Gooderham and Worts distillery into an arts and entertainment destination. Buildings were separated by streets to prevent the spread of fire.
Photo courtesy of Artscape www.torontoartscape.on.ca

year-round activity, especially in the winter. Restaurants have been hesitant to open there; the developer started its own eatery.

This project is privately developed and when work started, tax credits were not available for historic renovation. The developer has recently received a grant to work on the distillery building, and Artscape has received a grant for its rental. According to the developer, the project is a decade ahead of schedule. It opened two years after its purchase and is proposing to start on new residential towers at the perimeter of the site.

Endnotes

1. Whether because developers are enamored of their original use or not, a frequently converted building type is the chocolate factory. All over the world, the chocolate factory gets saved. In SoHo, New York, the former Tootsie Roll factory is the newly minted "Chocolate Factory Condominiums." In Moscow, it's a nightclub; in Long Island City, New York, it's a performance space; in Newark, New Jersey, a school; and in Blois, France, it's housing.
2. In *The New Waterfront,* p. 110.
3. A drama began between the redevelopment corporation's vision of the harbor and the federal highway proposal for a highway that would block waterfront access. The corporation worked with the agency through a design concept team to relocate the road.
4. In an interesting cross-cultural dialogue, as Americans look upon Amsterdam development in wonder, the Dutch claim to have gotten some of its inspiration from the public celebration of the waterfront from Baltimore's Inner Harbor festivities during the 1976 Tall Ships visit.
5. Jeroen den Uyl, "The Use of Public Ground Leases in European Cities," report by the Development Corporation of the City of Amsterdam, September 1, 2005, www.oga.amsterdam.nl/bijlagen/downloads/use_of_public_ground_lease_in_european_cities.pdf (accessed April 17, 2009); Frank Uffen, "Implementing Waterfront Redevelopment in Amsterdam and Havana," *Land Lines*: April 2004, vol. 16, no. 2; www.lincolninst.edu/pubs/PubDetail.aspx?pubid=888 (accessed April 21, 2009).
6. Frank Uffen, "Implementing Waterfront Redevelopment in Amsterdam and Havana," Land Lines: April 2004, vol. 16, no. 2; www.lincolninst.edu/pubs/PubDetail.aspx?pubid=888 (accessed April 21, 2009).
7. Floris Blom, Housing Department "Amsterdam Housing Policy, Situation, Goals and Instruments," published by the City of Amsterdam, undated. The planning for all the areas was done by the City government, with the exception of KNSM Island, where there was little to no public involvement in the plans because the areas were vacant or had few squatters. The artists and squatters on KNSM coalesced as a community and fought for some of the existing harbor buildings to remain.
8. The planning for all the areas was done by the City government, with the exception of KNSM Island, where there was little to no public involvement in the plans because the areas were vacant or had few squatters. The artists and squatters on KNSM coalesced as a community and fought for some of the existing harbor buildings to remain.
9. Rodolfo Machado, editor. *Residential Waterfront Borneo Sporenburg*, Harvard University Graduate School of Design, Cambridge, MA, 2005.
10. DETR (Department of the Environment, Transport and the Regions) Research Summery No. 12

Baseline Study: "The Condition of London Docklands in 1981." Accessed November 22, 2009. www.communities.gov.uk/archived/general-content/citiesandregions/condition/.

11. A subsequent agency, English Partnerships, is working with the Borough of Newham to develop the area around the Royal Docks.

12. www.lddc-history.org.uk/lddcachieve/index.html, London Docklands Development Corporation website, accessed November 22, 2009.

CHAPTER 9

OPEN SPACE AND PARKS

"Why can't it be a park?" These are the first words heard when abandoned urban land becomes available.

Since the creation of New York City's Central Park 150 years ago, urban parks have evolved from novelty to necessity. They have assumed wide-ranging roles over the years as their use, designs, and facilities reflect changes in their cities and inhabitants. Parks have inserted themselves into everyday urban life—as personal refuges from noisy, congested streets, as fields for organized softball games, as bike and skating paths snaking through cities, as arenas for outdoor concerts and movies. Good parks attest to civic pride and health. The development of new ones speak to the revived popularity and use of public spaces in major cities, in short, a renewed sense of community.

City officials and residents are increasingly earmarking the scarred sites of urban industrial abandonment as ripe for redevelopment as parks and open space. Well-maintained parks impart cachet to new neighborhoods as well as help turn old neighborhoods around. In addition to bolstering economic development as a result of construction and funding, parks attract people and contribute to the rise in real estate values of existing and formerly bereft neighborhoods. Isolated residential enclaves in the shadows of factories are now being transformed with the addition of open space amenities.

Recreational projects are easy to like, a popularity that seldom makes them easy to accomplish. What constitutes a park is different for everyone, and those distinctions raise aesthetic, financial, and public policy questions. Of all industrial conversions, parks are the most public in character and benefit. Privately held land is often transferred into some form of government ownership, demanding public-sector intervention, financing, and of course, public input and comment. Few private developers willingly invest in such purely philanthropic endeavors except as concessions to make their commercial ventures acceptable to surrounding neighborhoods. Government stewardship imposes a public process in which local and special-interest groups seek to exert pressure and influence over the location, use, and design of parks.

Community groups, concerned about what will or will not be built, demand participation in the development process. Advocates with strongly held opinions clash over the allocation of scarce urban amenities, especially when children, dogs, bicycles, strollers, loungers, and athletes vie for the same space. The sports clubs, marinas, restaurants, and other for-profit businesses that provide income as well as enliven parks and attract a broad range of people can be viewed as unwanted intrusions by park purists. Physical complexities of cleanup and design, combined with political realities, consume many years, even decades. Projects move ahead in fits and starts, as will be demonstrated in the examples that follow. It is not a process for the impatient or the faint of heart.

* * *

Public urban parks as we know them were a response to industry's harmful effects and the mass population movement into cities. Before the mid-1800s, countries were overwhelmingly rural, cities and towns small. In built-up areas, public open space mainly consisted of town squares. The countryside was nearby and easily reached. In general, urban landscaped open space and gardens belonged to private estates, whether of royalty in Europe or the well-to-do in America. The notion of a public park was nonexistent.

Development's rapid pace gave rise to fears that urbanization would obliterate all open land within cities. The attendant overbuilding and crowding increased incidences of communicative diseases and triggered deadly epidemics such as cholera and yellow fever. In addition to enhancing the public realm and physically expressing democratic ideals, parks were part and parcel of the Victorian reform movement's concern for public health and safety, along with civic improvements such as sewers and boards of health.

Many of today's established urban parks are themselves reclamations, time having obliterated their sites' unsavory histories from memory as land use changed and cities cleaned up sites in the path of urbanization. Even before the postwar, postindustrial age, urban parks were generally sited on land that was cheap or

Figure 9.1
Baseball and soccer players, roller skaters, and loungers use New York City's Riverside Park, created when Robert Moses decked over garbage dumps and railroad tracks between 1937 and 1941.
Carol Berens

inappropriate for building or profit-making endeavors. The present location of New York City's Central Park, formerly swampland riddled with rock outcroppings, was selected instead of more marketable eastside waterfront property. Parks were created from industrial land when cities encroached, driving unsanitary and noxious uses from the paths of their expansion. In New York City, Robert Moses decked over garbage-strewn waterfront land bisected by a rail line to create Riverside Park. The Trylon and Perisphere rose phoenix-like from the "valley of ashes," as F. Scott Fitzgerald called the 100-foot-high ash dump in *The Great Gatsby*. This area is now Flushing Meadows-Corona Park, home to the 1939 and 1964 World's Fairs and today to the Mets' CitiField Stadium, the U.S.T.A. National Tennis Center, and several museums.

By no means is New York alone. The small falls of Wissahickon Creek, now part of Philadelphia's Fairmont Park, powered paper mills during the early days of industrialization. During the late 1860s, the Fairmont Park Commission acquired land to protect the area's water supply and watershed. During the 1930s, the Works Progress Administration (WPA) built a natural-looking park, complete with log cabin outposts and pebbled trails, its former industrial life recalled only on park placards.

Figure 9.2
Wissahickon Creek's industrial past as the site for paper mills is recounted in placards installed when the WPA built Fairmont Park in Philadelphia, during the Depression.
J. Brooke Harrington

Figure 9.3
Commissioned by Napoleon III, the Parc des Buttes Chaumont is located on former limestone and gypsum mines. The park was created by Baron Haussmann and the engineer Jean-Charles Alphand in 1867, a team that remade the boulevards and parks of Paris. Its renown grottos, waterfalls, and hills are all man-made, formed from concrete.
Carol Berens

The Parc des Buttes Chaumont in Paris, one of the few nineteenth-century European parks not created from royal or private gardens, shows that industrial conversions are not new and are not only an American occurrence. Its extraordinary topography, fantastic grottos, and Romantic settings, belie the fact that this park once contained limestone mines, gallows, and a sanitary sewage dump, as well as a mass grave for those killed during civil unrest. Even park details are studies in artifice—steps built into the hills and log-like fences and bowers are all molded from concrete, not the trees they're imitating.

The list of the types of land to be converted grows longer as more types of industry relocate. While water is an obvious attraction, no site—even landfills, military bases, or railroad beds—has been deemed impossible to convert to recreational use. The detritus of daily life—whether it be present-day garbage or ash from nineteenth-century coal fires—has long been relegated to landfills (when it wasn't just dumped into rivers). The most famous, or perhaps the most visible, even from space, is the Fresh Kills Landfill on Staten Island, New York. Plans are underway to make this a park.

Railroads crisscrossed this country, and as some of them have become unused, a country-wide program dubbed Rails-to-Trails has instituted programs to help municipalities replace these rail beds with walking and jogging trails throughout the country. Most of these are not in urban areas. Ping Tom Memorial Park in Chicago is a new park created for that city's Chinatown community from a railroad maintenance yard that was formerly used by the Burlington Northern and Santa Fe Railway Company and was bought by the Trust for Public Land.

The decommissioning of military property, in both America and Canada, has added a large amount of parkland, usually combined with mixed-use developments and slightly apart from the urban fabric. Although land patterns resulting from abandoned military bases are not linear, these areas are generally extremely flat and visually uninteresting. Gateway National Park is a string of parkland woven through New Jersey and several boroughs of New York City. Miller Field in Staten Island still contains some original World War I–era airplane hangars to convey some of the history of the site. Those sites were converted in the 1970s, slightly earlier than the major military rollbacks of the 1990s. Even Canada experienced a military pullback, of which Toronto's Downsview Park, the subject of an international competition, is perhaps the most visible.

Canals such as the Erie Canal as well as those that thread through the Midwest that channeled the Ohio River were instrumental in the success of milled goods and manufacturing. In places such as Akron, the refurbishment of the previously lost canal waterfront has been important for the revival of those cities.

CREATING NEW PARKS—AN OVERVIEW

The present-day creation of new parks builds upon the public parks movement that began in England and America during the mid-1800s spearheaded by Liverpool's Birkenhead Park, London's Regent's Park, and New York City's Central Park. They remain critical points of reference, their influence difficult to overestimate. Much of the process, goals, and to some extent design of these parks and the impact upon their communities arise in the discussions concerning parks today.

SYMBOLS OF DEMOCRACY AND THE PUBLIC REALM

Many claims of parks' benefits heard today echo those voiced during the creation and design of New York City's Central Park. Considered the first American public landscaped park and conceived as a respite from the City, Central Park was billed as a haven from urban evils and insalubrious conditions. That park's principal designer and proponent, Frederick Law Olmsted, thought that the unmediated enjoyment of the country was needed to civilize urban life, help the city's poor, and, in no small part, physically express "American Democracy."

Andrew Jackson Downing, an early nineteenth-century American horticulturist, landscaper, and friend and mentor of Olmsted, proposed reserving large open spaces in cities where all people could mingle. Public parks, proclaimed Downing, should be "public enjoyments, open to all classes of people, provided at public cost, maintained at public expense, and enjoyed daily and hourly by all classes of persons."[1] Olmsted strove to implement Downing's social and landscaping ideas of nature's ability to calm and temper life in the city. Olmsted, along with his business partner, Calvert Vaux, reiterated and expanded those goals in the plan for Brooklyn's Prospect Park, by stating that parks were "for people to come together for the single purpose of enjoyment, unembarrassed by the limitations with which they are surrounded at home..."[2]

In America, many ideas that bolster park development and influence design reprise the urban-versus-rural debates that emerged at the country's beginning and pose a conflict between the city (bad) and the country (good). In the eyes of America's most notable agrarian proponent, Thomas Jefferson, nature was restorative and cities were deleterious to personal health and democracy. (Jefferson's desire to limit the expansion of industry in America is discussed in chapter 1.) Augmenting these theories, the nineteenth-century Transcendentalists, led by Henry David Thoreau and Ralph Waldo Emerson, extolled nature for its uplifting value and awe-inspiring beauty.

As Galen Cranz outlines in *The Politics of Park Design: A History of Urban Parks in America,*[3] the parks of the nineteenth century were created to be pure "pleasure grounds" for enjoying nature directly, unfettered by commercial intrusions or active sports. Park open space was thought to give moral uplift to its citizens and considered necessary for civic life. Nineteenth-century parks, of which Central Park was the model, were places to escape from the city to find the peace and quiet required to have a good life.

Since the opening of Central Park, wide-ranging social and moral ideologies have been ascribed to parks, which were variously promoted as vehicles to appreciate nature, alleviate disease, provide a "wholesome" alternative to amusement parks, spearhead social reform, enforce separation of groups, and provide active recreation and neighborhood services. What a park represents and how it is designed mirrors its era's political and social attitudes. Over time, views of urban parks seesawed from the positive, genteel country promenade to the negative, dangerous, untended no-man's land to symbols of citizens' inalienable "open space rights." Urban areas that were former centers of industry and distribution are now expected to overflow with amenities, including parks that cater to many needs and tastes, both athletic and cultural. Today's parks provide swimming pools, bike paths, indoor and outdoor basketball courts, skateboarding half-pipes; host opera, rock, and classical concerts; show movies; and support educational programs. Of course, there are also those who feel these activities intrude on their enjoyment of the outdoors and prefer nature *au naturel*.

Present-day debates about how to develop parks, how to maintain them, and what facilities to provide inevitably revolve around concepts of the public realm. Is the state responsible for the recreational needs of its citizens? If the answer is yes, what facilities are free and what are for a fee? If the answer is no, then who provides them? Are they still needed? Do people patronize parks to be with other people, that is, to be in public, or to find their own private worlds? Who cleans the sandboxes and who mends the broken benches? Should public design be exuberant, proud to proclaim the glory of the state, or should economy and practicality rule? Can public-private partnerships in vogue today be effective for parks that are not popular or are located in poor neighborhoods? These and other questions speak to the role of government and haunt public hearings and landscape architectural theory as much today as they did a century ago. The answers are complex and varied, as will be seen in the examples presented in this chapter.

LAND CONTROL, FINANCING AND MAINTENANCE

Whatever the political theory, the costs and issues associated with park development require that governments play an important role. From Central Park to today's Olympic Park in Seattle, Duisburg-Nord in Germany, and Hudson River Park in New York, in order to create a new park, land must be under uniform control by an entity—usually government, but not always—with sufficient power and financial resources. If, because of previous uses, government does not already own the land, it either purchases it or acquires it through the process of eminent domain. Central Park is again the template for development—the state legislature gave an independent Board of Commissioners the power to acquire land and the responsibility for choosing a design and managing construction.

Americans prefer the excitement of building to the responsibility of upkeep. From its beginning, Central Park proved no exception, its maintenance underfunded and consigned to political appointees and hacks. Several years after Central Park's completion, New York City wrested control of the park from the commission and created its own Department of Parks—a new entity for administering what had quickly become the latest civic requirement. Although cities have since operated their own parks departments, routine cleanup and maintenance often remains lax, and local social groups take up the slack.

In America, not-for-profit groups have reacted to neglected and run-down public spaces by not only preserving parks, but also redeveloping, and in some cases rebuilding and enhancing them as well. These public-private partnerships are often formed to help specific parks and again Central Park continues to be in the forefront. Epitomized by the Central Park Conservancy (created in 1980) which infused the park with private contributions and successfully implemented construction projects, these groups have been hailed as saviors of parks around the country, responsible for instilling pride in the public amenities. Other parks try to emulate this example, with varying success. Small neighborhood parks out of the limelight with an underserved public have a difficult time raising the necessary money and must rely on public-sector funds.

One approach to addressing such inequalities is the creation of a group that is not park-specific but rather charged with aiding all the municipality's public spaces. The Seattle Parks Foundation, an independent not-for-profit organization, was developed in 2001 to, as outlined in its Mission Statement, "improve, expand and create parks and greenspaces." It raises money and organizes projects to enhance parks throughout its city including planting trees, providing benches and swings, and focusing on underfunded neighborhood parks. It works with the city and is able to channel private donations to complete its projects.

Development of new American parks now address ongoing maintenance through often controversial income-generating programming and private fundraising, an outright acknowledgment of the fickleness of public funding. In some instances, parks are expected to pay for themselves, although schemes that include these facilities are often accused of selling the public's interest. As will be seen in the discussion of Hudson River Park later in this chapter, the inclusion of private enterprise within public parks to address the need for fees is often met with derision. The inclusion of commercial ventures in parks, however, adds a level of interest and activity that makes places inviting. As seen in the establishment of Granville Island in Vancouver, Canada, some people opposed the inclusion of different uses and wanted everything torn down for a simple park. Instead, with its diversity of uses, it is now considered a prime example of an interesting urban park.

In America, cities look to their states, and the states look to the federal government to supply capital costs for new park construction. There is substantial economic development value in recreation facilities, which have a significant impact on a city's economy. Because localities generally fund park creation with money not their own, parks are a way of channeling money into a municipality.

No one instinctively understood this better than Robert Moses, who rose to power in New York State through various park departments and authorities. After an early battle in his parks-building career, he shrewdly stated, "As long as you're on the side of parks, you're on the side of the angels. You can't lose."[4] During the Depression, he funneled federal money via the Civil Works Administration (CWA) and Works Progress Administration (WPA) into New York for the construction and renovation of local parks. (Post–WWII, federal money favored highways and housing, although today, some grant money is directed to local communities for recreational facilities through the Environmental Protection Agency.)

Many of the public parks in England and Europe are converted private and royal gardens, with the most famous exception being some of the public spaces created during Paris' transformation under Napoleon III. His administrator/city planner, Baron Haussmann, and engineer, J.C. Adolphe Alphand cut swaths through the medieval alleyways that constituted nineteenth-century Paris to create wide boulevards and neighborhood parks, integrating promenades and parks with the street network. Landscaped streets became integral to the public realm, their squares and plantings enhancing parks formed from former royal landscaped grounds such as the Tuilleries and the Luxembourg Gardens. In spite of the ubiquity of tree-lined boulevards, Paris throughout the twentieth century has had one of the lowest parkland areas per citizen in Europe, a problem that each succeeding master plan attempted to address.

REAL ESTATE VALUES AND CHANGING NEIGHBORHOODS

Over the years, various schemes have been invented to meet the major financial requirements for park land acquisition and construction. In the end, though, government generally ends up paying the bill through bond issues or appropriations. Liverpool's Birkenhead Park and London's Regent's Park were carved out from larger parcels of land and the surrounding land subdivided into lots for sale. It was assumed, in both cases falsely, that the sale proceeds would cover the parks' construction costs. Although this scheme did not work, real estate values of adjacent land rose, as it does around almost all parks.

To this day, private real estate concerns are never far from consideration when talk of developing parks starts. Ideas for parks unfold when land is still contaminated, city services and amenities scarce, and the surrounding neighborhood stagnant and struggling. A park's construction and completion greatly influence the life of the city and affect the value of adjacent property—whether from the creation of new neighborhoods, the refurbishment of the old, or the promise of unobstructed views in perpetuity. The history of the increased land value that park development brings is the basis of concern, not unfounded, about gentrification.

REDEVELOPMENT OF EASTERN PARIS

Developing parks can spearhead as well as reinforce efforts to improve whole neighborhoods or sections of cities while providing welcomed amenities. Over the past several decades, Paris inserted parks in some of its grim and neglected neighborhoods into the eastern districts in its drive to reinvigorate those suffering from the effects of deindustrialization. In 1977, the mayor of Paris obtained control over city projects previously managed by the state. Since then, more than 250 acres of parks and green space have been created. Now greenhouses replace assembly lines (Parc Citroen), vineyards grow on old slaughterhouse grounds (Parc Georges Brassens), boxed trees sit atop a former railway viaduct (Promenade Plantée).

CREATING NEW PARKS—AN OVERVIEW

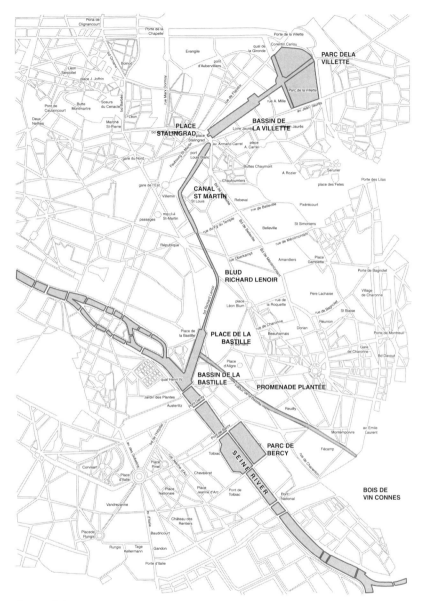

Figure 9.4
Eastern Paris had a dearth of parkland until the government started converting abandoned and underused industrial facilities and canals into parks to spark adjacent development. From the Parc de la Villette (former slaughterhouse) in the northeast one can now stroll down or kayak the Bassin de la Villette to the Canal St. Martin, where new restaurants have sprung up. At the Bastille, one can enjoy the Promenade Plantée (former railroad) or the Seine River at the revived Bassin de l'Arsenal. Adjacent to all these new parks, new development or renovation of old neighborhoods has occurred.

Paris's master plan positioned parks as keystones to new development and, building upon Alphand's ideas, connected them with promenades and landscaped canal quays. Barges which once conveyed goods into central Paris markets and the Seine River through a network of canals constructed under Napoleon I now transport weekenders and sightseers. Thus a walk or bike ride through eastern Paris's newly landscaped promenades and parks turns into an exploration of postindustrial Paris. The Parc de la Villette, formerly a slaughterhouse ominously dubbed the "City of Blood," feeds into the Bassin de la Villette, which in turn connects to the Canal St. Martin, which leads to Promenade Richard Lenoir, which brings one to the Bastille. At the Bastille, one either continues to the Seine by the banks of the Bassin de l'Arsenal or meanders to the nineteenth-century Bois de Vincennes over the Promenade Plantée.

Adjacent and surrounding areas have improved as a result of these newly created or refurbished public recreation and open space areas. Local controversies now revolve around gentrification, increased rents, and fear of the displacement of long-time residents rather than the continuing deterioration of abandoned vacant lots and weed-clogged waterways.

Paris's new parks are created through the lens of the past, often, but not always, with the land's former use palpable today. These are not romanticized versions of an unspoiled countryside beloved by the Americans and English, nor indeed are they chockablock with sports fields or tennis courts. It's only in the last few decades that walking on the grass has been allowed in some parks. Instead, the French evoke the memory of cultivated rows of agricultural fields and formal private gardens. These are parks for strolling and observing, created to please the senses and the intellect. In Paris, theme gardens refer not to cartoon characters, but to ideas and natural phenomena. Thus, the wind rustling through the Bamboo Garden at the Parc de La Villette appeals to hearing and the scented garden for the blind at Parc Georges Brassens appeals to smell.

PARK: PARC DE LA VILLETTE AND BASSIN DE LA VILLETTE

LOCATION: 19TH ARRONDISSEMENT, PARIS, FRANCE

FORMER USE: CATTLE MARKET AND SLAUGHTERHOUSE

DATES: 1980S AND EARLY 1990S

MAJOR GOALS: MIXED-USE PARK WITH MUSEUMS, CONSERVATORIES, THEATERS, AS WELL AS OPEN SPACE

KEY PLAYERS: CITY OF PARIS, BERNARD TSCHUMI, BERNARD HUET (BASSIN), ALEXANDRE CHEMETOV (BAMBOO GARDEN), REICHEN AND ROBERT (LA GRANDE HALLE RESTORATION), CHRISTIAN DE PORTZAMPARAC (CITY OF MUSIC)

As with all publicly funded projects in France today, each park's design was chosen by competition. The international competition for the conversion of La Villette (the first one in 1976 and the second in 1982), the former animal market and slaughterhouse in the 19th arrondissement in the northeast corner of Paris, where the city and country once met attracted over 470 entrants. The competition mandate was the creation of an innovative cultural urban park—a 24-hour center that combined a science museum and a center for music, as well as public open spaces. Bernard Tschumi's winning design, announced in 1982 and built between 1987–1991, reflected deconstructionist philosophy espoused by the French philosopher

Figure 9.5
The Grande Halle (originally designed by a disciple of Victor Baltard, the designer of Les Halles) at the Parc de la Villette in Paris was once a cattle market but now serves as the park's entrance and hosts spectacles and other events.
Carol Berens

Jacques Derrida. As a result, the park's design does not build upon the area's historical use or context but, with the exception of the renovation and reuse of some historic buildings by other architects, consists of an intellectual construct of three grids—points, lines, and curves—that are laid out independently and superimposed upon each other.

The most evident is the point grid, which is composed of 30 red "follies," structures that were designed before they had a use and positioned at the junctions of a 394-foot square grid (120 meters by 120 meters). These red structures measure 32.8 feet on each side (10 meters each side) with each being a different shape; some, claiming an aesthetic connection with forms from the Russian Constructivist movement, now host different functions such as a restaurant, concession stands, information booth, first aid stations, lookout points, among other uses. The Fog Garden, Bamboo Garden, and Garden of Mirrors are just some of the themed spaces designed by other architects or landscape architects. Despite, or perhaps because of this intellectual overlay, the Project for Public Spaces has put this park in its Hall of Shame and on a list of the worst parks in the world, stating that its "dull landscape [that] substitutes absurd sculpture and disproportionately scaled structures for playfulness and variety."[5]

Although the park is public space owned by the government, building revenue-generating venues or institutions within parks is common in Europe and does not lead to great controversies as it often does in America. Two major institutions—the Cité de la Musique (designed by Christian de Portzamparc in 1994) and the Cité des Science et de l'Industrie

Figure 9.6
At Paris's Parc de la Villette, red follies are installed on a grid system, one of three systems around which the design is based.
Carol Berens

(1986)—border the park on the south and north, respectively. A geodesic dome houses an IMAX-like movie theater. The cast-iron and glass *Grande Halle,* the site of the former animal market, is now an entertainment venue, just one of actively programmed spaces that host theater, spectacles, and shows to attract people to this former uninhabitable section of Paris. Regardless of the Project for Public Space's derision, the park is well used by the neighborhood, partly because of planned events, but also because it provides a large area of open space where none was before.

PARK: PARC DE BERCY AND ZAC BERCY

LOCATION: 12TH ARRONDISSEMENT, PARIS FRANCE

FORMER USE: WINE WAREHOUSES

DATES: 1990S

MAJOR GOALS: MIXED-USE PARK AND NEW NEIGHBORHOOD

KEY PLAYERS: CITY OF PARIS (MAYOR JACQUES CHIRAC), BERNARD HUET,

Figure 9.7
The Bassin de la Villette, originally constructed to bring goods into central Paris markets, has been restored as a promenade surrounded by theaters and restaurants. Sunbathing and boat rentals have become common weekend sights.
Carol Berens

(MARYLÈNE FERRAND, JEAN-PIERRE FEUGAS, AND BERNARD LEROY), IAN LE CAISNE AND PHILIPPE RAGUIN (LANDSCAPE); CHRISTIAN DE PORTZAMPARC (ZAC MASTER PLAN)

Not connected to the canal system but an integral part of the improvement of the eastern section is the Parc de Bercy. Barrels of wine were once rolled in from barges on the Seine to Bercy, a small enclave of cobblestone streets, low brick buildings, and majestic sycamores and chestnuts. Bercy, until recently home to wine warehouses, became an insular world encircled by expressways, railroads, and bridges. As the effort toward renovating the eastern half of the city continues, the Bercy area currently contains new housing, the Ministry of Finance, the Palais Omnisports, and the Frank Gehry-designed defunct American Center, which since 2005 houses the Cinémathèque Française.

Figure 9.8
Barrels of wine were stored at Bercy, the former wine warehouse of Paris, just feet from the Seine River. It is now one of the new eastern Paris parks.
Collection du Pavillon de l'Arsenal, Ville de Paris

Through a system called *Zones d'Aménagement Concertées*, or ZACs, a master planner is designated to plan the area's redevelopment and the elements within the plan are designed and executed by others. The ZAC Bercy's master planner, Christian de Portzamparc, created the new neighborhood with housing around a rectangular park, which also included the grass-sided Palais Omnisports, which hosts concerts, trade fairs, and sports events. In 2006, a pedestrian bridge, the Passerelle Simone de Beauvoir, opened and now connects Bercy to the new neighborhood being built near the Bibliothèque Nationale in the 12th arrondissement.

CREATING NEW PARKS—AN OVERVIEW

"Gardens of Memory," the winner of a 1987 Parc de Bercy design competition, whose ZAC-defined guidelines mandated that the design recall the history of the site, pays tribute not only to the past use of the site but also to traditional French landscape design. Paths, laid out in a grid and notched when they encountered any of the 400 existing trees, connect to surrounding streets and recall the old village. Three distinct types of gardens extend the length of the park parallel to the Seine. A great lawn with small stone structures, on axis with the Palais Omnisports, welcomes soccer players and loungers. Further east are nine large "parterres," or squares of formal French gardens showcasing roses, vegetables, and orchards, as well as abstract representations of the four seasons. The final, romantic garden manipulates water into canals, grottos, islands, and waterfalls.

Figure 9.9
The Parc de Bercy today is divided into several sections, many of which reflect the history of the site. Here, replanted vineyards reflect the area's history as a wine depot. The building in the rear is the Gehry-designed Cinémathèque Française.

Figure 9.10
The design of today's Parc de Bercy plays tribute to its past use by retaining some buildings, mature trees and the train tracks imbedded in the cobblestoned streets.
Julie Pecheur

Parks and the Public Process

Design and programming go hand in hand. The first step of park design, especially in the United States, has become the involvement of local neighborhoods. Urban parks are not merely inflated landscaped private gardens but public spaces designed and programmed to reflect the needs of the population, the site, and the surrounding neighborhood. Large-scale public meetings and small task forces that actively elicit opinions about what parks should provide are now commonplace. Open competitions, some international in scope, are held to stimulate ideas and generate excitement about new parks. Such competitions seek ideas, not designers, and strive to include as many people as possible. (See Chapter 3 for a discussion of Request for Proposals and Competitions.)

The rise in the number of actual and proposed conversions of industrial sites into parks in New York City has increased the public's awareness that it can have a say in what goes in its neighborhood. The web-based Gotham Gazette[6] created an interactive game titled "Plan Your Future Park," which presents critical issues about park building, funding, and local involvement. The steps outlined appear obvious, but failing to address any one can delay or prevent park creation. The multiple-choice interactive website asks participants questions such as the relationship between nature and recreation and the balance between children's playgrounds and adult ball fields, and indicates the ramifications of those decisions with respect to crime, upkeep, and neighborhood acceptance.

A new park needs broad civic support from adjacent neighbors and elected officials in order to identify funding sources such as private donors, not-for-profit foundations, and government. In addition, park policies with respect to such seemingly simple issues as dog runs or picnic areas have sociological implications concerning the ethnicity, age, and interests of users. Landscape architects and groups such as the Project for Public Places or the Trust for Public Land play important roles in guiding local groups to identify sites and community needs and translate them into physical design programs.

Retaining History through Design

All urban parks are studies in artifice. Whether containing seemingly random clumps of trees or formal parterres, all urban parks are man-made. Efforts to mimic the countryside are customarily accepted at face value by the American general public, perhaps because of its professed love of a nature apparently untouched. Europeans, living for centuries in cultivated landscapes, seldom have such illusions. It is difficult to overestimate Frederick Law Olmsted's influence on what Americans esthetically expect from parks. All sections of his parks, from Central Park, to Brooklyn's Prospect Park to Montreal's Mount Royal Park are manipulated landscapes. Parks reflect the ideals of their day, and Olmsted's was a romantic era that equated wild nature with true beauty. Americans have not totally forsaken this idea.

The high level of intervention required to create all parks—the ostensibly natural or formally landscaped—means the design process of industrial land conversions does not differ greatly from the creation of parks in general. With industrial conversions, however, designers and localities must also assess how much history to retain, what to remove and what to keep. Despite representing failed industries and containing toxic byproducts, the rusting hulks and skeletal relics of old factories are surprisingly evocative, if not beautiful. Because these sites are frequently contaminated and dangerous, destroying evidence of previous operations is sometimes unavoidable. The intense human contact with the land demands that environmental issues be addressed more thoroughly for parks than for sites on which buildings or parking lots are erected.

Today, as in the past, remnants of a site's history are often completely erased in order to make way for new uses and new design ideas. Conveying a site's history and meaning without appearing false or didactic requires skill and resourcefulness. In America, the public's preference for traditional design can lead to a safe, aesthetic homogeneity, usually nostalgically referencing early-twentieth-century forms and materials such as wooden benches with ornamental metal frames, gas-light-inspired street lamps, and hexagonal paving. It is the visionary administrator and thick-skinned landscape architect who can pull off a design that is a bit experimental. Innovative designs, even if conceptually accepted, rarely endure budgetary reviews and are often the first items to be pared.

Because many new parks are now located on waterfronts or former railroad beds, parks are often linear, posing further design challenges. Repetitiveness and uniformity are difficult to avoid in these constrained and narrow spaces. In addition, their length often transects different neighborhoods with conflicting needs and attitudes. Differences in treatment of the water's edge, seating, paving, and light fixtures, among other items, are subtle between parks, the view of the skyline on the horizon the only distinguishing feature.

GAS WORKS PARK

PARK: GAS WORKS PARK

LOCATION: SEATTLE, WASHINGTON

FORMER USE: GASIFICATION PLANT

DATES: 1970S

MAJOR GOALS: PARK

KEY PLAYERS: CITY OF SEATTLE, COUNCILWOMAN MYRTLE EDWARDS, RICHARD HAAG, LANDSCAPE ARCHITECT

Some projects are able to hold on to bits of industrial history and avoid its eradication. One of the first was Gas Works Park in Seattle, Washington. Living up to its name, this 20-acre park was built on a site formerly used by the Seattle Gas Light Company for its gasification plant in which coal, and then later oil, was converted to gas for lighting, heat, and other household purposes. The city's switch to natural gas in 1956 rendered the plant obsolete. The city of Seattle purchased the site with bond proceeds and a Department of Housing and Urban Development community development block grant. In 1970, the city hired landscape architect Richard Haag to design a park on the site. Haag proposed retaining portions of the manufacturing works and reusing the structures and the grounds rather than obliterating the site's history.

The site, capped and bioremediated, was opened as a park in 1975. There is a 60-foot-high hill composed of contaminated soil, which is now known as Kite Hill, or the "Great Mound." The most telling characteristics of the park are the gas work relics that remain as functional sculptures on the landscape. The boiler house is a picnic shelter with places for tables and grills. A children's playroom is in the former exhauster-compressor building which contains brightly colored machinery. While this approach does not seem radical today, it was at the time. Richard Haag was quoted as saying that when he started the design, he was going "to do something to the place" but as he worked on the land his intent changed to doing "something with it."[7] The required environmental remediation was greater than originally envisioned and the area is still monitored; however, Haag's approach to retaining remnants and interpreting past use of a site has influenced many designers after him.

Duisburg-Nord Landscape Park

Park: Duisburg-Nord Landscape Park

Location: Ruhr Valley, Germany

Former Use: Coal and steel production

Dates: 1990s; ongoing

Major Goals: Mixed-use park retaining existing structures

Key Players: Duisburg public development authorities, Latz + Partner

The International Building Exhibition Emscher Park (IBA) in Germany's Ruhr Valley retains the raw machinery of industry in about 100 projects encompassing almost 570 acres at what was once one of the most heavily industrialized areas of Western Europe. Duisburg-Nord Landscape Park, a section of the larger park, is an evocative design, which preserves items of the past while encouraging the natural transformation to recreational use. This scheme by the Kranzberg, Germany, landscape architecture firm of Latz + Partner won an international competition over a cerebral French design. (The French submission called for all reminders of the factories to be removed and replaced by three gardens that were to symbolize preindustrial, industrial, and postindustrial landscapes.)

Figure 9.11
At the Landscape Park Duisburg-Nord in Germany, the industrial past is palpable, changing either on its own or through phytoremediation. Wherever possible, existing elements were left in place, a reminder of the site's past.
© Latz + Partners

The former home of the Thyssen and iron smelting and zinc mines as well as the center of Germany's munitions district, this rustbelt area is now slowly, naturally, becoming decontaminated and turning green. The main thrust of the design called for allowing the remedial process to happen on its own. Wherever possible, existing elements were left in place, and areas where contamination could not be ameliorated were roped off. Phytoremediation, the using of plants to cleanse the soil and water, is used where possible. The Duisburg-Nord Landscape Park also doubles as a performing arts center, hosting theater festivals and events that utilize the former blast furnaces and facilities as backdrops for presentations and shows. Its design juxtaposes nature and artifice, benign neglect and manipulation.

The contrast between the crumbling vestiges of heavy production and growing vines and trees is striking. A plaza was created from the heavy iron plates that formerly covered casting molds. These plates, like all the manufacturing and foundry detritus, will continue to change as the materials react to usage and exposure to the elements. The park experience balances the

Figure 9.12
At the Landscape Park Duisburg-Nord, relics of factory buildings are actively used for recreation and sport—here former bunker walls are used for climbing.
© Latz + Partners

Figure 9.13
The old blast furnaces at Landscape Park Duisburg-Nord are haunting sculptures, reminders of the previous use of the site.
© Latz + Partners

learning about the industrial past with observing the healing of the landscape. Park activities as well as organized performances and exhibitions are interwoven within industrial ruins. Climbers scale old bunker walls, audiences gather in a former blast furnace, promenaders walk on a former elevated rail line, and bicyclists ride by recovering landscapes.

Lowell National Park

PARK/MUSEUM: LOWELL NATIONAL PARK

LOCATION: LOWELL, MASSACHUSETTS

FORMER USE: TEXTILE MILLS, INDUSTRIAL TOWN

DATES: LATE 1970S; ONGOING

MAJOR GOALS: ECONOMIC REDEVELOPMENT, HISTORIC PRESERVATION, RECREATION

KEY PLAYERS: LOCAL POLITICAL AND BUSINESS LEADERS, NATIONAL PARK SERVICE

One of the newest American national parks is located in Lowell, Massachusetts, location of one of the earliest mill towns. Containing over five miles of canals that harnessed the power of the Merrimack River, the park is an open air venue encompassing mill buildings, museums, and industrial canals. In the early 1970s, the decline of Lowell appeared inevitable. Following the traditional arc of pioneering industrial centers, people and factories departed, leaving in their wake abandoned mills and deteriorating infrastructure. Attempts at countering its 13 percent unemployment rate were ineffective, or when buildings were torn down, outright detrimental. Postwar urban design and public policy advocated destroying existing structures and using available federal money for urban renewal projects. When not left as empty lots, the replacement projects clashed with the nineteenth-century character of this once-proud town.

Local educator, Patrick J. Mogan, along with a group of civic leaders, developed a plan to revive Lowell while recalling its storied industrial and labor history. They proposed that the town infrastructure and form be considered as a whole rather than concentrating on individual historic buildings, many of which in Lowell were not intact. As a result, in 1978, with the urging of the local congressman Paul Tsongas, Congress established the Lowell National Historical Park and the Lowell Historic Preservation Commission. This marked a change in the National Park Service approach, which traditionally concentrated on wilderness and recreation or the restoration of individual structures. The goals of the new Lowell National Park were fourfold:

- Preservation of the social and physical aspects of the industrial revolution such as the canal system and mill buildings;
- Interpretation of the social economic and cultural forces of the nineteenth-century industrial community;
- Revitalization of Lowell by combining the resources of government and private sector; and
- Managing the environment and historic qualities of Lowell.[8]

The park was to showcase the city as an experience in which to participate, not merely observe. Now, the canals that once moved the waterwheels to make the cotton provide scenic pedestrian and bike paths. The Boott Cotton Mills Museum shows the weaving process and cultural centers demonstrate the history of the textile workers as well as recreate the boarding houses where "mill girls" lived. The park encompasses 141 acres including Lowell's downtown, canals, and surrounding areas. In addition to restoring buildings and infrastructure, several

Figure 9.14
Aerial view of the Swamp Locks area of Lowell National Park in Massachusetts, established in 1978 to revive this traditional textile town by restoring its infrastructure and buildings and using the park as an economic regenerator.
U.S. National Park Service, Jim Higgins, photographer Sept. 9, 2008

educational museums and institutions have been established. The New England Quilt Museum and the American Textile Museum build upon the textile heritage of Lowell, while new theaters and sports venues broaden the destinations. Restoration has been carefully calibrated to reflect the historical character of the town, not only relating to buildings but to the streetscape where brick sidewalks and iron streetlamps have been installed.

Building upon the goals of Lowell's National Historic Park, the Lowell Historic Preservation Commission created the Brush Art Gallery & Studios in 1982 to broaden Lowell's economic base as well as restore a former silk mill building. In addition to mounting special exhibitions, affordable studios are rented by painters, jewelers, sculptors, photographers, and illustrators, as well as fabric and ceramic artists among others. All are required to open their studios to the

Figure 9.15
At Lowell National Park, a row of boarding houses has been restored and now is home to an exhibit on mills girls and immigration. The streetscape has been renovated in accordance with nineteenth-century aesthetic and materials.
U.S. National Park Service, Jim Roberts, photographer Sept. 15, 2008

public, a policy that allows artists to engage with the visitors while also providing a forum to sell their art. In addition, artists are required to participate in running the gallery during their stay. This policy was modeled upon the Torpedo Factory in Alexandria, Virginia, and demonstrates that encouraging the arts is not a passive endeavor but one that requires defined programs and the active involvement of groups and individuals. As a result, Lowell schedules an annual Open Studios weekend in the autumn.

In 1998, in its continued effort to revive its downtown, Lowell created an Artists Overlay District to its zoning code to encourage all types of visual, literary, and performance artists. The overlay encourages artists to live and work in

Figure 9.16
The Boott Mill Museum in the Lowell National Park shows how textiles were made in the 1800s. This model demonstrates how close the looms were and how tight the working conditions were. Note the separate fire stair, typical of early mill buildings.
U.S. National Park Service, Jim Higgins, photographer Sept. 15, 2008

the downtown area, both in the city and in the National Park area. This overlay especially addresses the upper stories of downtown buildings, where offices and commercial uses may have left but which contain good spaces for artists to work. Several city-owned buildings that had been taken over for non payment of taxes have been converted for artists.

Another center of artist activity, the Western Avenue Studios, is a renovated mill building privately developed in 2005 that contains 143 working studios. The Loading Dock Gallery located with the Western Avenue Complex represents more than 50 members of the Western Avenue Studios Artist Association. In addition to participating in Lowell's annual programs, the

Figure 9.17
The weave room demonstrations at the Book Mill Museum in Lowell National Park. The original mill did not have air conditioning, however, the narrowness of the room with large windows in the facades let in as much light and air as possible.
U.S. National Park Service, Jim Higgins, photographer Sept. 15, 2008

RETAINING HISTORY THROUGH DESIGN 255

Figure 9.18
The park encompasses buildings as well as the canals and falls that powered the mills before electricity.
U.S. National Park Service, Jim Higgins, photographer Sept. 15, 2008

Figure 9.19
Building on its arts scene, Lowell, Massachusetts, celebrates its native son, Jack Kerouac, with annual events that take place in Kerouac Park, built in 1988. The stones contain excerpts from his writings.
U.S. National Parks Service, Jim Higgins, photographer, September 15, 2008

artists make their studios available to the public monthly during First Saturday Open Studios. The town is actively programmed with other destination events such as the Lowell Photography Weekend and Lowell Quilt Festival. In addition, a downtown square celebrates native son Jack Kerouac with sculptures as well as two annual festivals, educational and cultural activities sponsored by a not-for-profit group, Lowell Celebrates Kerouac! (LCK!).

Figure 9.20
Lowell National Park was also to be an economic development project and some mill buildings have been renovated into housing to encourage downtown living. This 2007 conversion of the Western Mills wing of the Boott Mill condominiums is by Bruner/Cott.
Bruner/Cott, 2007

WATERFRONT PARKS

As was discussed in Chapter 1, industry and trade relied heavily on waterways whether oceans, rivers, or man-made canals. As a result, coastlines around the world were lined with commercial or industrial properties, privately owned and often contaminated after generations of use. Sealed off from their cities by highways, warehouse buildings, or dilapidated piers, this waterfront property is viewed as a valuable recreation and residential amenity. The conversion of these derelict waterfront areas pose many challenges as the public's growing conviction of its right of access often conflicts with the ability to get to the water, whether physically or legally, because of ownership patterns.

Two stories about the development of new parks on either side of the American continent show the stamina and resources needed to provide these city-wide amenities without the wherewithal of federal government help as in Europe. On the east coast in New York City, although money to build as well as maintain a major new park was and is difficult to raise, neighborhood resistance to change and conflicting visions of the city were the biggest hurdles. As one of the first industrialized ports in America, New York's waterfront was intensely developed, and its shoreline presented an impenetrable fortress of industrial, warehouse, and port uses. Although Manhattan is an island, New York typified many American cities' relationship with water. Its residents could look at it from tall buildings, roadways, and a few elevated parks and promenades. They could ride on it in ferries and cruise ships. But for the main part, they could not get near it: Roads ringed the island, railroads hugged the shore, and cyclone fences cut off venturesome and intrepid explorers and stopped them in their tracks.

The ongoing transformation of America's waterfronts over the last decades is unparalleled and is critical to the revival of the nation's cities and how their public spaces are viewed and treated. The 30-year saga to develop the Hudson River Park, although tortuous and at times quite parochial, has broader significance than the petty fights that constitute it. It traced how cities have changed economically and redefined what the public realm should provide and what the "good" urban life is. It started at a time when citizens and governments assumed that large cities could not thrive, that their infrastructure was doomed to failure, and that government could not or should not be responsible for public space nor pay for amenities. During this time span New York City went from a city where public spaces were physically and financially shunned to one whose ambitious goal is to make much of its considerable waterfront public and accessible.

On the west coast, Seattle was also a city that had made its living from the ocean—whether in trade or in fishing. Over the same time span that New York was redefining itself, Seattle became the home of several of the country's newly minted moguls, beneficiaries of the computer and Internet industry. The new city elite turned its attention to art and their city's public realm and the resulting park is privately owned. Getting to it, however, proved to be the major obstacle. Realizing that both rail and motor transportation facilities that hugged the shoreline would remain and couldn't be moved, the new park had to "jump over" these impediments to get to the water. The resulting linear (with a few jigs and jags) park provides city views otherwise impossible.

HUDSON RIVER PARK

PARK: HUDSON RIVER PARK

LOCATION: WEST SIDE OF MANHATTAN, NEW YORK

FORMER USE: WORKING HARBOR

DATES: 1980s; ONGOING

MAJOR GOALS: CONSTRUCTION AND MAINTENANCE OF NEW RIVERSIDE PARK

KEY PLAYERS: CITIZEN GROUPS BOTH FOR AND AGAINST PARK DEVELOPMENT, STATE AND CITY GOVERNMENTS, HUDSON RIVER PARK TRUST, A CITY-STATE DEVELOPMENT AUTHORITY

Hudson River Park's story starts with a road; specifically, the elevated West Side Highway, which paralleled the river and blocked the island's western view from any cross-street south of 57th Street. The original 1930s highway was

Figure 9.21
View toward New York City with the elevated West Side Highway and Empire State Building in the background from pier 49 in 1975.
© Shelley Seccombe

in such poor condition that in late 1973, in a fitting cautionary tale, a truck en route to repair the road instead triggered the collapse of a 60-foot section. As soon as that segment of the roadway was closed to traffic, people reclaimed it as recreational space by jogging or skating on it, or just viewing the city and river. A few years later, as in Baltimore, the waterfront drew thousands of people during the July 1976 Bicentennial celebration to witness the highly successful OpSail parade of tall ships from around the world.

Plans were already being drawn to replace the dilapidated highway with Westway, a road that would connect to the interstate highway system. Envisioned as a six-lane expressway sunk under landfill in the harbor, Westway was a $1.7 billion mixed-use project containing land for housing, parks, and mass transit.[9] A vocal and active group banded together to thwart Westway's construction and initiated a 14-year-long political and legal battle of legendary proportions, which ended in 1985 when a judge halted the project in a fabled ruling claiming that the landfill required would destroy the habitat of striped bass. (That the Hudson River at that time actually contained live fish came as a surprise to most New Yorkers.)

Figure 9.22
Despite being surrounded by crumbling infrastructure, the piers along the Hudson River during the mid-1970s were a favorite place to loll away an afternoon.
© Shelley Seccombe

While the battle of Westway was raging in the courts, what was left of the West Side Highway became increasingly unsafe. Its rusty hulk was completely torn down and a large swath of New York City's waterside came within reach. At the same time, ships were abandoning the harbor and several piers opened to the public as ad-hoc recreation places, well-used though bereft of amenities. Meanwhile, during years of debate, redesign, and lawsuits, the state had acquired land and rights-of-way over the piers for the building of Westway. The City-State West Side Task Force created in 1985 proposed an on-grade thoroughfare with parks along the riverfront and piers. The city negotiated with the federal government to retain the interstate highway funds by allocating 60 percent of the $1.7 billion to mass transit, with the remainder going to the rebuilding of a replacement road.

Around the same time, Battery Park City, after a tentative start, began building housing, as well as a promenade and park with extraordinary views of the harbor, the Statue of Liberty, and Ellis Island. It was a turning point in modern park construction for New York, a beacon of pride for both its design and continuing maintenance. Being part of Battery Park City meant that it was public in use, but private in ownership and upkeep with homeowner association dues keeping the park clean and well-tended. But more importantly, it created a template of what a modern waterfront park could be in New York City.

In 1992, the city and state created the Hudson River Park Conservancy ("HRPC") to be the vehicle for planning and building a park according to the Task Force's vision of redeveloping public piers for active and passive recreation, with a bike path and walkway, which would in part be funded by leasing some of the land and piers to businesses. This being New York, however, controversy from a myriad of constituencies erupted immediately. A columnist for the weekly newspaper, *The Village Voice*, expressed concern that a park would not benefit the forgotten and marginal people—the homeless who sought refuge under the old elevated highway and on the piers, as well as the gays, whose famed cruising spots would most likely be eradicated. Good government groups complained that HRPC was a state entity and therefore would not be responsive to local concerns, notwithstanding the fact that this was the mechanism for creating New York City's more successful parks—Central Park and Battery Park City Park. Local council members and vocal opponents rallied against a park as planned, claiming that any commercial intrusion was unnecessary and that the less done the better.

Meanwhile, HRPC, without the promise of any construction funds, developed a master plan with the design team of Quennell Rothschild Associates/Signe Nielsen. The potential park spanned five miles, contained 13 piers, and encompassed five neighborhoods. Working with three community boards with distinctly different characteristics and priorities, a concept plan was drawn up by consulting with small groups and holding many public meetings. The master plan's introduction thanks over 150 people, various working groups, associations, and residents and indicates that more than 150 meetings were held to hear the concerns and needs of the community.

By 1995, a deadly combination of local antagonism and official indifference threatened the future park's funding and construction. HRPC started leasing piers to various users such as a sports center and golf driving range, called Chelsea Piers, and the city began planning new sanitation facilities on the Gansevoort Pier (the location of the office of a former customs inspector, Herman Melville). Upset by the potential loss of a park and embarrassed that local infighting made everyone look like fools, a coalition of environmental, planning, and civic groups and individuals formed the Hudson River Park Alliance in 1996 and prodded the state and city to commit funds for the construction of the park. In 1998, state legislation was passed formally creating and funding the park as a state and city partnership. Shortly thereafter, the Hudson River Park was officially designated and is being developed and maintained by the Hudson River Park Trust (HRPT) with a committed budget of $200 million. All that was left to do was to work with the 13 agencies that have jurisdiction over the land, including the Army Corps of Engineers, Department of Transportation (City and State), the Federal Environmental Protection Agency, the Coast Guard, the New York State Department of Environmental Conservation, among many others.

The park is now under construction, its main obstacle being the on-grade multilaned highway, now called Route 9A. Referred to as a tree-lined boulevard, in reality it remains a large-scale impediment to getting to the park. Difficult to cross during the time span of one traffic light, it

Figure 9.23
The old piers along New York City's Hudson River were so rotted that it was cheaper to rebuild than to restore. The old wooden piers are kept, as they are good environments for aquatic life.
Carol Berens

has become a mental as well as physical barrier, separating the park from the city. This situation has led some to question whether the success of killing Westway was really a victory. In fact, for a while some plans revisited the idea of burying the road in conjunction with the rebuilding of the World Trade Center site, but the plans were abandoned.

Construction of Hudson River Park is an ongoing process with funding an ever-constant problem. State and city money is allocated with prodding not only from HRPT but from the successor organization of the Alliance, Friends of Hudson River Park. After the initial funding, another $200 million was received; however, it is estimated that about that same amount is needed to continue construction. Walking up the waterfront one comes upon a series of incidences—a trapeze school, a miniature golf range, piers for kayaking, and an environmental boat with maritime experiments—not yet a unified design. New York's waterfront parks have always been promenades—the Brooklyn Heights Promenade and the Battery Park City park follow through with this idea. The Greenwich Village section at 10th Street opened in 2003. As with Battery Park City park, it is a picture of manicured bliss with little recollection of its earlier hardscrabble and rowdy days.

Figure 9.24
The new piers that jut into the Hudson River are refuges from the city and contain shaded areas as well as those fully exposed to the river and the sun.
Carol Berens

The park consists of two main parts—the upland area that hugs the shore and abuts the road, and the piers that spectacularly jut out into the river affording views of both the harbor and the city. The master plan for the park calls for each of the seven segments (which roughly relate to different neighborhoods) to be designed by different architectural teams using certain common design elements such as railing, lighting, and pavement treatments to create a uniform identity. Design teams for each segment met with community groups to develop programs and specific elements.

The upland area will be a continuous esplanade with granite and bluestone pavement and plantings between the road and the promenade. Plaza spaces occur at park entrances and at the piers. Although the esplanade and some

Figure 9.25
The upland promenade of the Hudson River Park is an active zone.
Carol Berens

of the piers are designed for passive use, much of the park reflects the recreational needs of the communities such as playfields and tennis courts, a skate park that includes a bowl and a mini half-pipe, kayaking, a trapeze school, playgrounds, and cultural programs such as summer night movie screenings. Many of the activities take place on the piers, many of which were in such terrible shape it was cheaper to tear them down and start anew.[10]

True to park developments, the adjacent area, formerly home to dingy by-the-hour hotels and leather bars, has been spiffed up. Banners advertise sales and rentals of renovated residential loft buildings, including three modern, impeccably detailed glass-and-white-metal towers designed by Richard Meier. Surrounding buildings are under construction, creating a bund-like feeling along the Hudson. This development has given rise to local preservation groups, such as the Preserve Greenwich Village Waterfront Federation, which vocally protest any proposed neighborhood changes and rezoning.

Figure 9.26
At New York's Hudson River Park, as with the creation of all new parks, development has become upscale, as evidenced from these new Richard Meier-designed modernist towers.
Carol Berens

In September 2008, The Friends of Hudson River Park released a study[11] based on research by the Regional Plan Association confirming that the property values in the area have risen as a result of the park. The study specifically concentrated on the completed Greenwich Village segment and attributed a gain of $200 million in property value in the two blocks across from the Greenwich Village section that cost $75 million. In contrast to the High Line's effect on property values, the announcement in 1990 that a park was going to be built had no influence on values and it wasn't until construction began in 1997 that a change could be discerned. As a result of the findings, the Friends floated the idea of creating a Hudson River Park Business Improvement District, or BID, to access surrounding property owners to fund ongoing maintenance of the park through HRPT.

Olympic Sculpture Park

PARK/MUSEUM: OLYMPIC SCULPTURE PARK

LOCATION: SEATTLE, WASHINGTON

FORMER USE: OIL TRANSFER STATION

DATES: OPENED 2007

MAJOR GOALS: DISPLAY OF LARGE-SCALE OUTDOOR SCULPTURE, ACCESS TO WATERFRONT

KEY PLAYERS: SEATTLE ART MUSEUM, WEISS/MANFREDI ARCHITECTS, TRUST FOR PUBLIC LAND, LOCAL PHILANTHROPISTS

The conversion of a nine-acre strip of polluted Seattle waterfront into a public park by a private institution took over seven years. Although the project was much smaller and the process not as convoluted as the Hudson River Park, it presented distinct challenges. The expansion of the Seattle Art Museum into an outdoor park on the site of the former Union Oil of California's (Unocal) oil transfer station was apparently drama-free compared to the battles on the East Coast. Originally slated to be a condo development, Unocal agreed to sell the land to the Museum for $17 million. The Seattle Art Museum, whose city is home to Microsoft, Amazon.com, and Starbucks,

Figure 9.27
Seattle's Olympic Sculpture Park affords park-goers unusual vistas of the city as well as the Olympic Mountains and Puget Sound.
© Lara Swimmer

Figure 9.28
Construction of Seattle's Olympic Sculpture Park was a massive undertaking as it zigzagged its way from the city to the shore, bridging over a highway and railroad tracks.
© Lara Swimmer

was able to raise the money from private donors as well as the Trust for Public Land. The goal was to build an outdoor sculpture park that not only gives the museum a place to exhibit its large-scale work but also connects downtown with this long-polluted section of the waterfront.

The waterfront is separated from the city center by active railroad tracks and a multilane highway. On the city side of the park is an entrance pavilion that also doubles as an outdoor terrace, café, public performance space, as well as meeting and gallery space. The park, designed by the New York architectural firm Weiss/Manfredi selected by competition, manages a 40-foot drop from downtown to the shoreline over those barriers through a zigzag, 2,200-foot-long path. Vistas from the park of Puget Sound, its islands, and the Olympic Mountains change as one progresses either down or up the path. Outdoor sculptures by Alexander Calder, Mark Di Suvero, and Richard Serra, among others, are placed throughout the length of the park, whose irregular path turns the difficulties of its site to an advantage. In addition to the sculpture, the park is landscaped by Charles Anderson Landscape Architecture to represent the different regional environments from meadows to evergreens to aspen forest and shoreline sand, rocks, and driftwood.

The contamination on this site, although extensive, was cleaned up by Unocal in coordination with the state of Washington's Department of Ecology or capped with a low-permeability clay liner. Costs as well as contamination were contained by using the fill that was needed to create the park, much of which was obtained from the concurrent $85 million expansion of the Seattle Art Museum.[12]

ENDNOTES

1. In *Parks, Green Spaces in European Cities*, Topos (Basel: Birkhauser, 2002) p. 75.
2. Witold Rybczynski, *A Clearing in the Distance* (New York: Scribner, 1999) p. 271.
3. Galen Cranz, *The Politics of Park Design: A History of Urban Parks in America* (Cambridge: MIT Press, 1982).
4. Robert Caro. *The Power Broker*, p. 218.
5. www.pps.org/great_public_spaces/one?public_place_id=369, accessed November 7, 2009.
6. www.gothamgazette.com, a website sponsored by the Citizen Union Foundation of the City of New York, self-described as a nonprofit research and education affiliate of a good government group.
7. As quoted in *Richard Haag: Bloedel Reserve and Gas Works Park*. Elizabeth K. Meyer, "Seized by Sublime Sentiments," p. 7.
8. Description of the founding of Lowell was based upon Dennis Frenchman and Jonathan S. Lane's *Discussion White Paper: Assessment of Preservation and Development in Lowell National Historical Park at its 30-Year Anniversary. Where Have We been and Where Should We be Going?* 2003.
9. For a vivid description of the fight for and against Westway see Phillip Lopate's *Waterfront: A Journey Around Manhattan* (New York: Crown Publishers, 2004).
10. The old piers are made of wood and their stubs can still be seen. Although they can be good habitats for fish, one of the reasons the piers are collapsing is that the water of the Hudson River is cleaner than it's been in decades, affording marine borers a better habitat. The park has kept some of the piles as an important element of its estuarine sanctuary, providing homes for the famous striped bass.
11. "Friends of Hudson River Park releases study, confirms park's value as public investment," September 25, 2008, Press release.
12. The Seattle Art Museum's expansion was designed by Allied Works Architecture and was part of a 12-story building jointly developed with its then-neighbor Washington Mutual.

AFTERWORD

There are many lessons to be learned about how cities are changing from hubs of industry to redefined urban centers. While it's obvious that what works for one doesn't work for all, certain principles crop up throughout many of the projects. Whether the remaking of a harbor or the rebuilding of a dilapidated building, the redevelopment of industrial sites requires incredible perseverance, knowledge, and, yes, a bit of luck. The projects covered in the book are also the stories of those who had the vision or the ability to implement the following process.

Be or find a committed project advocate. There is one item that can't be "ordered" or easily replicated but is critical to the success of almost all the projects in this book: the energy and vision of an individual who sees the void in the neighborhood and pursues solutions to address it. These projects span years, even decades, and obviously require a strong team to achieve their goals, however, the person who first saw the need and then had the tenacity to see the process through is critical. This is the person who never takes "no" for an answer and when confronted with adversity devises another method.

Some of the earliest projects that changed the way people think about urban centers, the role of art in economic development, or the creation of new parks developed from the goals of individuals who happened upon projects that they thought would be a good idea. I'm thinking about William Matson Roth who bought Ghirardelli Square because he thought that a rambling industrial building should be saved. He then hired one of the best landscape architects at the time, Lawrence Halprin, to design an urban plaza that encouraged people to use urban spaces when political leaders and academics saw no future in American cities as viable entities. Or Marian Van Landingham, who needed a place to show art and used the sweat equity of her group's members to renovate a building that no one wanted so that she and others had a place to paint and sell their art. The resulting Torpedo Factory is still a viable template for the creation of artist studios and their relationship to the public around America. Or Bart Blatsein, a private developer who sought to revive an underserved area and created a vibrant center at Philadelphia's Piazza at Schmidts. Or Joshua David and Robert Hammond, who attended a community board meeting, disagreed with the proposed tearing down of an elevated railroad in Manhattan, and spent the next 10 years gathering support for a new park in New York City.

The list goes on. If the answer to successful redevelopment were more mechanical, it would be easier, but it is not. In the end, it all comes down to people. Obviously, money and good ideas are necessary, but both follow in importance the energy and will of project advocates.

Create a project with multiple uses. A multiplicity of uses to attract tourists as well as encourage residents to return again and again often translates into successful projects. If possible, create centers that not only have different activities but also create places to live, work, play, and shop. In America, zoning tends to favor the strict separation of uses and, as aresult, infusing projects with the right mix of uses can be difficult. Have the patience to work with city officials to institute overlays of allowable uses, a method that keeps existing zoning but injects some flexibility. This has worked well with artist overlays, especially in creating live/work spaces.

Park purists are often opponents of this approach and try to keep all commercial uses out of parks. While big box stores or large shopping centers might not be the best park neighbors, cafes, sports venues, and other commercial ventures enhance parks. The 30-year-old Granville Island shows that highly programmed parks, including space for simple enjoyment of nature are not only viable, but quite successful places, both financially and in terms of experience. At this park, the diversity of uses is extreme and includes an existing concrete plant.

This is one area where Americans need to learn from Europe where mixed-use spaces are the norm. Many European residential areas not only have retail on the ground floor, but also contain educational and office uses mixed with housing units on the floors above. Its lively public spaces filled with cafés, concessions as well as venues for spectacles and plays are some of the reasons Americans profess to enjoy going to Europe. Yet getting those same multiplicity of uses in parks remains difficult in America.

Build upon the strengths of the existing site. Some of the most compelling projects are the ones that enhance their sites or their buildings. Historic renovation is becoming financially possible as tax credit programs have made them more feasible in America (although they create several approval levels). These reminders of what was, newly polished and reinvented, maintain cohesiveness of their surrounding neighborhoods. If it's a waterfront site, build upon the water-related uses and the natural draw of water. Some of Amsterdam's new housing projects such as Silodam which looks like a container barge set loose on the sea, or Sporenburg where the inlet is treated as a front lawn, are good examples. If it's a difficult site, make a design feature of the difficulty—a trip to Seattle's Olympic Sculpture Park and Pittsburgh's Allegheny River Park should prove that no site is impossible to build upon.

Be flexible and resourceful. Find the best consultants or learn how to intrigue the development community to participate in your project. Development has gotten quite complicated today and good ideas need to be supported by people who know what they're doing.

Encourage a willing public sector. Some of the infrastructure issues, especially near waterfronts or at large, self-contained factories, need access and services that only public financing can provide. Improvements in roads, transportation, and utilities connect these projects to the existing city and are made with public funds such as bonds and allocations.

Work through special purpose entities. Almost all large-scale projects were accomplished though special-purpose entities. These entities, while often controversial, can streamline the development process and, by creating their own project plans, can provide the multiplicity of uses that makes projects interesting.

Be lucky.

APPENDIX: RESOURCES

INFORMATION AND GRANTS

In America, governments at all levels provide support through grants, awards, and technical help. The first place to start is the United States Environmental Protection Agency (EPA) (www.epa.gov/brownfields), which devotes resources and focus to brownfields and their redevelopment issues. For the past decade it has conferred Phoenix Awards, the aptly named program that honors projects that have developed brownfields and revived abandoned sites and buildings. In addition, each state has its own policies, programs, and grants, which are published on their websites.

PRESERVATION AND STUDY OF THE INDUSTRIAL HERITAGE

- International Congress for Conservation of Industrial Heritage (www.mnactec.cat/ticcih/)
- The Association for Industrial Archaeology promotes the study, preservation, and presentation of Britain's industrial heritage (www.industrial-archaeology.org)
- Society for the Preservation of Old Mills SPOOM (www.spoom.org)
- Society for Industrial Archeology (www.siahq.org)
- The National Trust for Preservation (www.preservationnation.org)
- The Library of Congress's Prints and Photographs Division contains a great repository of drawings and photographs of historic sites around the country. The Department of the Interior's National Park Service has, through its Historic Architectural Building Survey and the Historic American Engineering Record (HABS/HAER), documented many sites, often before their destruction; many images are digitized.
- Lawyers' Committee for Cultural Heritage Preservation (www.culturalheritagelaw.org) is a source of education and advocacy revolving around historic preservation issues.
- European Route of Industrial Heritage (www.erih.net) is an Internet-based tourist network of important industrial sites throughout Europe.

Planning and Public Outreach

- International Association for Public Participation (www.iap2.org), 13762 Colorado Blvd, Suite 124 PMB 54, Thronton, CO 80602 USA, 303-254-5642 or 800-644-4273
- New England Environmental Finance Center, 34 Bedford Street, Portland, ME 04104-9300, 207-228-8594 (http://efc.muskie.usm.maine.edu) for information on consensus building and smart growth
- National Charrette Institute, 1028 SE Water Avenue, Suite 245, Portland, Oregon 97214, 503-233-8486, www.charretteinstitute.org for information, advice, and training in community planning and public involvement
- Project for Public Places, 700 Broadway, 4th Floor, New York, New York 10003, 212-620-5660 (www.pps.org)
- Trust for Public Land (www.tpl.org) is a nonprofit organization that works to conserve parks, land, and historic sites.

Public Policy

- The Americans for the Arts website www.artsusa.org/information_services/research/services/economic_impact/005.asp contains its "Arts & Economic Prosperity III" calculator to download and estimate the economic impact of nonprofit arts and cultural organizations and their audiences on the community.
- International Economic Development Council (www.iedconline.org) helps local economic developers with information to enhance their communities and advance the profession.
- National Association of Local Government Environmental Professionals (NALGEP) (www.nalgep.org) helps local governments with environmental compliance and implementation of environmental policies and programs.
- LINC—Leveraging Investments in Creativity (www.lincnet.org) is a national organization whose goal is to improve conditions for artists.
- Both Toronto Artscape (www.torontoartscape.on.ca) and the Minneapolis-based Artspace (www.artspace.org) have good track records of providing artist housing and resources.
- The Greenpoint Manufacturing and Design Center (www.gmdconline.org), created an interesting path for retaining artisan manufacturing space in New York City.

Financing and Development

- National Trust Community Investment Corporation (Subsidiary of National Trust for Historic Preservation)
- Council of Development Finance Agencies, 818 Superior Avenue, Suite 1301, Cleveland, Ohio 44114, 216-920-3073, www.dcfa.net (TIF)
- Urban Land Institute (www.uli.org) provides support and information concerning real estate development through its staff, publications, and conferences.
- There are national not-for-profit organizations that specialize in the acceptance of preservation easements including the Trust for Architectural Easements (www.architecturaltrust.org) which specializes in preservation easements as well as educational outreach programs to promote historic preservation as well as the Preservation Easement Trust (www.preservationeasement.org). Many states and cities have local organizations that do the same for their areas.

BIBLIOGRAPHY

Banham, Reyer. *Concrete Atlantis: U.S. Industrial Building and European Modern Architecture, 1900–1925.* Cambridge, MA: MIT Press, 1986.

Bergeron, Louis and Maria Teresa Maiullari-Pontois. *Industry, Architecture, and Engineering.* New York: Harry N. Abrams, Inc. 2000.

Blom, Floris. Amsterdam Housing Policy, Situation, Goals and Instruments. Undated. http://ary.fi/aineisto/Amsterdam_Housing_Policy_220508.pdf, accessed May 9, 2009.

Bone, Kevin, editor. *The New York Waterfront: Evolution and Building Culture of the Port and Harbor.* New York: The Monacelli Press, 1997.

Bradley, Betsy Hunter. *The Works: The Industrial Architecture of the United States.* Oxford University Press, 1998.

Breen, Ann and Dick Rigby. *Waterfronts: Cities Reclaim Their Edge.* New York: McGraw-Hill, Inc., 1994.

Breen, Ann and Dick Rigby. *The New Waterfronts: A Worldwide Urban Success Story.* New York: McGraw-Hill, Inc., 1996.

Bairoch, Paul. *Cities and Economic Development.* Chicago: Univeristy of Chicago Press, 1988.

Bucci, Federico. *Albert Kahn: Architect of Ford.* New York: Princeton Architectural Press, 2002.

Buttenwieser, Ann L. *Manhattan Water-Bound. Planning and Developing Manhattan's Waterfront from the Seventeenth Century to the Present.* New York: New York University Press, 1987.

Caro, Robert A. *The Power Broker Robert Moses and the Fall of New York.* New York: Vintage Books, 1975.

Clemens, Marilyn. "Industrial Evolution," *Landscape Architecture.* Jan. 1989, v. 79. no. 1, pp. 25–30.

Cranz, Galen. *The Politics of Park Design: A History of Urban Parks in America.* Cambridge, MA: MIT Press, 1982.

Darley, Gilliam. *Factory.* London: Reaktion Books, 2003.

Floriida, Richard. *The Rise of the Creative Class: And How It's Transforming Work, Leisure, Community and Everyday Life.* New York: Basic Books, 2002.

Gastil, Raymond W. *Beyond the Edge: New York's New Waterfront.* New York: Van Alen/Princeton Architectural Press, 2002.

Hall, Peter Geoffrey. *Cities in Civilizations.* New York: Pantheon Books, 1998.

Hambourg, Serge. *Mills and Factories of New England.* New York: Hanover, NH: H.N. Abrams; Hood Museum of Art, Dartmouth College, 1988.

Hildebrand, Grant. *Designing for Industry: The Architecture of Albert Kahn.* Cambridge, MA: The MIT Press, 1974.

Jaeggi, Annemarie. *Fagus: Industrial Culture from Werkbund to Bauhaus.* New York: Princeton Architectural Press. 2000. (Translated from the German by Elizabeth M. Schwaiger.)

Kirkwood, Niall (ed.). *Manufactured Sites Rethinking the Post-Industrial Landscape.* London and New York: Spon Press, 2001.

Kostelanetz, Richard. *SoHo: The Rise and Fall of an Artist's Colony.* New York: Routledge, 2003.

Kron, Joan and Suzanne Slesin. *High-Tech.* New York: Clarkson N. Potter, Inc., 1978.

Laborde, Marie Francoise. *Architecture industrielle Paris & alentours* (2nd ed.). Paris: Parisgramme, 2003.

Lootsma, Bart. *Super Dutch*. New York: Princeton Architectural Press. 2000.

Jolles, Allard, Erik Klusman and Ben Teunissen, editors. *Planning Amsterdam: Scenarios for Urban Development 1928–2003*. Rotterdam: Nai Publishers, 2003

Machado, Rodolfo. *Residential Waterfront, Borneo Sporenburg, Amsterdam*, Cambridge, MA: Harvard University Graduate School of Design, 2005.

Malone, Patrick. *City, Capital, and Water*. London and New York: Routledge, 1996.

Melet, Ed, editor. *Eastern Harbour District Amsterdam*. Amsterdam: Nai Publishers, 2007.

Miller, Sara Cedar. *Central Park, an American Masterpiece: A Comprehensive History of the Nation's First Urban Park*. New York: Harry N. Abrams, 2003.

Millspaugh, Martin L. "The Inner Harbor Story." *Urban Land*. April 2003, vol. 62, no. 4, pp. 36–41.

Nelson, George. *Industrial Architecture of Albert Kahn, Inc.* New York: Architectural Book Publishing Company, Inc., 1939.

Project for Public Spaces, Inc., Kathy Madden, project director. Public Parks, Private Partners, 2000.

Rybczynski, Witold. *A Clearing in the Distance*. New York: Scribner. 2000.

Saunders, William S., editor. *Richard Haag: Bloedel Reserve and Gas Works Park*. New York: Princeton Architectural Press with the Harvard University Graduate School of Design, 1998.

Schuiling, Dick and Jeroen van der Veer. "Governance in Housing in Amsterdam and the Role of Housing Associations." Paper for the International Housing Conference in Hong Kong 2004, organized by the Hong Kong Housing Authority, February 2–4, 2004. www.kei-centrum.nl/websites/kei//files/kei2003/documentatie/urban_renewal/schuiling-veer_governance-in-housing-amsterdam_2004.pdf. Accessed April 19, 2009.

Schwartz, Frederic J. *The Werkbund: Design Theory and Mass Culture before the First World War*. New Haven: Yale University Press. 1997.

Tate, Alan. *Great City Parks*. London: Spon Press, 2001.

Topos Parks: *Green Spaces in European Cities*. Basel: Birkhauser, 2002.

INDEX

A

Agnelli, Giovanni, 58–59
Allegheny River Bridge, Pittsburgh, Pennsylvania, 190–192
Alumnae Valley, Wellesley, Massachusetts, 127–129
AMD&ART, Vintondale, Pennsylvania, 123–127
American Brewery Building, Baltimore, Maryland, 133–137
Amsterdam Eastern Harbor District, the Netherlands, 192–205
Architectural Heritage Foundation, 138
Artist housing/studios
    Distillery District, Toronto, Canada, 223–226
    Les Frigos, Paris, France, 108, 110–111
    Northern warehouse (Artspace), St. Paul, Minnesota, 97–99
    Piano Craft Guild, Boston, Massachusetts, 106–107
    Tilsner warehouse (Artspace), St. Paul, Minnesota, 97–99
    Torpedo Factory, Alexandria, Virginia, 108–110
    Traffic Zone, Minneapolis, Minnesota, 99
    Westbeth Artist Housing, New York, New York, 102–106, 113n
    Western Avenue Studios, Lowell, Massachusetts, 253
    Wychwood Barns, Toronto, Canada, 100–101
Artist incentives, 112
    Artists overlay district, Lowell, Massachusetts, 252
    Artist Space Inititive (Boston), 112
    Artist Tax Free District, 112

Artist incentives (*Continued*)
    Northeast Minneapolis Arts Association (NEMAA), 96
    Partnership for Creative Industrial Space, Providence, Rhode Island, 88
    Supporting Diverse Art Spaces Initiative (Ford Foundation), 95
Artscape Toronto, 100–102, 225–226
Artspace, 97–100
Audax Textile Museum, Tilburg, the Netherlands, 154–156
Austin, Nichols & Co. warehouse, Brooklyn, New York, 140–144

B

Baltard, Victor, 56–57
Baltimore Inner Harbor, 185–189
Baltimore, Maryland, 64–65
    American Brewery Builidng, 133–137
    Baltimore Inner Harbor, 185–189
    The Can Company, 119–121
    Tide Point, 64–65
Bargmann, Julie (D.I.R.T.), 94, 126
Bassin de l'Arsenal, Paris, 241
Behrens, Peter, AEG turbine factory, Berlin, Germany, 33–34, 34f
Bilbao, Spain, 150, 214–215
Birmingham, Alabama
    Sloss Furnaces National Historic Landmark, 162–165
Blatstein, Bart, 61–64
Boott Mill Museum, Lowell, Massachusetts, 250, 253–254
Boott Mill, Lowell, Massachusetts, 8, 257
Borneo and Sporenburg, Amsterdam, the Netherlands, 197–204
Bridgewater Canal, England, 18
Brownfield legislation, 117–118
Brownfields Voluntary Cleanup Programs, 118–120
Bruner/Cott, 106–107, 152, 173–174, 257
Buffalo, New York, grain elevators, 35–39

C

Canada Lands, 221
(The) Can Company, Baltimore, Maryland, 119–121

canals, 17–18
Cast iron construction, 23–25, 41n
Central Park, New York, New York, 229, 231, 233–235, 245, 261
Centre Pompidou, Paris, France, 40–41
cepezed, 154
Charles River Musuem of Industry and Innovation, Waltham, Massachusetts, 150, 170
Charrettes, 46, 47, 48, 73n
Chimney Pot Houses, Salford, England, 15
Cho Benn Holback + Associates, 133–137
Chocolate factories, 226n
Cité Industrielle, 4t, 14, 17f
Cityscape Development Corporation, 224
Coenen, Jo, 197
Colgate sign, 86–87
Comp, T. Allan, 123–127
Comprehensive Environmental Response, Compensation and Liability Act (CERCLA), 116
Conservation Easements, 140
Container City, London Docklands, England, Figure C-20
Cranz, Galen, 234
Crown and Eagle Mill, North Uxbridge, Massachusetts, 152

D

Deutscher Werkbund, 32
Dia:Beacon, Beacon, New York, 177–179
Diller + Scofidio & Renfo, 68
Distillery District, Toronto, Canada, 223–226
Domino Sugar sign, 87
Duisburg-Nord Landscape Park, Ruhr Valley, Germany, 247–249

E

E.R.A. Architects, 224
Eminent domain, 50, 73n–74n
Erdy McHenry Archtiecture, 61–64
Erie Canal, 17–18
European Route of Industrial Heritage, 151, 154, 166

F

Factory housing, 6–9, 14, 252
Factory Insurance Association guidelines, 22
Fiat Lingotto Factory, Turin, Italy, 58–61
Field Operations, 68
Ford's River Rouge factory, 31
Foss Waterway, Tacoma, Washington, 215
Frank O. Ghery and Associates, 176

G

Garden Cities of Tomorrow, 4t, 14, 16f
Garnier, Tony—Cité Industrielle, 4t, 14, 17f
Gas Works Park, Seattle, Washington, 246
Geffen Contemporary at MOCA, Los Angeles, 176
Georgetown Land Development Company (Gilbert & Bennett Manufacturing Company), 48–49
Geuze, Adriaan, *See* West 8 Urban Design & Landscape Architecture
Ghirardelli Square, San Francisco, California, 184–185
Gilbert, Cass, 140–141
Gooderham & Worts Distillery, *See* Distillery District
Grain elevators, 35–39
Granville Island, Vancouver, Canada, 50–53
Green Museum, 124, 129n
Greenpoint Manufacturing and Design Center, 89–92
Greenpoint-Williamsburg, Brooklyn, New York, 78–83
Gropius, Walter, 33, 35, 41n
Groupe Cardinal Hardy, 218–221

H

Heikkinen-Komonen Architects, 38–39
Helsinki, Finland, office conversion, 37–38
High Line, New York City, 66–70, 74n. *See also* Parks
Hotson Bakker Boniface Haden, 50
Housing
    Austin, Nichols & Co. warehouse, Brooklyn, New York, 140–144
    Boott Mill, Lowell, Massachusetts, 257

    Borneo and Sporenburg, Amsterdam, the Netherlands, 197–204
    Chimney Pot Houses, Salford, England, 15
    Container City, London Docklands, England, Figure C-20
    Crown and Eagle Mill, North Uxbridge, Massachusetts, 152
    Java Island, Amsterdam, the Netherlands, 198
    KNSM Island, Amsterdam, the Netherlands, 197, 226n
    Northern warehouse (Artspace), St. Paul, Minnesota, 97–99
    Piano Craft Guild, Boston, Massachusetts, 106–107
    Piazza at Schmidts, Philadelphia, Pennsylvania, 61–64
    Redpath Lofts, Montreal, Canada, 218–221
    Silodam, Amsterdam, the Netherlands, 204–205
    Tilsner warehouse (Artspace), St. Paul, Minnesota, 97–99
    Washington Mills Building No. 1, Lawrence, Massachusetts, 137–139
    Westbeth Artist Housing, New York, New York, 102–106, 113n
Howard, Ebenezer, 4t, 14, 16f
Hudson River Park, New York, New York, 258–265. *See also* Parks
Humanim, 133–137. *See also* American Brewery Building

I

Industrial Revolution, 3, 6, 19
Industrial towns with housing
    Lowell, Massachusetts, 8–10, 250–257
    Noisiel, France, 13–14
    Paterson, New Jersey (SUM), 4–6
    Pullman, Illinois, 11–14
    Waltham, Massachusetts, 6–8

J

Java Island, Amsterdam, the Netherlands, 198

K

Kahn, Albert, 28–30, 41n
Kerouac Park, Lowell, Massachusetts, 256
KNSM Island, Amsterdam, the Netherlands, 197, 226n

L

Lachine Canal, Montreal, Canada, 17–18, 218–219, 221
LEED, 112, 121–122
Les Frigos, Paris, France, 108, 110–111
Les Halles, Paris, France, 54–57
Leveraging Investments in Creativity (LINC), 112
London Docklands, 206–213
Loos, Adolf, 22t, 33, 35
Love Canal, New York, 116
Lowell National Park, Lowell, Massachusetts, 250–257
Lowell, Massachusetts, 8–10, 250–257
Lowell System, 7

M

Mass MoCA, North Adams, Massachusetts, 171–175
Meier, Richard, 265, 105
Menier Chocolate factory, 14, 25–26
Meyer, Scherer & Rockcastle Ltd., 93–94, 157–161
Michael Van Valkenburgh Associates, 127–129, 192
Mill City Museum, Minneapolis, Minnesota, 156–161
Mill girls, 6, 7–8
Mills (early), 21–23
Minneapolis, Minnesota
    Mill City Museum, 156–161
    Artspace, 97–100
    Northeast Minneapolis Arts Association, 96
Montreal, Canada, 216
    Canada Lands, 221
    Lachine Canal, 18, 218–219, 221
    Old Port of Montreal Corporation, 216
    Redpath Lofts, 218–221
Municipal Arts Society, New York, 82
Museums
    Audax Textile Museum, Tilburg, the Netherlands, 154–156
    Charles River Musuem of Industry and Innovation, Waltham, Massachusetts, 70
    Dia:Beacon, Beacon, New York, 177–179
    Geffen Contemporary at MOCA, Los Angeles, 176
    Mass MoCA, North Adams, Massachusetts, 171–175

INDEX

    Mill City Museum, Minneapolis, Minnesota, 156–161
    Museum of Contemporary Art Detroit (MOCAD), 179–181
    Museum of Glass, Tacoma, Washington, 118–119
    National Waterfront Museum, Swansea, Wales, 166–170
    Nemo Science Musuem, Amsterdam, the Netherlands, 205
    Sloss Furnaces National Historic Landmark, Birmingham, Alabama, 162–165
    Tate Modern, London, England, 212
Museum of Contemporary Art Detroit (MOCAD), 179–181
Museum of Glass, Tacoma, Washington, 118–119
MVRDV, 205

N

National Heritage Corridors (U.S. Parks Service), 151
National Trust for Historic Preservation, 82
National Trust Loan Fund, 136
National Waterfront Museum, Swansea, Wales, 166–170
Nemo Science Musuem, Amsterdam, the Netherlands, 205
New Urbanism, 73n
New York Industrial Retention Network (NYIRON), 88
New York, New York
    Central Park, 229, 231, 233–235, 245, 261
    Domino Sugar sign, 87
    Greenpoint Manufacturing and Design Center, 89–92
    Greenpoint-Williamsburg rezoning, 78–83
    Hudson River Park, 258–265
    Red Hook, Brooklyn, 83–85
    Riverside Park, 230
    SoHo, 24, 75–78
    Westbeth Artist Housing, 102–106, 113n
Noisiel, France, 13–14
Northeast Minneapolis Arts Association, 96
Northern warehouse (Artspace), St. Paul, Minnesota, 97–99

O

O'Connell, Greg, 83–85
Old Port of Montreal Corporation, 216

Olmsted, Frederick Law, 233–234
Olympic Sculpture Park, Seattle, Washington, 266–268
Olympic venues, 213

P

Parc de Bercy, Paris, France, 240–244. *See also* Parks
Parc de La Villette, Paris, France, 238–240. *See also* Parks
Parc des Buttes Chaumont, Paris, France, 232–233. *See also* Parks
Parks
    AMD&ART, Vintondale, Pennsylvania, 123–127
    Central Park, New York, New York, 229, 231, 233–235, 245, 261
    Design issues, 234, 245–246
    Duisburg-Nord Landscape Park, Ruhr Valley, Germany, 247–249
    Early reclamations, 203–233
    Eastern Paris—change through building of parks, 236–238
    Financing of, 235–236
    Gas Works Park, Seattle, Washington, 246
    Granville Island, Vancouver, Canada, 50–53
    High Line, New York City, 66–70, 74n
    Hudson River Park, New York, New York, 258–265
    Impact on real estate values and neighborhoods, 236
    Kerouac Park, Lowell, Massachusetts, 256
    Les Halles, Paris, France, 54–57
    Lowell National Park, Lowell, Massachusetts, 250–257
    National Heritage Corridors (U.S. Parks Service), 151
    Olympic Scupture Park, Seattle, Washington, 266–268
    Parc de Bercy, Paris, France, 240–244
    Parc de La Villette, Paris, France, 238–240
    Parc des Buttes Chaumont, Paris, France, 232–233
    Promenade Plantee, Paris, France, 73
    Riverside Park, New York, New York, 230
    Tom McCall Waterfront Park, Portland, Oregon, 189–190
    Wissahickon Creek, Philadelphia, Pennsylvania, 231
Paris, France
    Bassin de l'Arsenal, 241
    Centre Pompidou, 40–41
    Les Frigos, 108, 110–11
    Les Halles, 54–57
    Parc de Bercy, 240–244

    Parc de La Villette, 238–240
    Parc des Buttes Chaumont, 232–233
    Promenade Plantee, 73
Partnership for Creative Industrial Space, Providence, Rhode Island, 88
Paterson, New Jersey, 4
PepsiCo Bottling sign, 86
Philadelpia Industrial Development Corporation, 92
Philadelphia Navy Yard, 92–94
Philadelphia, Pennsylvania
    Wissahickon Creek, 231
    Urban Outfitters, 93–94
    Piazza at Schmidts, 61–64
Phytoremdiation, 126, 128
Piano Craft Guild, Boston, Massachusetts, 106–107
Piazza at Schmidts, Philadelphia, Pennsylvania, 61–64
Portland, Oregon—Tom McCall Waterfront Park, 189–190
Project for Public Spaces, 52, 54
Promenade Plantée, Paris, France, 71f, 72. *See also* Parks
Providence, Rhode Island, 112
Pullman, Illinois, 11–14

R

Ransome, Ernest L., 30–32
Red Hook, Brooklyn, New York, 83–85
Redding, Connecticut, 48
Redpath Lofts, Montreal, Canada, 218–221
Reinforced concrete construction, 27–30
Renzo Piano Building Workshop, 58–61
Requests for Proposals, 46–48
Riverside Park, New York, New York, 230
Robert A.M. Stern Architects, 92

S

St. Katharine's Dock, London, England, 210
St. Paul, Minesota Tilsner and Northern warehouses (Artspace), 97–99
San Francisco, California rezoning, 88
Seattle Parks Foundation, 235

Seattle, Washington
    Gas Works Park, 246
    Olympic Sculpture Park, 266–268
Silodam, Amsterdam, the Netherlands, 204–205
Sloss Furnaces National Historic Landmark, Birmingham, Alabama, 162–165
Smart Growth, 121–122
Society for Establishing Useful Manufactures (SUM), 4–6
SoHo, New York, 24, 75–78
Struever Bros. Eccles & Rouse, 64–65, 119, 133
Sweeney, David, 89

T

Tacoma, Washington
    Foss Waterway, 215
    Museum of Glass, 118–119
Tate Modern, London, England, 212
Tax programs
    Historic tax credits and incentives, 132, 133 136, 140
    Rehabilitation tax credits, 132–133, 136
    New Markets tax credits, 133
    Tax Increment Financing, 144
Thames River Walk, London, England, 209
Tide Point, Baltimore, Maryland, 64–65
Tilsner warehouse (Artspace), St. Paul, Minnesota, 97–99
Times Beach, Missouri, 116
Tom McCall Waterfront Park, Portland, Oregon, 189–190
Torpedo Factory, Alexandria, Virginia, 108–110
Traffic Zone, Minneapolis, Minnesota, 99
Trust for Architectural Easements, 140–143
Trust for Public Land, 266
Turin, Italy, 58–61

U

United Shoe Company , Beverly, Massachusetts, 30–32
Urban Outfitters, Philadelphia, Pennsylvania, 93–94

V

Van Landingham, Marian, 108–110
Vintondale, Pennsylvania, *See* AMD&ART

W

Waltham, Massachusetts, 6–8, 150
Waltham System, 7
Washington Mills Building No. 1, Lawrence, Massachusetts, 137–139
West 8 Urban Design & Landscape Architecture, 195, 198–202, 205
Westbeth Artist Housing, New York, New York, 102–106, 113n
Western Avenue Studios, 253
Wilkinson Eyre Architects, 167
Wissahickon Creek, Philadelphia, Pennsylvania, 231
Wychwood Barns, Toronto, 100–101

Z

Zago Architecture, 18